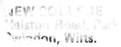
CASEBOO...

D1135892

JANE AU. E...
JANE AUSTEN:
JANE AUSTEN: *'Sense a...*
  B. C. Southam
BECKETT: *Waiting for Godot* Ruby Cohn
WILLIAM BLAKE: *Songs of Innocence and Experience* Margaret Bottrall
CHARLOTTE BRONTE: *'Jane Eyre' & 'Villette'* Miriam Allott
EMILY BRONTE: *Wuthering Heights* (Revised) Miriam Allott
BROWNING: *'Men and Women' & Other Poems* J. R. Watson
CHAUCER: *The Canterbury Tales* J. J. Anderson
COLERIDGE: *'The Ancient Mariner' & Other Poems* Alun R. Jones & W. Tydeman
CONRAD: *'Heart of Darkness', 'Nostromo' & 'Under Western Eyes'* C. B. Cox
CONRAD: *The Secret Agent* Ian Watt
DICKENS: *Bleak House* A. E. Dyson
DICKENS: *'Hard Times', 'Great Expectations' & 'Our Mutual Friend'* Norman Page
DICKENS: *'Dombey and Son' & 'Little Dorrit'* Alan Shelston
DONNE: *Songs and Sonets* Julian Lovelock
GEORGE ELIOT: *Middlemarch* Patrick Swinden
GEORGE ELIOT: *'The Mill on the Floss' & 'Silas Marner'* R. P. Draper
T. S. ELIOT: *Four Quartets* Bernard Bergonzi
T. S. ELIOT: *'Prufrock', 'Gerontion' & 'Ash Wednesday'* B. C. Southam
T. S. ELIOT: *The Waste Land* C. B. Cox & Arnold P. Hinchliffe
T. S. ELIOT: *Plays* Arnold P. Hinchliffe
HENRY FIELDING: *Tom Jones* Neil Compton
E.M. FORSTER: *A Passage to India* Malcolm Bradbury
WILLIAM GOLDING: *Novels 1954–64* Norman Page
HARDY: *The Tragic Novels* (Revised) R. P. Draper
HARDY: *Poems* James Gibson & Trevor Johnson
HARDY: *Three Pastoral Novels* R. P. Draper
GERARD MANLEY HOPKINS: *Poems* Margaret Bottrall
HENRY JAMES: *'Washington Square' & 'The Portrait of a Lady'* Alan Shelton
JONSON: *Volpone* Jonas A. Barish
JONSON: *'Every Man in his Humour' & 'The Alchemist'* R. V. Holdsworth
JAMES JOYCE: *'Dubliners' & 'A Portrait of the Artist as a Young Man'* Morris Beja
KEATS: *Odes* G.S. Fraser
KEATS: *Narrative Poems* John Spencer Hill
D.H. LAWRENCE: *Sons and Lovers* Gamini Salgado
D.H. LAWRENCE: *'The Rainbow' & 'Women in Love'* Colin Clarke
LOWRY: *Under the Volcano* Gordon Bowker
MARLOWE: *Doctor Faustus* John Jump
MARLOWE: *'Tamburlaine the Great', 'Edward II' & 'The Jew of Malta'* J. R. Brown
MARLOWE: *Poems* Arthur Pollard
MAUPASSANT: *In the Hall of Mirrors* T. Harris
MILTON: *Paradise Lost* A. E. Dyson & Julian Lovelock
O'CASEY: *'Juno and the Paycock', 'The Plough and the Stars' & 'The Shadow of a
  Gunman'* Ronald Ayling
EUGENE O'NEILL: *Three Plays* Normand Berlin
JOHN OSBORNE: *Look Back in Anger* John Russell Taylor
PINTER: *'The Birthday Party' & Other Plays* Michael Scott
POPE: *The Rape of the Lock* John Dixon Hunt
SHAKESPEARE: *A Midsummer Night's Dream* Antony Price
SHAKESPEARE: *Antony and Cleopatra* (Revised) John Russell Brown
SHAKESPEARE: *Coriolanus* B. A. Brockman

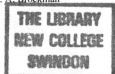

SHAKESPEARE: *Early Tragedies* Neil Taylor & Bryan Loughrey
SHAKESPEARE: *Hamlet* John Jump
SHAKESPEARE: *Henry IV Parts I and II* G.K. Hunter
SHAKESPEARE: *Henry V* Michael Quinn
SHAKESPEARE: *Julius Caesar* Peter Ure
SHAKESPEARE: *King Lear* (Revised) Frank Kermode
SHAKESPEARE: *Macbeth* (Revised) John Wain
SHAKESPEARE: *Measure for Measure* C. K. Stead
SHAKESPEARE: *The Merchant of Venice* John Wilders
SHAKESPEARE: *'Much Ado About Nothing' & 'As You Like It'* John Russell Brown
SHAKESPEARE: *Othello* (Revised) John Wain
SHAKESPEARE: *Richard II* Nicholas Brooke
SHAKESPEARE: *The Sonnets* Peter Jones
SHAKESPEARE: *The Tempest* (Revised) D. J. Palmer
SHAKESPEARE: *Troilus and Cressida* Priscilla Martin
SHAKESPEARE: *Twelfth Night* D. J. Palmer
SHAKESPEARE: *The Winter's Tale* Kenneth Muir
SPENSER: *The Faerie Queene* Peter Bayley
SHERIDAN: *Comedies* Peter Davison
STOPPARD: *'Rosencrantz and Guildenstern are Dead', 'Jumpers' & 'Travesties'*
    T. Bareham
SWIFT: *Gulliver's Travels* Richard Gravil
SYNGE: *Four Plays* Ronald Ayling
TENNYSON: *In Memoriam* John Dixon Hunt
THACKERAY: *Vanity Fair* Arthur Pollard
TROLLOPE: *The Barsetshire Novels* T. Bareham
WEBSTER: *'The White Devil' & 'The Duchess of Malfi'* R. V. Holdsworth
WILDE: *Comedies* William Tydeman
VIRGINIA WOOLF: *To the Lighthouse* Morris Beja
WORDSWORTH: *Lyrical Ballads* Alun R. Jones & William Tydeman
WORDSWORTH: *The 1807 Poems* Alun R. Jones
WORDSWORTH: *The Prelude* W. J. Harvey & Richard Gravil
YEATS: *Poems 1919–35* Elizabeth Cullingford
YEATS: *Last Poems* Jon Stallworthy

Issues in Contemporary Critical Theory Peter Barry
Thirties Poets: 'The Auden Group' Ronald Carter
Tragedy: Developments in Criticism R.P. Draper
The Epic Ronald Draper
Poetry Criticism and Practice: Developments since the Symbolists A.E. Dyson
Three Contemporary Poets: Gunn, Hughes, Thomas A.E. Dyson
Elizabethan Poetry: Lyrical & Narrative Gerald Hammond
The Metaphysical Poets Gerald Hammond
Medieval English Drama Peter Happé
The English Novel: Developments in Criticism since Henry James Stephen Hazell
Poetry of the First World War Dominic Hibberd
The Romantic Imagination John Spencer Hill
Drama Criticism: Developments since Ibsen Arnold P. Hinchliffe
Three Jacobean Revenge Tragedies R.V. Holdsworth
The Pastoral Mode Bryan Loughrey
The Language of Literature Norman Page
Comedy: Developments in Criticism D.J. Palmer
Studying Shakespeare John Russell Brown
The Gothic Novel Victor Sage
Pre-Romantic Poetry J.R. Watson

Shakespeare
Hamlet

A CASEBOOK

EDITED BY

JOHN JUMP

MACMILLAN

First published 1968 by
THE MACMILLAN PRESS LTD
Houndmills, Basingstoke, Hampshire RG21 2XS
and London
Companies and representatives
throughout the world

ISBN 0-333-09309-7

Twelfth reprint 1994

Printed in Hong Kong

CONTENTS

6   *Contents*

ACKNOWLEDGEMENTS

T. S. Eliot, *Selected Essays, 1917–1932* (Faber & Faber Ltd, Harcourt, Brace & World Inc.); G. Wilson Knight, *The Wheel of Fire* (Methuen & Co. Ltd); Caroline F. Spurgeon, *Leading Motives in the Imagery of Shakespeare's Tragedies* (Cambridge University Press); L. L. Schücking, *The Meaning of Hamlet* (Oxford University Press); J. Dover Wilson, *What Happens in Hamlet* (Cambridge University Press); Harley Granville-Barker, *Prefaces to Shakespeare: Third Series*, Hamlet (Field Roscoe & Co.); George Bernard Shaw, *Back to Methuselah* (The Public Trustee and The Society of Authors); Ernest Jones, *Hamlet and Oedipus* (Victor Gollancz Ltd); Wolfgang H. Clemen, '*Hamlet*', from *The Development of Shakespeare's Imagery* (Methuen & Co. Ltd); D. G. James, 'The New Doubt', from *The Dream of Learning* (The Clarendon Press); Maynard Mack, 'The World of Hamlet', from the *Yale Review*, xli (Yale University Press Inc.; © Yale University Press); H. D. F. Kitto, '*Hamlet*', from *Form and Meaning in Drama* (Methuen & Co. Ltd); T. S. Eliot, 'Poetry and Drama', from *On Poetry and Poets* (Faber & Faber Ltd, Farrar, Straus & Giroux Inc.); Harry Levin, 'The Antic Disposition', from *The Question of Hamlet* (Oxford University Press Inc.); Helen Gardner, 'The Historical Approach', from *The Business of Criticism* (The Clarendon Press); L. C. Knights, *An Approach to 'Hamlet'* (Chatto & Windus Ltd, Stanford University Press); John Holloway, '*Hamlet*', from *The Story of the Night* (Routledge & Kegan Paul Ltd, The University of Nebraska Press); Patrick Cruttwell, 'The Morality of Hamlet – "Sweet Prince" or "Arrant Knave"?', from *Hamlet*, ed. J. R. Brown and Bernard Harris, *Stratford-upon-Avon Studies*, 5 (Edward Arnold (Publishers) Ltd); Jan Kott, '*Hamlet* of the

Mid-century', from *Shakespeare Our Contemporary* (Methuen &
Co. Ltd, Doubleday & Co. Inc.; © Panstwowe Wydawnictwo
Naukowe 1964).

GENERAL EDITOR'S PREFACE

EACH of this series of Casebooks concerns either one well-known and influential work of literature or two or three closely linked works. The main section consists of critical readings, mostly modern, brought together from journals and books. A selection of reviews and comments by the author's contemporaries is also included, and sometimes comments from the author himself. The Editor's Introduction charts the reputation of the work from its first appearance until the present time.

What is the purpose of such a collection? Chiefly, to assist reading. Our first response to literature may be, or seem to be, 'personal'. Certain qualities of vigour, profundity, beauty or 'truth to experience' strike us, and the work gains a foothold in our mind. Later, an isolated phrase or passage may return to haunt or illuminate. Where did we hear that? we wonder – it could scarcely be better put.

In these and similar ways appreciation begins, but major literature prompts to very much more. There are certain facts we need to know if we are to understand properly. Who were the author's original readers, and what assumptions did he share with them? What was his theory of literature? Was he committed to a particular historical situation, or to a set of beliefs? We need historians as well as critics to help us with this. But there are also more purely literary factors to take account of: the work's structure and rhetoric; its symbols and archetypes; its tone, genre and texture; its use of language; the words on the page. In all these matters critics can inform and enrich our individual responses by offering imaginative recreations of their own.

For the life of a book is not, after all, merely 'personal'; it is more like a tripartite dialogue, between a writer living 'then', a reader living 'now', and whatever forces of survival and honour link the two. Criticism is the public manifestation of this dialogue, a witness to the continuing power of literature to arouse and excite. It illuminates the possibilities and regards of the dialogue, pushing 'interpretation' as far forward as it can go.

And here, indeed, is the rub: how far can it go? Where does 'interpretation' end and nonsense begin? Why is one interpretation superior to another, and why does each age need to interpret for itself? The critic knows that his insights have value only in so far as they serve the text, and that he must take account of views differing sharply from his own. He knows that his own writing will be judged as well as the work he writes about, so that he cannot simply assert inner illumination or a differing taste.

The critical forum is a place of vigorous conflict and disagreement, but there is nothing in this to cause dismay. What is attested is the complexity of human experience and the richness of literature, not any chaos or relativity of taste. A critic is better seen, no doubt, as an explorer than as an 'authority', but explorers ought to be, and usually are, well equipped. The effect of good criticism is to convince us of what C. S. Lewis called 'the enormous extension of our being which we owe to authors'. A Casebook will be justified only if it helps to promote the same end.

A single volume can represent no more than a small selection of critical opinions. Some critics have been excluded for reasons of space, and it is hoped that readers will follow up the further suggestions in the Select Bibliography. Other contributions have been severed from their original context, to which some readers may wish to return. Indeed, if they take a hint from the critics represented here, they certainly will.

A. E. DYSON

INTRODUCTION

SHAKESPEARE'S *Hamlet* is one of those rich and complex works of art that convey different meanings in different generations and to different individuals.

For a hundred years after it was written, no one seems to have made it the subject of an extended critical analysis; but frequent allusions to it, and echoes of it, show that it already enjoyed great popularity. Seventeenth-century playgoers and readers apparently conceived Hamlet himself as 'primarily a bitterly eloquent and princely avenger'.[1] They did not ask themselves why he delayed so long before killing Claudius. In fact, they gave no sign of noticing that he delayed at all.

Their successors during the early and middle decades of the eighteenth century began to ascribe to the prince a greater delicacy and a more '*melancholy Cast*'; and David Garrick's interpretation of the role gave memorable form to this revised conception. But Hamlet was not yet seen as lacking initiative and resolution. He was 'an active prince with a task on his hands, a task which in due time he carried out successfully'.[2]

In 1736, however, the writer of the first detailed critical study of *Hamlet*, possibly Thomas Hanmer, recognized the hero's procrastination. He explained it as forced on Shakespeare by the necessities of his craft; if Hamlet had not delayed, he said, 'there would have been an End of our Play'. Hanmer seems also to have made the earliest recorded protest against Hamlet's cruelty – 'so unworthy of a Hero' – in sparing Claudius at prayer in the hope of destroying his soul as well as his body on some future

[1] Paul S. Conklin, *A History of Hamlet Criticism, 1601–1821* (1947) p. 26.
[2] Conklin, p. 43.

occasion. Dr Johnson echoed this protest in 1765. Towards the close of the eighteenth century such particular observations on Hamlet's character became increasingly common. Critics grew more aware of his complexity; they pondered his procrastination and his assumed or real madness; and the more sentimentally inclined – Henry Mackenzie, for example, and Goethe – saw in him a reflection of tendencies they felt in themselves.

As they developed and refined their psychological analysis, some of them began to prefer the play as they might read it in a library to the play as they might watch it in a theatre. Such a preference became widespread during the Romantic period. Wordsworth and Leigh Hunt doubted whether any contemporary actor could make a tolerable Hamlet; and Coleridge, Lamb and Hazlitt believed that no actor, living or dead, would be adequate in the role.

In its turn, the increasing acceptance of the work as a literary text suited for private study permitted psychological analysis of the characters, and especially of the protagonist, to become more and more subtle. Lamb described a 'shy, negligent, retiring Hamlet'. Coleridge imagined a prince whose great and splendid activity of intellect necessarily incapacitated him for meeting the demands of action; he detected 'a smack of Hamlet' in himself. Hazlitt fused this philosophical Hamlet with the sentimentalized Hamlet of some of the late eighteenth-century commentators and found the prince 'the most amiable of misanthropes'.

For nineteenth-century students of the play, character-analysis became the standard critical method. Hartley Coleridge defined it in its most extreme development when he invited his readers to 'put Shakspeare out of the question, and consider Hamlet as a real person, a recently deceased acquaintance'. Agreement was fairly general that Hamlet delayed inordinately. Debate centred on the reasons for his delay. How grave were the external obstacles to his fulfilment of the Ghost's command? Was he deterred by moral scruples? Did an extraordinary sensitiveness, or even neurosis, render him unfit for the task? Or was he disabled by a reflective or speculative habit of mind? Such questions as these engaged the attention of critics as different from one another as Taine and Bradley, Dowden and George Bernard Shaw.

Meanwhile Matthew Arnold and others were recognizing that Hamlet had acquired, in the imagination of mankind, a very special status. Like Faust, for example, or Helen of Troy, he had come to be seen as a powerfully representative, or even mythical, figure. James Russell Lowell indicated the significance of this figure by remarking 'how prophetically typical the character is of that introversion of mind which is so constant a phenomenon of these latter days, of that over-consciousness which wastes itself in analysing the motives of action instead of acting'.

The finest product of the Victorian approach to Shakespeare by way of character-analysis is generally agreed to have been A. C. Bradley's *Shakespearean Tragedy* (1904). This remains influential, and deservedly so. But the present century has witnessed a number of reactions against it. Many critics today dislike abstracting the characters from a complete work in order to discuss them almost as if they were real persons, or recently deceased acquaintances. They feel that they can discuss a work more profitably if they regard it, in G. Wilson Knight's words, 'as a visionary whole, close-knit in personification, atmospheric suggestion, and direct poetic-symbolism'. They dwell upon its poetry, and especially its poetic imagery. Caroline Spurgeon's investigations are of service to them, and the interpretations of Wilson Knight himself are immensely suggestive.

Admittedly, some of their interpretations of the plays as symbolist poems are as remote from theatrical reality as were any of the nineteenth-century character-analyses. But the twentieth century has received also some very useful reminders of the need to keep sight of this reality. The fullest of Harley Granville-Barker's *Prefaces to Shakespeare* is that devoted to *Hamlet*. While his general interpretation represents no sharp break with Victorian tradition, his lively sense of theatrical values makes his study constantly illuminating in detail. A. J. A. Waldock, in *Hamlet: A Study in Critical Method* (1931), invokes our experience of the play in performance in order to challenge the most widespread assumption of Romantic and subsequent criticism.

He argues that in the theatre Hamlet's procrastination is hardly noticeable and that critics of the play ought therefore to concentrate less exclusively upon their leading question, 'Why does he delay?'

Other twentieth-century critics have tried to correct their predecessors by adopting a more historical approach to Shakespeare's work. E. E. Stoll, L. L. Schücking, and Lily B. Campbell are prominent among these. But the most influential attempt to describe a genuinely Elizabethan *Hamlet* has been J. Dover Wilson's *What Happens in Hamlet* (1935). Dover Wilson argues that the Ghost is an ambiguous figure and that Hamlet has good reason to doubt whether it is his father's spirit or a devil taking that shape to tempt him to murder; that, in ordering him to kill Claudius without compromising Gertrude, it sets him an extraordinarily difficult task; that Hamlet in II ii overhears Polonius's scheme to 'loose' Ophelia to him; and that Shakespeare intended the audience, but not Claudius, to heed the dumb-show preceding *The Mousetrap*. Dover Wilson does not break with Bradley, any more than Granville-Barker does. But certain of his contentions serve to emphasize the difficulties confronting Hamlet and to imply that up to a point his delay is prudent. In this way, they discourage us from seeing the play too exclusively as concerned with a man who could not make up his mind.

Recent critics have challenged also the traditional notion of Hamlet as a character of some sweetness and nobility. Wilson Knight sees him as a sick, cynical and inhuman prince corrupting a world that is, 'except for the original murder of Hamlet's father . . . one of healthy and robust life, good-nature, humour, romantic strength, and welfare'. It seems fair to retort that the murder is a rather large exception for dismissal in a parenthetical phrase. L. C. Knights refrains from praise of Claudius but is no less severe on Hamlet. 'His attitudes of hatred, revulsion, self-complacence and self-reproach . . . are, in their one-sided insistence, forms of escape from the difficult process of complex adjustment which normal living demands and which Hamlet finds beyond his powers.'

Of the brief extracts which in the present volume represent *Hamlet* criticism down to 1945, some have been chosen for their historical significance. Others have been included because they embody especially penetrating comments, still others because they contain the idiosyncratic observations of highly individual thinkers. As far as possible, extracts have been selected which refer to various parts or aspects of the play. Between them, they raise most of the questions discussed in the complete essays and essay-length passages from longer works, published since 1945, which compose the main part of this book.

The first of these larger extracts represents an application of the modern technique of psycho-analysis to the solution of the problem which so preoccupied the nineteenth-century critics: 'Why does Hamlet delay?' As early as 1900, Freud himself ascribed the revenger's irresolution to an Oedipus complex. Ernest Jones, his most distinguished British disciple and his biographer, elaborates this view in a study of the play which he published in several versions before issuing it in its finally revised form in 1949. At this date, the reaction against the approach to Shakespeare's plays by way of character-analysis was widespread, and it caused many readers to be less than fair to a book which does, after all, provide a vigorous and coherent discussion of a central component of the tragedy.

D. G. James also focuses upon Hamlet himself and asks why he delays. But with his interpretation of him as a character afflicted by doubt he couples a recognition 'that we must not see the play as merely an affair of the character of its hero'.

Many who share this recognition have chosen approaches which seem to promise a more comprehensive view of the tragedy. W. H. Clemen proceeds by way of an analysis of the language and, more especially, of the imagery. Maynard Mack shows himself well aware of what can be discovered from this angle when he sets about describing the very world of the play, that is, the whole imaginative environment that it invites us to enter when we read it or go to see it. This world cannot be described without resort to religious ideas. So there is nothing surprising in the fact that both H. D. F. Kitto and John Holloway should, in different ways, see *Hamlet* as a religious drama. To Kitto, Shakespeare's theme is the corroding influence of sin, the insidious power with which evil, once started on its course, so works as to attack and overthrow impartially the good and the bad. To Holloway, the developing spectacle is that of a diseased society deferring to, and placing in distinguished isolation, the revenger who has reluctantly undertaken the role of its purifier, which Providence has forced upon him. Such commentators aim at nothing less than a formulation of the total significance of the work.

They are naturally concerned that their interpretations should be historically plausible. Helen Gardner, justifying the historical approach, points out that in Elizabethan revenge-plays generally the initiator of the action is the initiator of its resolution, that the villain, in other words, is to some extent the involuntary agent of his own destruction. This being so, the revenging hero does not so much create an opportunity as wait for the one that his victim will unintentionally provide. Hamlet is typical in that he has this waiting role. His guilelessness in it wins our affection, his constancy our approval. Talk of his delay is largely, though not entirely, beside the point.

In opposition to Helen Gardner and many others, L. C. Knights has elaborated, with some modifications, the disparaging view of Hamlet already quoted from his essay of 1940. Where Helen Gardner appreciates Hamlet's constancy in awaiting his opportunity, Knights detects only 'a sterile concentration on death and evil'. His case, sensitively and subtly argued though it is, has provoked considerable opposition. One of the more genial and persuasive retorts comes from Patrick Cruttwell, who follows Helen Gardner in stressing the prince's constancy and other soldierly virtues. When Knights mentions Hamlet's 'murder' of Rosencrantz and Guildenstern, Cruttwell protests that Hamlet was engaged in a just war such as might be held to sanction extreme measures. What Hamlet really is, summarizes Cruttwell at the end of his essay, 'is a conscript in a war. He has done things, as we all do in wars, he would rather not have done; but he believes it to be a just war, and all in all, he has borne himself well.'

A conviction that Hamlet is in some sense a 'conscript' finds many spokesmen in recent criticism. Maynard Mack reminds us that his situation is 'mainly not of his own manufacture, as are the situations of Shakespeare's other tragic heroes'; Helen Gardner repeats that this 'horrible . . . intolerable' situation is one 'for which he has no responsibility'; and John Holloway stresses that his role is something thrust upon him which he undertakes with distinct reluctance and repugnance. Jan Kott, writing in Poland, a country which has experienced modern political totalitarianism in a variety of forms, sees *Hamlet* as a political play in which not only the prince but also Laertes, Ophelia and Fortinbras play parts 'imposed on them from outside'. Kott's purpose is to portray Hamlet for our own times. This is no less the purpose of Helen Gardner and Patrick Cruttwell. But, whereas they try to see him historically, in relation to the Elizabethan Age, before suggesting his significance for the twentieth century, Kott proceeds more directly to choose his twentieth-century Hamlet from those which he knows to be realizable on the stage. His intimacy with the theatre gives him his principal strength as a critic.

Other critics have focused upon particular aspects or parts of the play. Harry Levin examines Hamlet's 'antic disposition' against the background of other treatments of real or assumed madness in Elizabethan drama. T. S. Eliot, in a passage originally forming part of a pre-war lecture but first printed in 1951 in a new context, analyses the verse of the opening scene of *Hamlet* from the point of view of a practising poetic dramatist. D. G. James, discussing moral and metaphysical uncertainty in *Hamlet*, bases his discussion upon a careful reading of the most famous of the soliloquies.

It would be foolish to try to sum up the findings of recent criticism in a single comprehensive formula. At the same time, four prominent trends deserve notice. In the first place, character-analysis is today even less relied upon than it was a generation ago; and, when the character of the hero has to be investigated, the question 'Why does he delay?' is even less often regarded as central. In the second place, contemporary critics seem unwilling

to let the strictures of a few scrupulous moralists outweigh the
testimony of a vast majority of the readers and theatre-goers of
three and a half centuries to the effect that Hamlet is a highly
sympathetic character. In the third place, certain of the more
recent critics describe this sympathetic character primarily as a
man upon whom an almost intolerable burden has been laid, the
action of the tragedy being largely the outcome of his reluctant
but dutiful shouldering of it. Finally, the world in which Hamlet
has to act is seen as one in which there is little or no certainty,
and the society with which he is involved is seen as sinking into
decay.

For the convenience of readers, all quotations from *Hamlet*
occurring in the essays and other items reprinted in this volume
have been brought into line with the text of a single well-known
edition of the play, and references have been revised wherever
necessary to make them applicable to that edition. J. Dover
Wilson's 'New Cambridge' text has been used for this purpose.
But in one or two cases where a critic's argument depends upon
a reading found in some other text, but not in the 'New Cambridge', that reading has been allowed to stand. Apart from a few
brief cuts, indicated in the usual way, no changes have been made
in the various critics' own writing, and each of them has been
allowed to retain his national or personal preferences in the
matter of spelling.

PART ONE

Extracts from Earlier Critics, 1710-1945

ANTHONY ASHLEY COOPER,
EARL OF SHAFTESBURY

TH A T Piece of his [The Tragedy of *Hamlet*], which appears to
have most affected *English* Hearts, and has perhaps been oftnest
acted of any which have come upon our Stage, is almost one
continu'd *Moral*; a Series of deep Reflections, drawn from *one*
Mouth, upon the Subject of *one* single Accident and Calamity,
naturally fitted to move Horror and Compassion. It may be
properly said of this Play, if I mistake not, that it has only ONE
Character or *principal Part*.

(from *Soliloquy, or Advice to an Author*, 1710)

JOSEPH ADDISON

TH E Appearance of the Ghost in *Hamlet* is a Masterpiece in its
kind, and wrought up with all the Circumstances that can create
either Attention or Horrour. The Mind of the Reader is wonder-
fully prepared for his Reception by the Discourses that precede
it: His dumb Behaviour at his first Entrance, strikes the Imagination very strongly; but every Time he enters, he is still more
terrifying. Who can read the Speech with which young *Hamlet*
accosts him, without trembling?

(from *The Spectator*, 20 April 1711)

ANONYMOUS
(attributed to Thomas Hanmer)

N o w I am come to mention *Hamlet*'s Madness, I must speak my
Opinion of our Poet's Conduct in this Particular. To conform to
the Ground-work of his Plot, *Shakespeare* makes the young

Prince feign himself mad. I cannot but think this to be injudicious; for so far from Securing himself from any Violence which he fear'd from the Usurper, which was his Design in so doing, it seems to have been the most likely Way of getting himself confin'd, and consequently, debarr'd from an Opportunity of Revenging his Father's Death, which now seem'd to be his only Aim; and accordingly it was the occasion of his being sent away to *England*. Which Design, had it taken effect upon his Life, he never could have revenged his Father's Murder. To speak Truth, our Poet, by keeping too close to the Ground-work of his Plot, has fallen into an Absurdity; for there appears no Reason at all in Nature, why the young Prince did not put the Usurper to Death as soon as possible, especially as *Hamlet* is represented as a Youth so brave, and so careless of his own Life.

The Case indeed is this: Had *Hamlet* gone naturally to work, as we could suppose such a Prince to do in parallel Circumstances, there would have been an End of our Play. The Poet therefore was obliged to delay his Hero's Revenge; but then he should have contrived some good Reason for it.

Hamlet's Speech upon seeing the King at Prayers, has always given me great Offence. There is something so very Bloody in it, so inhuman, so unworthy of a Hero, that I wish our Poet had omitted it. To desire to destroy a Man's Soul, to make him eternally miserable, by cutting him off from all hopes of Repentance; this surely, in a Christian Prince, is such a Piece of Revenge, as no Tenderness for any Parent can justify. To put the Usurper to Death, to deprive him of the Fruits of his vile Crime, and to rescue the Throne of *Denmark* from Pollution, was highly requisite: But there our young Prince's Desires should have stop'd, nor should he have wished to pursue the Criminal in the other World.

(from *Some Remarks on the Tragedy of Hamlet*, 1736)

VOLTAIRE

ENGLISHMEN believe in ghosts no more than the Romans did, yet they take pleasure in the tragedy of *Hamlet*, in which the ghost of a king appears on the stage. . . . Far be it from me to justify everything in that tragedy; it is a vulgar and barbarous drama, which would not be tolerated by the vilest populace of France, or Italy. Hamlet becomes crazy in the second act, and his mistress becomes crazy in the third; the prince slays the father of his mistress under the pretence of killing a rat, and the heroine throws herself into the river; a grave is dug on the stage, and the grave-diggers talk quodlibets worthy of themselves, while holding skulls in their hands; Hamlet responds to their nasty vulgarities in silliness no less disgusting. In the meanwhile another of the actors conquers Poland. Hamlet, his mother, and his father-in-law, carouse on the stage; songs are sung at table; there is quarrelling, fighting, killing – one would imagine this piece to be the work of a drunken savage. But amidst all these vulgar irregularities, which to this day make the English drama so absurd and so barbarous, there are to be found in *Hamlet*, by a *bizarrerie* still greater, some sublime passages, worthy of the greatest genius. It seems as though nature had mingled in the brain of Shakespeare the greatest conceivable strength and grandeur with whatsoever witless vulgarity can devise that is lowest and most detestable.

(from 'Dissertation sur la Tragédie', in *Semiramis*, 1748)

SAMUEL JOHNSON

IF the dramas of *Shakespeare* were to be characterised, each by the particular excellence which distinguishes it from the rest, we must allow to the tragedy of *Hamlet* the praise of variety. The incidents are so numerous, that the argument of the play would make a long tale. The scenes are interchangeably diversified with merriment and solemnity; with merriment that includes judicious and instructive observations, and solemnity, not strained by poetical violence above the natural sentiments of man. New characters appear from time to time in continual succession, exhibiting various forms of life and particular modes of conversation. The pretended madness of *Hamlet* causes much mirth, the mournful distraction of *Ophelia* fills the heart with tenderness, and every personage produces the effect intended, from the apparition that in the first act chills the blood with horror, to the fop in the last, that exposes affectation to just contempt.

The conduct is perhaps not wholly secure against objections. The action is indeed for the most part in continual progression, but there are some scenes which neither forward nor retard it. Of the feigned madness of *Hamlet* there appears no adequate cause, for he does nothing which he might not have done with the reputation of sanity. He plays the madman most, when he treats *Ophelia* with so much rudeness, which seems to be useless and wanton cruelty.

Hamlet is, through the whole play, rather an instrument than an agent. After he has, by the stratagem of the play, convicted the King, he makes no attempt to punish him, and his death is at last effected by an incident which *Hamlet* has no part in producing.

The catastrophe is not very happily produced; the exchange of weapons is rather an expedient of necessity, than a stroke of art. A scheme might easily have been formed, to kill *Hamlet* with the dagger, and *Laertes* with the bowl.

The poet is accused of having shewn little regard to poetical justice, and may be charged with equal neglect of poetical probability. The apparition left the regions of the dead to little purpose; the revenge which he demands is not obtained but by the death of him that was required to take it; and the gratification which would arise from the destruction of an usurper and a murderer, is abated by the untimely death of *Ophelia*, the young, the beautiful, the harmless, and the pious.

(from his edition of Shakespeare's plays, 1765)

HENRY MACKENZIE

THAT gaiety and playfulness of deportment and of conversation, which *Hamlet* sometimes not only assumes, but seems actually disposed to, is, I apprehend, no contradiction to the general tone of melancholy in his character. That sort of melancholy which is the most genuine, as well as the most amiable of any, neither arising from natural sourness of temper, nor prompted by accidental chagrin, but the effect of delicate sensibility, impressed with a sense of sorrow, or a feeling of its own weakness, will, I believe, often be found indulging itself in a sportfulness of external behaviour, amidst the pressure of a sad, or even the anguish of a broken heart. Slighter emotions affect our ordinary discourse; but deep distress, sitting in the secret gloom of the soul, casts not its regard on the common occurrences of life, but suffers them to trick themselves out in the usual garb of indifference, or of gaiety, according to the fashion of the society around it, or the situation in which they chance to arise. The melancholy man feels in himself (if I may be allowed the expression) a sort of double person; one which, covered with the darkness of its imagination, looks not forth into the world, nor takes any concern in vulgar objects or frivolous pursuits; another, which he lends, as it were, to ordinary men, which can accommodate itself to their tempers and manners, and indulge, without feeling any degradation from the indulgence, a smile with the cheerful, and a laugh with the giddy.

The conversation of *Hamlet* with the *Grave-digger* seems to me to be perfectly accounted for under this supposition; and, instead of feeling it counteract the tragic effect of the story, I never see him in that scene, without receiving, from his transient jests with the clown before him, an idea of the deepest melancholy being rooted at his heart. The light point of view in which he places serious and important things, marks the power of that great impression, which swallows up every thing else in his mind, which makes *Cæsar* and *Alexander* so indifferent to him, that he can trace their remains in the plaster of a cottage, or the stopper of a beer-barrel.

(from *The Mirror*, 22 April 1780)

J. W. VON GOETHE

The time is out of joint, O curséd spite,
That ever I was born to set it right!

In these words, I imagine, will be found the key to Hamlet's whole procedure. To me it is clear that Shakspeare meant, in the present case, to represent the effects of a great action laid upon a soul unfit for the performance of it. In this view the whole piece seems to me to be composed. There is an oak-tree planted in a costly jar, which should have borne only pleasant flowers in its bosom; the roots expand, the jar is shivered.

A lovely, pure, noble and most moral nature, without the strength of nerve which forms a hero, sinks beneath a burden which it cannot bear and must not cast away. All duties are holy for him; the present is too hard. Impossibilities have been required of him; not in themselves impossibilities, but such for him. He winds, and turns, and torments himself; he advances and recoils; is ever put in mind, ever puts himself in mind; at last does all but lose his purpose from his thoughts; yet still without recovering his peace of mind.

(from *Wilhelm Meister's Apprenticeship*, 1795–6)

A. W. VON SCHLEGEL

W ITH respect to Hamlet's character: I cannot, as I understand the poet's views, pronounce altogether so favourable a sentence upon it as Goethe does. He is, it is true, of a highly cultivated mind, a prince of royal manners, endowed with the finest sense of propriety, susceptible of noble ambition, and open in the highest degree to an enthusiastic admiration of that excellence in others of which he himself is deficient. He acts the part of madness with unrivalled power, convincing the persons who are sent to examine into his supposed loss of reason, merely by telling them unwelcome truths, and rallying them with the most caustic wit. But in the resolutions which he so often embraces and always leaves unexecuted, his weakness is too apparent: he does himself only justice when he implies that there is no greater dissimilarity than between himself and Hercules. He is not solely impelled by necessity to artifice and dissimulation, he has a natural inclination for crooked ways; he is a hypocrite towards himself; his far-fetched scruples are often mere pretexts to cover his want of determination: thoughts, as he says on a different occasion, which have

> but one part wisdom,
> And ever three parts coward.

He has been chiefly condemned both for his harshness in re-pulsing the love of Ophelia, which he himself had cherished, and for his insensibility at her death. But he is too much overwhelmed with his own sorrow to have any compassion to spare for others.

(from *Dramatic Art and Literature*, 1809–11)

CHARLES LAMB

T H E character of Hamlet is perhaps that by which, since the days of Betterton, a succession of popular performers have had the greatest ambition to distinguish themselves. The length of the part may be one of their reasons. But for the character itself, we find it in a play, and therefore we judge it a fit subject of dramatic representation. The play itself abounds in maxims and reflexions beyond any other, and therefore we consider it as a proper vehicle for conveying moral instruction. But Hamlet himself – what does he suffer meanwhile by being dragged forth as a public school-master, to give lectures to the crowd! Why, nine parts in ten of what Hamlet does, are transactions between himself and his moral sense, they are the effusions of his solitary musings, which he retires to holes and corners and the most sequestered parts of the palace to pour forth; or rather, they are the silent meditations with which his bosom is bursting, reduced to *words* for the sake of the reader, who must else remain ignorant of what is passing there. These profound sorrows, these light-and-noise-abhorring ruminations, which the tongue scarce dares utter to deaf walls and chambers, how can they be represented by a gesticulating actor, who comes and mouths them out before an audience, making four hundred people his confidants at once? I say not that it is the fault of the actor so to do; he must pronounce them *ore rotundo*, he must accompany them with his eye, he must insinuate them into his auditory by some trick of eye, tone, or gesture, or he fails. *He must be thinking all the while of his appearance, because he knows that all the while the spectators are judging of it.* And this is the way to represent the shy, negligent, retiring Hamlet.

(from 'On the Tragedies of Shakspeare', in *The Reflector*, 1811)

WILLIAM HAZLITT

HAMLET is a name; his speeches and sayings but the idle coinage of the poet's brain. What then, are they not real? They are as real as our own thoughts. Their reality is in the reader's mind. It is *we* who are Hamlet. This play has a prophetic truth, which is above that of history. Whoever has become thoughtful and melancholy through his own mishaps or those of others; whoever has borne about with him the clouded brow of reflection, and thought himself 'too much i' th' sun'; whoever has seen the golden lamp of day dimmed by envious mists rising in his own breast, and could find in the world before him only a dull blank with nothing left remarkable in it; whoever has known 'the pangs of despised love, the insolence of office, or the spurns which patient merit of the unworthy takes'; he who has felt his mind sink within him, and sadness cling to his heart like a malady, who has had his hopes blighted and his youth staggered by the apparitions of strange things; who cannot be well at ease, while he sees evil hovering near him like a spectre; whose powers of action have been eaten up by thought, he to whom the universe seems infinite, and himself nothing; whose bitterness of soul makes him careless of consequences, and who goes to a play as his best resource to shove off, to a second remove, the evils of life by a mock representation of them – this is the true Hamlet. . . .

He is the prince of philosophical speculators; and because he cannot have his revenge perfect, according to the most refined idea his wish can form, he declines it altogether. So he scruples to trust the suggestions of the ghost, contrives the scene of the play to have surer proof of his uncle's guilt, and then rests satisfied with this confirmation of his suspicions, and the success of his experiment, instead of acting upon it. Yet he is sensible of his own weakness, taxes himself with it, and tries to reason himself out of it. . . .

Still he does nothing; and this very speculation on his own infirmity only affords him another occasion for indulging it. It is not from any want of attachment to his father or of abhorrence of his murder that Hamlet is thus dilatory, but it is more to his taste to indulge his imagination in reflecting upon the enormity of the crime and refining on his schemes of vengeance, than to put them into immediate practice. His ruling passion is to think, not to act: and any vague pretext that flatters this propensity instantly diverts him from his previous purposes.

We do not like to see our author's plays acted, and least of all, *Hamlet*. There is no play that suffers so much in being transferred to the stage. Hamlet himself seems hardly capable of being acted. Mr. Kemble unavoidably fails in this character from a want of ease and variety. The character of Hamlet is made up of undulating lines; it has the yielding flexibility of 'a wave o' th' sea'. Mr. Kemble plays it like a man in armour, with a determined inveteracy of purpose, in one undeviating straight line, which is as remote from the natural grace and refined susceptibility of the character, as the sharp angles and abrupt starts which Mr. Kean introduces into the part. Mr. Kean's Hamlet is as much too splenetic and rash as Mr. Kemble's is too deliberate and formal. His manner is too strong and pointed. He throws a severity, approaching to virulence, into the common observations and answers. There is nothing of this in Hamlet. He is, as it were, wrapped up in his reflections, and only *thinks aloud*. There should therefore be no attempt to impress what he says upon others by a studied exaggeration of emphasis or manner; no *talking at* his hearers. There should be as much of the gentleman and scholar as possible infused into the part, and as little of the actor. A pensive air of sadness should sit reluctantly upon his brow, but no appearance of fixed and sullen gloom. He is full of weakness and melancholy, but there is no harshness in his nature. He is the most amiable of misanthropes.

(from *Characters of Shakespear's Plays*, 1817)

S. T. COLERIDGE

In Hamlet he seems to have wished to exemplify the moral necessity of a due balance between our attention to the objects of our senses, and our meditation on the workings of our minds, – an *equilibrium* between the real and the imaginary worlds. In Hamlet this balance is disturbed: his thoughts, and the images of his fancy, are far more vivid than his actual perceptions, and his very perceptions, instantly passing through the *medium* of his contemplations, acquire, as they pass, a form and a colour not naturally their own. Hence we see a great, an almost enormous, intellectual activity, and a proportionate aversion to real action, consequent upon it, with all its symptoms and accompanying qualities. This character Shakspeare places in circumstances, under which it is obliged to act on the spur of the moment: – Hamlet is brave and careless of death; but he vacillates from sensibility, and procrastinates from thought, and loses the power of action in the energy of resolve. Thus it is that this tragedy presents a direct contrast to that of Macbeth; the one proceeds with the utmost slowness, the other with a crowded and breathless rapidity.

The effect of this overbalance of the imaginative power is

beautifully illustrated in the everlasting broodings and superfluous activities of Hamlet's mind, which, unseated from its
healthy relation, is constantly occupied with the world within,
and abstracted from the world without, – giving substance to
shadows, and throwing a mist over all commonplace actualities.

(from *Lectures*, 1818)

HAMLET'S character is the prevalence of the abstracting and
generalizing habit over the practical. He does not want courage,
skill, will, or opportunity; but every incident sets him thinking;
and it is curious, and, at the same time strictly natural, that
Hamlet, who all the play seems reason itself, should be impelled,
at last, by mere accident to effect his object. I have a smack of
Hamlet myself, if I may say so.

A maxim is a conclusion upon observation of matters of fact,
and is merely retrospective: an Idea, or, if you like, a Principle,
carries knowledge within itself, and is prospective. Polonius is a
man of maxims. Whilst he is descanting on matters of past
experience, as in that excellent speech to Laertes before he sets
out on his travels, he is admirable; but when he comes to advise
or project, he is a mere dotard. You see, Hamlet, as the man of
ideas, despises him.

A man of maxims only is like a Cyclops with one eye, and that
eye placed in the back of his head.

(from *Table Talk*, 24 June 1827)

HARTLEY COLERIDGE

LET us, for a moment, put Shakspeare out of the question, and
consider Hamlet as a real person, a recently deceased acquaintance. In real life, it is no unusual thing to meet with characters
every whit as obscure as that of the Prince of Denmark; men
seemingly accomplished for the greatest actions, clear in thought,
and dauntless in deed, still meditating mighty works, and urged
by all motives and occasions to the performance, – whose
existence is nevertheless an unperforming dream; men of noblest,

warmest affections, who are perpetually wringing the hearts of those whom they love best; whose sense of rectitude is strong and wise enough to inform and govern a world, while their acts are the hapless issues of casualty and passion, and scarce to themselves appear their own. We cannot conclude that all such have seen ghosts; though the existence of ghost-seers is as certain, as that of ghosts is problematical. But they will generally be found, either by a course of study and meditation too remote from the art and practice of life, – by designs too pure and perfect to be executed in earthly materials, – or from imperfect glimpses of an intuition beyond the defined limits of communicable knowledge, to have severed themselves from the common society of human feelings and opinions, and become as it were ghosts in the body. Such a man is Hamlet; an habitual dweller with his own thoughts, – preferring the possible to the real, – refining on the ideal forms of things, till the things themselves become dim in his sight, and all the common doings and sufferings, the obligations and engagements of the world, a weary task, stale and unprofitable. By natural temperament he is more a thinker than a doer. His abstract intellect is an overbalance for his active impulses. The death of his father, his mother's marriage, and his own exclusion from the succession, – sorrow for one parent, shame for another, and resentment for himself, – tend still further to confirm and darken a disposition, which the light heart of happy youth had hitherto counteracted. Sorrow contracts around his soul, and shuts it out from cheerful light, and wholesome air.

(from *Blackwood's Edinburgh Magazine*, November 1828)

MATTHEW ARNOLD

I INTENDED to delineate the feelings of one of the last of the Greek religious philosophers, one of the family of Orpheus and Musaeus, having survived his fellows, living on into a time when the habits of Greek thought and feeling had begun fast to change, character to dwindle, the influence of the Sophists to prevail. Into the feelings of a man so situated there entered much that we are accustomed to consider as exclusively modern; how much, the fragments of Empedocles himself which remain to us are sufficient at least to indicate. What those who are familiar only with the great monuments of early Greek genius suppose to be its · exclusive characteristics, have disappeared; the calm, the cheerfulness, the disinterested objectivity have disappeared: the dialogue of' the mind with itself has commenced; modern problems have presented themselves; we hear already the doubts, we witness the discouragement, of Hamlet and of Faust.

(from Preface to *Poems*, 1853)

G. H. LEWES

Hamlet, in spite of a prejudice current in certain circles that if now produced for the first time it would fail, is the most popular play in our language. It *amuses* thousands annually, and it stimulates the minds of millions. Performed in barns and minor theatres oftener than in Theatres Royal, it is always and everywhere attractive. The lowest and most ignorant audiences delight in it. The source of the delight is twofold: First, its reach of thought on topics the most profound; for the dullest soul can *feel* a grandeur which it cannot *understand*, and will listen with hushed awe to the out-pourings of a great meditative mind obstinately questioning fate; Secondly, its wondrous dramatic variety. Only consider for a moment the striking effects it has in the Ghost; the tyrant murderer; the terrible adulterous queen; the melancholy hero, doomed to so awful a fate; the poor Ophelia, broken-hearted and dying in madness; the play within a play, entrapping the conscience of the King; the ghastly mirth of the gravediggers; the funeral of Ophelia interrupted by a quarrel over her grave betwixt her brother and her lover; and, finally, the horrid bloody dénouement. Such are the figures woven in the tapestry by passion and poetry. Add thereto the absorbing fascination of profound thoughts. It may indeed be called the tragedy of thought, for there is as much reflection as action in it; but the reflection itself is made dramatic, and hurries the breathless audience along, with an interest which knows no pause. Strange it is to notice in this work the indissoluble union of refinement with horrors, of reflection with tumult, of high and delicate poetry with broad, palpable, theatrical effects. The machinery is a machinery of horrors, physical and mental: ghostly apparitions – hideous revelations of incestuous adultery and murder – madness – Polonius killed like a rat while listening behind the arras – gravediggers casting skulls upon the stage and desecrating the churchyard with their mirth – these and other horrors form the machinery by which moves the highest, the grandest, and the most philosophic of tragedies.

(from *Life and Works of Goethe*, 1855)

H. A. TAINE

THIS heated imagination, which explains Hamlet's nervous disease and his moral poisoning, explains also his conduct. If he hesitates to kill his uncle, it is not from horror of blood or from our modern scruples. He belongs to the sixteenth century. On board ship he wrote the order to behead Rosencrantz and Guildenstern, and to do so without giving them 'shriving-time'. He killed Polonius, he caused Ophelia's death, and has no great remorse for it. If for once he spared his uncle, it was because he found him praying, and was afraid of sending him to heaven. He thought he was killing him, when he killed Polonius. What his imagination robs him of, is the coolness and strength to go quietly and with premeditation to plunge a sword into a breast. He can only do the thing on a sudden suggestion; he must have a moment of enthusiasm; he must think the king is behind the arras, or else, seeing that he himself is poisoned, he must find his victim under his foil's point. He is not master of his acts; occasion dictates them; he cannot plan a murder, but must improvise it. A too lively imagination exhausts energy, by the accumulation of images and by the fury of intentness which absorbs it. You recognise in him a poet's soul, made not to act, but to dream, which is lost in contemplating the phantoms of its creation, which sees the imaginary world too clearly to play a part in the real world; an artist whom evil chance has made a prince, whom worse chance has made an avenger of crime, and who, destined by nature for genius, is condemned by fortune to madness and unhappiness. Hamlet is Shakespeare.

(from *History of English Literature*, 1863–4)

EDWARD DOWDEN

WHEN *Hamlet* was written Shakspere had passed through his years of apprenticeship, and become a master-dramatist. In point of style the play stands midway between his early and his latest works. The studious superintendence of the poet over the development of his thought and imaginings, very apparent in Shakspere's early writings, now conceals itself; but the action of imagination and thought has not yet become embarrassing in its swiftness and multiplicity of direction. Rapid dialogue in verse, admirable for its combination of verisimilitude with artistic metrical effects occurs in the scene in which Hamlet questions his friends respecting the appearance of the ghost (I ii); the soliloquies of Hamlet are excellent examples of the slow, dwelling verse which Shakspere appropriates to the utterance of thought in solitude; and nowhere did Shakspere write a nobler piece of prose than the speech in which Hamlet describes to Rosencrantz and Guildenstern his melancholy. But such particulars as these do not constitute the chief evidence which proves that the poet had now attained maturity. The mystery, the baffling, vital obscurity of the play, and in particular of the character of its chief person, make it evident that Shakspere had left far behind him that early stage of development when an artist obtrudes his intentions, or distrusting his own ability to keep sight of one uniform design, deliberately and with effort holds that design persistently before him. When Shakspere completed *Hamlet* he must have trusted himself and trusted his audience; he trusts himself to enter into relation with his subject, highly complex as that subject was, in a pure, emotional manner. *Hamlet* might so easily have been manufactured into an enigma, or a puzzle; and then the puzzle, if sufficient pains were bestowed, could be completely taken to pieces and explained. But Shakspere created it a mystery, and therefore it is for ever suggestive; for ever suggestive, and never wholly explicable.

(from *Shakspere: A Critical Study of his Mind and Art*, 1875)

A. C. SWINBURNE

I TRUST it will be taken as no breach of my past pledge to abstain from all intrusion on the sacred ground of Gigadibs and the Germans, if I venture to indicate a touch inserted by Shakespeare for no other perceptible or conceivable purpose than to obviate by anticipation the indomitable and ineradicable fallacy of criticism which would find the keynote of Hamlet's character in the quality of irresolution. I may observe at once that the misconception involved in such a reading of the riddle ought to have been evident even without this episodical stroke of illustration. In any case it should be plain to any reader that the signal characteristic of Hamlet's inmost nature is by no means irresolution or hesitation or any form of weakness, but rather the strong conflux of contending forces. That during four whole acts Hamlet cannot or does not make up his mind to any direct and deliberate action against his uncle is true enough; true, also, we may say, that Hamlet had somewhat more of mind than another man to make up, and might properly want somewhat more time than might another man to do it in; but not, I venture to say in spite of Goethe, through innate inadequacy to his task and unconquerable weakness of the will; not, I venture to think in spite of Hugo, through immedicable scepticism of the spirit and irremediable propensity to nebulous intellectual refinement. One practical point in the action of the play precludes us from accepting so ready a solution of the riddle as is suggested either by the simple theory of half-heartedness or by the simple hypothesis of doubt. There is absolutely no other reason, we might say there was no other excuse, for the introduction or intrusion of an else superfluous episode into a play which was already, and which remains even after all possible excisions, one of the longest plays on record. The compulsory expedition of Hamlet to England, his discovery by the way of the plot laid against his life, his interception of the King's letter and his forgery of a substitute for it against the lives of the King's agents, the ensuing adventure of the sea-fight, with Hamlet's daring act of hot-headed personal intrepidity, his capture and subsequent release on terms giving no less patent proof of his cool-headed and ready-witted courage and resource than the attack had afforded of his physically impulsive and even impetuous hardihood – all this serves no purpose whatever but that of exhibiting the instant and almost unscrupulous resolution of Hamlet's character in time of practical need. But for all that he or Hamlet has got by it, Shakespeare might too evidently have spared his pains; and for all this voice as of one crying in a wilderness, Hamlet will too surely remain to the majority of students, not less than to all actors and all editors and all critics, the standing type and embodied emblem of irresolution, half-heartedness, and doubt.

That Hamlet should seem at times to accept for himself, and even to enforce by reiteration of argument upon his conscience and his reason, some such conviction or suspicion as to his own character, tells much rather in disfavour than in favour of its truth. A man whose natural temptation was to swerve, whose inborn inclination was to shrink and skulk aside from duty and from action, would hardly be the first and last person to suspect his own weakness, the one only unbiassed judge and witness of sufficiently sharp-sighted candour and accuracy to estimate aright his poverty of nature and the malformation of his mind. But the high-hearted and tender-conscienced Hamlet, with his native bias towards introspection intensified and inflamed and directed and dilated at once by one imperative pressure and oppression of unavoidable and unalterable circumstance, was assuredly and exactly the one only man to be troubled by any momentary fear that such might indeed be the solution of his riddle, and to feel or to fancy for the moment some kind of ease

and relief in the sense of that very trouble. A born doubter
would have doubted even of Horatio; hardly can all positive and
almost palpable evidence of underhand instigation and inspired
good intentions induce Hamlet for some time to doubt even of
Ophelia.

(from *A Study of Shakespeare*, 1880)

A. C. BRADLEY

LET me try to show now, briefly, how much this melancholy
accounts for.

It accounts for the main fact, Hamlet's inaction. For the
immediate cause of that is simply that his habitual feeling is one
of disgust at life and everything in it, himself included, – a
disgust which varies in intensity, rising at times into a longing
for death, sinking often into weary apathy, but is never dispelled
for more than brief intervals. Such a state of feeling is inevitably
adverse to *any* kind of decided action; the body is inert, the mind
indifferent or worse; its response is, 'it does not matter', 'it is not
worth while', 'it is no good'. And the action required of Hamlet
is very exceptional. It is violent, dangerous, difficult to accomplish perfectly, on one side repulsive to a man of honour and
sensitive feeling, on another side involved in a certain mystery
(here come in thus, in their subordinate place, various causes of
inaction assigned by various theories). These obstacles would
not suffice to prevent Hamlet from acting, if his state were
normal; and against them there operate, even in his morbid state,
healthy and positive feelings, love of his father, loathing of his
uncle, desire of revenge, desire to do duty. But the retarding
motives acquire an unnatural strength because they have an ally
in something far stronger than themselves, the melancholic
disgust and apathy; while the healthy motives, emerging with
difficulty from the central mass of diseased feeling, rapidly sink
back into it and 'lose the name of action'. We *see* them doing so;
and sometimes the process is quite simple, no analytical reflection
on the deed intervening between the outburst of passion and the

relapse into melancholy. But this melancholy is perfectly consistent also with that incessant dissection of the task assigned, of which the Schlegel–Coleridge theory makes so much. For those endless questions (as we may imagine them), 'Was I deceived by the Ghost? How am I to do the deed? When? Where? What will be the consequence of attempting it – success, my death, utter misunderstanding, mere mischief to the State? Can it be right to do it, or noble to kill a defenceless man? What is the good of doing it in such a world as this?' – all this, and whatever else passed in a sickening round through Hamlet's mind, was not the healthy and right deliberation of a man with such a task, but otiose thinking hardly deserving the name of thought, an unconscious weaving of pretexts for inaction, aimless tossings on a sick bed, symptoms of melancholy which only increased it by deepening self-contempt.

(from *Shakespearean Tragedy*, 1904)

T. S. ELIOT

THE only way of expressing emotion in the form of art is by finding an 'objective correlative'; in other words, a set of objects, a situation, a chain of events which shall be the formula of that *particular* emotion; such that when the external facts, which must terminate in sensory experience, are given, the emotion is immediately evoked. If you examine any of Shakespeare's more successful tragedies, you will find this exact equivalence; you will find that the state of mind of Lady Macbeth walking in her sleep has been communicated to you by a skilful accumulation of imagined sensory impressions; the words of Macbeth on hearing of his wife's death strike us as if, given the sequence of events, these words were automatically released by the last event in the series. The artistic 'inevitability' lies in this complete adequacy of the external to the emotion; and this is precisely what is deficient in *Hamlet*. Hamlet (the man) is dominated by an emotion which is inexpressible, because it is in *excess* of the facts as they appear. And the supposed identity of Hamlet with his author is genuine to this point: that Hamlet's bafflement at the absence of objective equivalent to his feelings is a prolongation of the bafflement of his creator in the face of his artistic problem. Hamlet is up against the difficulty that his disgust is occasioned by his mother, but that his mother is not an adequate equivalent for it; his disgust envelops and exceeds her. It is thus a feeling which he cannot understand; he cannot objectify it, and it therefore remains to poison life and obstruct action. None of the possible actions can satisfy it; and nothing that Shakespeare can do with the plot can express Hamlet for him. And it must be noticed that the very nature of the *données* of the problem precludes objective equivalence. To have heightened the criminality of Gertrude would have been to provide the formula for a totally different emotion in Hamlet; it is just *because* her character is so negative and insignificant that she arouses in Hamlet the feeling which she is incapable of representing.

(from 'Hamlet' (1919), *Selected Essays 1917–1932*, 1932)

G. WILSON KNIGHT

CLAUDIUS, as he appears in the play, is not a criminal. He is – strange as it may seem – a good and gentle king, enmeshed by the chain of causality linking him with his crime. And this chain he might, perhaps, have broken except for Hamlet, and all would have been well. But, granted the presence of Hamlet – which Claudius at first genuinely desired, persuading him not to return to Wittenberg as he wished – and granted the fact of his original crime which cannot now be altered, Claudius can hardly be blamed for his later actions. They are forced on him. As King, he could scarcely be expected to do otherwise. Hamlet is a danger to the state, even apart from his knowledge of Claudius' guilt. He is an inhuman – or superhuman – presence, whose consciousness – somewhat like Dostoievsky's Stavrogin – is centred on death. Like Stavrogin, he is feared by those around him. They are always trying in vain to find out what is wrong with him. They cannot understand him. He is a creature of another world. As

King of Denmark he would have been a thousand times more dangerous than Claudius. The end of Claudius' prayer is pathetic:

> What then? what rests?
> Try what repentance can – what can it not?
> Yet what can it, when one can not repent?
> O wretched state! O bosom black as death!
> O liméd soul, that struggling to be free,
> Art more engaged; help, angels! Make assay,
> Bow stubborn knees, and heart, with strings of steel,
> Be soft as sinews of the new-born babe –
> All may be well.   (III iii 64–72)

Set against this lovely prayer – the fine flower of a human soul in anguish – is the entrance of Hamlet, the late joy of torturing the King's conscience still written on his face, his eye a-glitter with the intoxication of conquest, vengeance in his mind; his purpose altered only by the devilish hope of finding a more damning moment in which to slaughter the King, next hastening to his mother to wring her soul too. Which then, at this moment in the play, is nearer the Kingdom of Heaven? Whose words would be more acceptable of Jesus' God? Which is the embodiment of spiritual good, which of evil? The question of the relative morality of Hamlet and Claudius reflects the ultimate problem of this play.

(from *The Wheel of Fire*, 1930)

CAROLINE F. E. SPURGEON

[THE distinctive atmosphere of *Hamlet*] is partly due to the number of images of sickness, disease, or blemish of the body in the play, and . . . the idea of an ulcer or tumour, as descriptive of the unwholesome condition of Denmark morally, is, on the whole, the dominating one.

Hamlet speaks of his mother's sin as a blister on the 'fair forehead of an innocent love', and as in *Lear*, the emotion is so strong and the picture so vivid, that the metaphor overflows into the verbs and adjectives; heaven's face, he tells her, is *thought-sick* at the act; her husband is a *mildewed ear, blasting* his *wholesome* brother, and to have married him her sense must be not only *sickly* but *apoplexed*, and at the end of that terrific scene (III iv) he implores her not to soothe herself with the belief that his father's apparition is due to her son's madness and not to her own guilt, for that

> will but skin and film the ulcerous place,
> Whiles rank corruption mining all within
> Infects unseen.

So also, later, he compares the unnecessary fighting between Norway and Poland to a kind of tumour which grows out of too much prosperity. He sees the country and the people in it alike in terms of a sick body needing medicine or the surgeon's knife. When he surprises Claudius at his prayers, he exclaims

> This physic but prolongs thy sickly days,

and he describes the action of conscience in the unforgettable picture of the healthy, ruddy countenance turning pale with sickness (III i 85). A mote in the eye, a 'vicious mole', a galled chilblain, a probed wound and purgation, are also among Hamlet's images; and the mind of Claudius runs equally on the same theme....

Thus, to Shakespeare's pictorial imagination, the problem in *Hamlet* is not predominantly that of will and reason, of a mind too philosophic or a nature temperamentally unfitted to act quickly; he sees it pictorially, *not as the problem of an individual at all*, but as something greater and even more mysterious, as a *condition* for which the individual himself is apparently not responsible, any more than the sick man is to blame for the cancer which strikes and devours him, but which, nevertheless, in its course and development impartially and relentlessly annihilates him and others, innocent and guilty alike. That is the tragedy of Hamlet, as it is, perhaps, the chief tragic mystery of life.

(from *Leading Motives in the Imagery of Shakespeare's Tragedies*, 1930)

L. L. SCHÜCKING

T H E play is remarkable for its powerful internal movement. The characters are continually changing before our eyes. Hamlet's melancholy, for ever waxing and waning, reaches its crises in varying moods of passionate excitement that alternate with dull brooding, and comes to a climax during the 'fit' at Ophelia's graveside, after which it abates in intensity, giving place to a certain apathy towards the end of the play. The King, at the outset calm and certain of himself, loses something of his self-confidence as his position grows more difficult; in the end he is forced to drop the mask of honesty which he has so long successfully worn, and to appear in all his villainy. The Queen, her peace of mind and untroubled conscience ruthlessly assailed, becomes uneasy, even bitter (IV v 109). We see Laertes falling a victim to the King's wiles – a drama within a drama – and agreeing to act against his better nature, a surrender that, from the psychological point of view, is not altogether convincing. The passive Ophelia treads her terrible path to mental derangement. But such inner movement is not in itself unusual in dramatic art. Here it is the tempo, forced to the uttermost, that is so characteristic. Ophelia, for instance, is not simply grieved at the death of her father; she loses her reason. Laertes does not merely thirst for revenge, but at once becomes a murderer. The character of Hamlet himself is typical of this dramatic technique, in which the intensification of emotion is carried to the verge of 'ecstatic' passion. Never before in Shakespeare's work had the cry of a tortured soul so wrung the hearts of his audience. It would seem that the first principle of this art is that life should be represented, as Shakespeare characteristically makes the 'poet' in *Timon* say, as 'livelier than life'. In other words, emotion is not allowed to take its usual course, but is shown as an overwhelming torrent hurling the human spirit to the very brink of destruction – or beyond. . . . *Hamlet* resembles other great Shakespearian tragedies in that it cannot be comprehended except as a study of passion. The presentation of emotion as the chief aim of the stage had indeed become such a matter of course to Shakespeare that, when Hamlet is giving instructions to the players at the Court of Elsinore, his attention is exclusively directed to this one aspect of theatrical art. Of all that might be said on the subject he singles out 'passion' alone (except for some remarks about the duties of the clown). And 'passion' is certainly not used here in the sense still current in the eighteenth century – that is to say, as a mere equivalent of 'feeling' – because Hamlet speaks of the 'very torrent, tempest ... whirlwind of passion' and warns the players not to 'tear it to tatters, to very rags'. Such vehemence is in accordance with the taste of the Elizabethans, who liked to be 'transported' (one of the favourite expressions of the time was 'ecstacy') and who demanded that art, in moments of intense emotion, should so carry them away that the mind might all but lose mastery over itself, and the 'very faculties of eyes and ears' – as Hamlet on occasion says – be 'amazed', i.e. put in confusion.

(from *The Meaning of Hamlet*, 1935)

J. DOVER WILSON

Hamlet is the greatest of popular dramas, and has held the stage for three centuries just because of that. Yet it is also full of 'necessary points' for which 'barren spectators' had no use but which its creator was most anxious that clowning and overacting should not be permitted to obscure for the judicious. There is, for instance, Hamlet's quibbling, much of it, with double or triple point, beyond the comprehension of even the nimblest-witted among the groundlings. Its existence proves that Shakespeare could count upon a section of the audience at the Globe, nobles, inns-of-court men and the like, capable in swiftness of apprehension and sustained attention of almost any subtlety he cared to put them to, and moreover armed like Hamlet himself with their 'tables' to set down matters which they could not at once understand or wished especially to remember. The quibbles did not worry the prentice-boys, because they, like many modern editors, took them as the nonsensical utterances of a madman; but the longer the judicious pondered them the more they found, though it is doubtful whether anyone even in Shakespeare's day ever got to the bottom of everything Hamlet says. And so too with other matters and with the play as a whole. *Hamlet* is a dramatic essay in mystery; that is to say it is so constructed that the more it is examined the more there is to discover. The character of the Prince is, of course, the central mystery: Shakespeare expressly dared his critics from the first to 'pluck out the heart of' that. But there are points, many points, in the plot also to which the majority of even the original audience probably gave little heed or which they entirely passed over. The main outline is clear enough and sufficed both for them and for their successors down to our own day. But within this framework, binding it together and filling it out with delightful dramatic filigree, lies a whole network of finer effects.

(from *What Happens in Hamlet*, 1935)

HARLEY GRANVILLE-BARKER

THE action of *Hamlet* is concentrated at Elsinore; and this though there is much external interest, and the story abounds in journeys. As a rule in such a case, unless they are mere messengers, we travel with the travellers. But we do not see Laertes in Paris, nor, more surprisingly, Hamlet among the pirates; and the Norwegian affair is dealt with by hearsay till the play is two-thirds over. This is not done to economise time, or to leave space for more capital events. Scenes in Norway or Paris or aboard ship need be no longer than the talk of them, and Hamlet's discovery of the King's plot against him is a capital event. Shakespeare is deliberately concentrating his action at Elsinore. When he does at last introduce Fortinbras he stretches probability to bring him and his army seemingly to its very suburbs; and, sooner than that Hamlet should carry the action abroad with him, Horatio is left behind there to keep him in our minds. On the other hand he still, by allusion, makes the most of this movement abroad which he does not represent; he even adds to our sense of it by such seemingly superfluous touches as tell us that Horatio has journeyed from Wittenberg, that Rosencrantz and Guildenstern have been 'sent for' – and even the Players are travelling.

The double dramatic purpose is plain. Here is a tragedy of inaction; the centre of it is Hamlet, who is physically inactive too, has 'foregone all custom of exercises', will not 'walk out of the air', but only, book in hand, for 'four hours together, here in the lobby'. The concentration at Elsinore of all that happens enhances the impression of this inactivity, which is enhanced again by the sense also given us of the constant coming and going around Hamlet of the busier world without. The place itself, moreover, thus acquires a personality, and even develops a sort of sinister power; so that when at last Hamlet does depart from it (his duty still unfulfilled) and we are left with the conscience-sick Gertrude and the guilty King, the mad Ophelia, a Laertes set on his own revenge, among a

> people muddied,
> Thick and unwholesome in their thoughts and whispers . . .

we almost seem to feel it, and the unpurged sin of it, summoning him back to his duty and his doom.

(from *Prefaces to Shakespeare: Third Series, Hamlet*, 1937)

GEORGE BERNARD SHAW

H E took up an old play about the ghost of a murdered king who haunted his son crying for revenge, with comic relief provided by the son pretending to be that popular curiosity and laughing-stock, a village idiot. Shakespear, transfiguring this into a tragedy on the ancient Athenian level, could not have been quite unconscious of the evolutionary stride he was taking. But he did not see his way clearly enough to save the tons of ink and paper and years of 'man's time' that have been wasted, and are still being wasted, on innumerable volumes of nonsense about the meaning of Hamlet, though it is now as clear as daylight. Hamlet as a prehistoric Dane is morally bound to kill his uncle, politically as rightful heir to the usurped throne, and filially as 'the son of a dear father murdered' and a mother seduced by an incestuous adulterer. He has no doubt as to his duty in the matter. If he can convince himself that the ghost who has told him all this is really his father's spirit and not a lying devil tempting him to perdition, then, he says, 'I know my course'.

But when fully convinced he finds to his bewilderment that he cannot kill his uncle deliberately. In a sudden flash of rage he can and does stab at him through the arras, only to find that he has killed poor old Polonius by mistake. In a later transport, when the unlucky uncle poisons not only Hamlet's mother but his own accomplice and Hamlet himself, Hamlet actually does at last kill his enemy on the spur of the moment; but this is no solution of his problem: it cuts the Gordian knot instead of untying it, and makes the egg stand on end only by breaking it. In the soliloquy beginning 'O, what a rogue and peasant slave am I' Shakespear described this moral bewilderment as a fact (he must have learnt it from his own personal development); but he did not explain it, though the explanation was staring him in the face as it stares in mine. What happened to Hamlet was what had happened fifteen hundred years before to Jesus. Born into the vindictive morality of Moses he has evolved into the Christian perception of the futility and wickedness of revenge and punishment, founded on the simple fact that two blacks do not make a white. But he is not philosopher enough to comprehend this as well as apprehend it. When he finds he cannot kill in cold blood he can only ask 'Am I a coward?' When he cannot nerve himself to recover his throne he can account for it only by saying 'I lack ambition'. Had Shakespear plumbed his play to the bottom he would hardly have allowed Hamlet to send Rosencrantz and Guildenstern to their death by a forged death warrant without a moment's scruple.

(from Postscript (1945) to *Back to Methuselah*, 1921)

PART TWO

Recent Studies

Ernest Jones

HAMLET AND OEDIPUS (1949)

W H A T we are essentially concerned with is the psychological understanding of the dramatic effect produced by Hamlet's personality and behaviour. That effect would be quite other were the central figure in the play to represent merely a 'case of insanity'. When that happens, as with Ophelia, such a person passes beyond our ken, is in a sense no more human, whereas Hamlet successfully claims our interest and sympathy to the very end. Shakespeare certainly never intended us to regard Hamlet as insane, so that the 'mind o'erthrown' must have some other meaning than its literal one. Robert Bridges[1] has described the matter with exquisite delicacy:

> Hamlet himself would never have been aught to us, or we
> To Hamlet, wer't not for the artful balance whereby
> Shakespeare so gingerly put his sanity in doubt
> Without the while confounding his Reason.

I would suggest that in this Shakespeare's extraordinary powers of observation and penetration granted him a degree of insight that it has taken the world three subsequent centuries to reach. Until our generation (and even now in the juristic sphere) a dividing line separated the sane and responsible from the irresponsible insane. It is now becoming more and more widely recognized that much of mankind lives in an intermediate and unhappy state charged with what Dover Wilson[2] well calls 'that sense of frustration, futility and human inadequacy which is the burden of the whole symphony' and of which Hamlet is the supreme example in literature. This intermediate plight, in the toils of which perhaps the greater part of mankind struggles and suffers, is given the name of psychoneurosis, and long ago the genius of Shakespeare depicted it for us with faultless insight.

Extensive studies of the past half century, inspired by Freud, have taught us that a psychoneurosis means a state of mind where the person is unduly, and often painfully, driven or thwarted by the 'unconscious' part of his mind, that buried part that was once the infant's mind and still lives on side by side with the adult mentality that has developed out of it and should have taken its place. It signifies *internal* mental conflict. We have here the reason why it is impossible to discuss intelligently the state of mind of anyone suffering from a psychoneurosis, whether the description is of a living person or an imagined one, without correlating the manifestations with what must have operated in his infancy and is *still operating*. That is what I propose to attempt here.

For some deep-seated reason, which is to him unacceptable, Hamlet is plunged into anguish at the thought of his father being replaced in his mother's affections by someone else. It is as if his devotion to his mother had made him so jealous for her affection that he had found it hard enough to share this even with his father and could not endure to share it with still another man. Against this thought, however, suggestive as it is, may be urged three objections. First, if it were in itself a full statement of the matter, Hamlet would have been aware of the jealousy, whereas we have concluded that the mental process we are seeking is hidden from him. Secondly, we see in it no evidence of the arousing of an old and forgotten memory. And, thirdly, Hamlet is being deprived by Claudius of no greater share in the Queen's affection than he had been by his own father, for the two brothers made exactly similar claims in this respect – namely, those of a loved husband. The last-named objection, however, leads us to the heart of the situation. How if, in fact, Hamlet had in years gone by, as a child, bitterly resented having had to share his mother's affection even with his own father, had regarded him as a rival, and had secretly wished him out of the way so that he might enjoy undisputed and undisturbed the monopoly of that affection? If such thoughts had been present in his mind in childhood days they evidently would have been 'repressed', and all traces of them obliterated, by filial piety and other educative influences. The actual realization of his early wish in the death of his father at the hands of a jealous rival would then have stimulated into activity these 'repressed' memories, which would have produced, in the form of depression and other suffering, an obscure aftermath of his childhood's conflict. This is at all events the mechanism that is actually found in the real Hamlets who are investigated psychologically.[3]

The explanation, therefore, of the delay and self-frustration exhibited in the endeavour to fulfil his father's demand for vengeance is that to Hamlet the thought of incest and parricide combined is too intolerable to be borne. One part of him tries to carry out the task, the other flinches inexorably from the thought of it. How fain would he blot it out in that 'bestial oblivion' which unfortunately for him his conscience contemns. He is torn and tortured in an insoluble inner conflict. . . .

As a child Hamlet had experienced the warmest affection for his mother, and this, as is always so, had contained elements of a disguised erotic quality, still more so in infancy. The presence of two traits in the Queen's character accord with this assumption, namely her markedly sensual nature and her passionate fondness for her son. The former is indicated in too many places in the play to need specific reference, and is generally recognized. The latter is also manifest: Claudius says, for instance (IV vii), 'The queen his mother Lives almost by his looks'. Nevertheless Hamlet appears to have with more or less success weaned himself from her and to have fallen in love with Ophelia. The precise nature of his original feeling for Ophelia is a little obscure. We may assume that at least in part it was composed of a normal love for a prospective bride, though the extravagance of the language used (the passionate need for absolute certainty, etc.) suggests a somewhat morbid frame of mind. There are indications that even here the influence of the old attraction for the mother is still exerting itself. Although some writers,[4] following Goethe,[5] see in Ophelia many traits of resemblance to the Queen, perhaps just as striking are the traits contrasting with those of the Queen. Whatever truth there may be in the many German conceptions of Ophelia as a sensual wanton – misconceptions that have been

questioned by Loening and others – still the very fact that it
needed what Goethe happily called the 'innocence of insanity'
to reveal the presence of any such libidinous thoughts demon-
strates in itself the modesty and chasteness of her habitual de-
meanour. Her naïve piety, her obedient resignation, and her
unreflecting simplicity sharply contrast with the Queen's
character, and seem to indicate that Hamlet by a characteristic
reaction towards the opposite extreme had unknowingly been
impelled to choose a woman who should least remind him of his
mother. A case might even be made out for the view that part of
his courtship originated not so much in direct attraction for
Ophelia as in an unconscious desire to play her off against his
mother, just as a disappointed and piqued lover so often has
resort to the arms of a more willing rival. It would not be easy
otherwise to understand the readiness with which he later throws
himself into this part. When, for instance, in the play scene he
replies to his mother's request to sit by her with the words 'No,
good mother, here's metal more attractive' and proceeds to lie at
Ophelia's feet, we seem to have a direct indication of this attitude;
and his coarse familiarity and bandying of ambiguous jests with
the woman he has recently so ruthlessly jilted are hardly intelli-
gible unless we bear in mind that they were carried out under the
heedful gaze of the Queen. It is as if his unconscious were trying
to convey to her the following thought: 'You give yourself to
other men whom you prefer to me. Let me assure you that I can
dispense with your favours and even prefer those of a woman
whom I no longer love.' His extraordinary outburst of bawdiness
on this occasion, so unexpected in a man of obviously fine
feeling, points unequivocally to the sexual nature of the underlying turmoil.

   Now comes the father's death and the mother's second marriage. The association of the idea of sexuality with his mother,
buried since infancy, can no longer be concealed from his
consciousness. As Bradley[6] well says: 'Her son was forced to see
in her action not only an astounding shallowness of feeling, but
an eruption of coarse sensuality, "rank and gross", speeding
post-haste to its horrible delight'. Feelings which once, in the

infancy of long ago, were pleasurable desires can now, because of his repressions, only fill him with repulsion. The long 'repressed' desire to take his father's place in his mother's affection is stimulated to unconscious activity by the sight of someone usurping this place exactly as he himself had once longed to do. More, this someone was a member of the same family, so that the actual usurpation further resembled the imaginary one in being incestuous. Without his being in the least aware of it these ancient desires are ringing in his mind, are once more struggling to find conscious expression, and need such an expenditure of energy again to 'repress' them that he is reduced to the deplorable mental state he himself so vividly depicts.

There follows the Ghost's announcement that the father's death was a willed one, was due to murder. Hamlet, having at the moment his mind filled with natural indignation at the news, answers normally enough with the cry (i v):

> Haste me to know 't, that I with wings as swift
> As meditation or the thoughts of love,
> May sweep to my revenge.

The momentous words follow revealing who was the guilty person, namely a relative who had committed the deed at the bidding of lust.* Hamlet's second guilty wish had thus also been realized by his uncle, namely to procure the fulfilment of the first – the possession of the mother – by a personal deed, in fact by murder of the father. The two recent events, the father's death and the mother's second marriage, seemed to the world to have no inner causal relation to each other, but they represented ideas which in Hamlet's unconscious fantasy had always been closely associated. These ideas now in a moment forced their way to conscious recognition in spite of all 'repressing forces', and found immediate expression in his almost reflex cry: 'O, my prophetic soul! My uncle?' The frightful truth his unconscious had already intuitively divined, his consciousness had now to assimilate as

* It is not maintained that this was by any means Claudius' whole motive, but it was evidently a powerful one and the one that most impressed Hamlet.

best it could. For the rest of the interview Hamlet is stunned by the effect of the internal conflict thus re-awakened, which from now on never ceases, and into the essential nature of which he never penetrates.

One of the first manifestations of the awakening of the old conflict in Hamlet's mind is his reaction against Ophelia. This is doubly conditioned by the two opposing attitudes in his own mind. In the first place, there is a complex reaction in regard to his mother. As was explained above, the being forced to connect the thought of his mother with sensuality leads to an intense sexual revulsion, one that is only temporarily broken down by the coarse outburst discussed above. Combined with this is a fierce jealousy, unconscious because of its forbidden origin, at the sight of her giving herself to another man, a man whom he had no reason whatever either to love or to respect. Consciously this is allowed to express itself, for instance after the prayer scene, only in the form of extreme resentment and bitter reproaches against her. His resentment against women is still further inflamed by the hypocritical prudishness with which Ophelia follows her father and brother in seeing evil in his natural affection, an attitude which poisons his love in exactly the same way that the love of his childhood, like that of all children, must have been poisoned. He can forgive a woman neither her rejection of his sexual advances nor, still less, her alliance with another man. Most intolerable of all to him, as Bradley well remarks, is the sight of sensuality in a quarter from which he had trained himself ever since infancy rigorously to exclude it. The total reaction culminates in the bitter misogyny of his outburst against Ophelia, who is devastated at having to bear a reaction so wholly out of proportion to her own offence and has no idea that in reviling her Hamlet is really expressing his bitter resentment against his mother.* 'I

---

* His similar tone and advice to the two women show plainly how closely they are identified in his mind. Cf. 'Get thee to a nunnery, why wouldst thou be a breeder of sinners?' (III i) with 'Refrain to-night, And that shall lend a kind of easiness To the next abstinence' (III iv). The identification is further demonstrated in the course of the play by Hamlet's killing the men who stand between him and these women (Claudius and Polonius).

have heard of your paintings too, well enough. God hath given you one face and you make yourselves another, you jig, you amble, and you lisp, and nickname God's creatures, and make your wantonness your ignorance; go to, I'll no more on 't, it hath made me mad' (III i). On only one occasion does he for a moment escape from the sordid implication with which his love has been impregnated and achieve a healthier attitude towards Ophelia, namely at the open grave when in remorse he breaks out at Laertes for presuming to pretend that his feeling for her could ever equal that of her lover. Even here, however, as Dover Wilson[7] has suggested, the remorse behind his exaggerated behaviour springs not so much from grief at Ophelia's death as from his distress at his bad conscience that had killed his love – he acts the lover he fain would have been.

Hamlet's attitude towards Ophelia is still more complex. Dover Wilson[8] has adduced good evidence for thinking that Hamlet is supposed to have overheard the intrigue in which Polonius 'looses' his daughter to test her erstwhile lover, a suggestion which had previously been made by Quincy Adams.[9] This is probably an echo of the old (Saxo) saga in which the girl is employed by the king to test his capacity for sexual love and so decide whether he is an imbecile or a cunning enemy. It certainly helps to explain the violence with which he attacks her feminine charms and treats her worse than a paid prostitute. He feels she is sent to lure him on and then, like his mother, to betray him at the behest of another man. The words 'Get thee to a nunnery'* thus have a more sinister connotation, for in Elizabethan, and indeed in later, times this was also a term for a brothel; the name 'Covent Garden' will elucidate the point to any student of the history of London.

The underlying theme relates ultimately to the splitting of the mother image which the infantile unconscious effects into two opposite pictures: one of a virginal Madonna, an inaccessible saint

* This exhortation (with its usual connotation of chastity) may be equated with the one addressed later to his mother, 'Go not to my uncle's bed', indicating Hamlet's identification of the two women in his feelings.

towards whom all sensual approaches are unthinkable, and the other of a sensual creature accessible to everyone. Indications of this dichotomy between love and lust (Titian's 'Sacred and Profane Love') are to be found later in most men's sexual experiences. When sexual repression is highly pronounced, as with Hamlet, then both types of women are felt to be hostile: the pure one out of resentment at her repulses, the sensual one out of the temptation she offers to plunge into guiltiness. Misogyny, as in the play, is the inevitable result.

The intensity of Hamlet's repulsion against woman in general, and Ophelia in particular, is a measure of the powerful 'repression' to which his sexual feelings are being subjected. The outlet for those feelings in the direction of his mother has always been firmly dammed, and now that the narrower channel in Ophelia's direction has also been closed the increase in the original direction consequent on the awakening of early memories tasks all his energy to maintain the 'repression'. His pent-up feelings find a partial vent in other directions. The petulant irascibility and explosive outbursts called forth by his vexation at the hands of Guildenstern and Rosencrantz, and especially of Polonius, are evidently to be interpreted in this way, as also is in part the burning nature of his reproaches to his mother. Indeed, towards the end of his interview with his mother the thought of her misconduct expresses itself in that almost physical disgust which is so characteristic a manifestation of intensely 'repressed' sexual feeling.

> Let the bloat king tempt you again to bed,
> Pinch wanton on your cheek, call you his mouse,
> And let him for a pair of reechy kisses,
> Or paddling in your neck with his damned fingers,
> Make you to ravel all this matter out.   (III iv)

Hamlet's attitude towards Polonius is highly instructive. Here the absence of family tie and of other similar influences enables him to indulge to a relatively unrestrained extent his hostility towards what he regards as a prating and sententious dotard.* The analogy he effects between Polonius and Jephthah† is in this connection especially pointed. It is here that we see his fundamental attitude towards moralizing elders who use their power to thwart the happiness of the young, and not in the over-drawn and melodramatic portrait in which he delineates his father: 'A combination and a form indeed, Where every god did seem to set his seal To give the world assurance of a man'.

It will be seen from the foregoing that Hamlet's attitude towards his uncle-father is far more complex than is generally supposed. He of course detests him, but it is the jealous detestation of one evil-doer towards his successful fellow. Much as he hates him, he can never denounce him with the ardent indignation that boils straight from his blood when he reproaches his mother, for the more vigorously he denounces his uncle the more powerfully does he stimulate to activity his own unconscious and 'repressed' complexes. He is therefore in a dilemma between on the one hand allowing his natural detestation of his uncle to have free play, a consummation which would stir still further his own horrible wishes, and on the other hand ignoring the imperative call for the vengeance that his obvious duty demands. His own 'evil' prevents him from completely denouncing his uncle's, and in continuing to 'repress' the former he must strive to ignore, to condone, and if possible even to forget the latter; *his moral fate is bound up with his uncle's for good or ill.* In reality his uncle incorporates the deepest and most buried part of his own personality, so that he cannot kill him without also killing himself. This solution, one closely akin to what Freud[10] has shown

* It is noteworthy how many producers and actors seem to accept Hamlet's distorted estimate of Polonius, his garrulity being presumably an excuse for overlooking the shrewdness and soundness of his worldly wisdom. After all, his diagnosis of Hamlet's madness as being due to unrequited love for Ophelia was not so far from the mark, and he certainly recognized that his distressful condition was of sexual origin.

† What Shakespeare thought of Jephthah's behaviour towards his daughter may be gathered from a reference in *3 Henry VI*, v i. See also on this subject Charles Wordsworth, *On Shakespeare's Knowledge and Use of the Bible* (1864) p. 67.

to be the motive of suicide in melancholia, is actually the one that Hamlet finally adopts. The course of alternate action and inaction that he embarks on, and the provocations he gives to his suspicious uncle, can lead to no other end than to his own ruin and, incidentally, to that of his uncle. Only when he has made the final sacrifice and brought himself to the door of death is he free to fulfil his duty, to avenge his father, and to slay his other self – his uncle.

There are two moments in the play when he is nearest to murder, and it is noteworthy that in both the impulse has been dissociated from the unbearable idea of incest. The second is of course when he actually kills the King, when the Queen is already dead and lost to him for ever, so that his conscience is free of an ulterior motive for the murder. The first is more interesting. It is clear that Hamlet is a creature of highly charged imagination; Vischer,[11] for instance, quite rightly termed him a 'Phantasie-mensch'. As is known, the danger then is that phantasy may on occasion replace reality. Now Otto Rank,[12] who uses the same term, has plausibly suggested that the emotionally charged play scene, where a nephew kills his uncle (!), and when there is no talk of adultery or incest, is in Hamlet's imagination an equivalent for fulfilling his task.* It is easier to kill the King when there is no ulterior motive behind it, no talk of mother or incest. When the play is over he is carried away in exultation as if he had really killed the King himself, whereas all he has actually done is to warn him and so impel him to sign a death warrant. That his pretext for arranging the play – to satisfy himself about Claudius' guilt and the Ghost's honesty – is specious is plain from the fact that *before* it he had been convinced of both and was reproaching himself for his neglect. When he then comes on the King praying,

* There is a delicate point here which may appeal only to psycho-analysts. It is known that the occurrence of a dream within a dream (when one dreams that one is dreaming) is always found when analysed to refer to a theme which the person wishes were 'only a dream', i.e. not true. I would suggest that a similar meaning attaches to a 'play within a play', as in *Hamlet*. So Hamlet (as nephew) can kill the King in his imagination since it is 'only a play' or 'only in play'.

and so to speak finds him surprisingly still alive, he realizes that his task is still in front of him, but can only say 'Now *might* I do it' (not 'will'). He then expresses openly the unconscious thoughts of his infancy – the wish to kill the man who is lying with his mother ('in th' incestuous pleasure of his bed') – but he knows only too well that his own guilty motive for doing so would always prevent him. So there is no way out of the dilemma, and he blunders on to destruction.

The call of duty to kill his stepfather cannot be obeyed because it links itself with the unconscious call of his nature to kill his mother's husband, whether this is the first or the second; the absolute 'repression' of the former impulse involves the inner prohibition of the latter also. It is no chance that Hamlet says of himself that he is prompted to his revenge 'by heaven and hell'.

In this discussion of the motives that move or restrain Hamlet we have purposely depreciated the subsidiary ones – such as his exclusion from the throne where Claudius has blocked the normal solution of the Oedipus complex (to succeed the father in due course) – which also play a part, so as to bring out in greater relief the deeper and effective ones that are of preponderating importance. These, as we have seen, spring from sources of which he is quite unaware, and we might summarize the internal conflict of which he is the victim as consisting in a struggle of the 'repressed' mental processes to become conscious. The call of duty, which automatically arouses to activity these unconscious processes, conflicts with the necessity of 'repressing' them still more strongly; for the more urgent is the need for external action the greater is the effort demanded of the 'repressing' forces. It is his moral duty, to which his father exhorts him, to put an end to the incestuous activities of his mother (by killing Claudius), but his unconscious does not want to put an end to them (he being identified with Claudius in the situation), and so he cannot. His lashings of self-reproach and remorse are ultimately because of this very failure, i.e. the refusal of his guilty wishes to undo the sin. By refusing to abandon his own incestuous wishes he perpetuates the sin and so must endure the stings of torturing conscience. And yet killing his mother's husband would be equivalent to committing the original sin himself, which would if anything be even more guilty. So of the two impossible alternatives he adopts the passive solution of letting the incest continue vicariously, but at the same time provoking destruction at the King's hand. Was ever a tragic figure so torn and tortured!

Action is paralysed at its very inception, and there is thus produced the picture of apparently causeless inhibition which is so inexplicable both to Hamlet* and to readers of the play. This paralysis arises, however, not from physical or moral cowardice, but from that intellectual cowardice, that reluctance to dare the exploration of his inmost soul, which Hamlet shares with the rest of the human race. 'Thus conscience does make cowards of us all.'

* The situation is perfectly depicted by Hamlet in his cry (IV iv):
> I do not know
> Why yet I live to say 'This thing's to do,'
> Sith I have cause, and will, and strength, and means,
> To do't.

With greater insight he could have replaced the word 'will' by 'pious wish', which it obviously means.

NOTES

1. Robert Bridges, *The Testament of Beauty*, I 577.
2. J. Dover Wilson, *What Happens in Hamlet* (1935) p. 261.
3. See, for instance, Wulf Sachs, *Black Hamlet* (1937).
4. e.g. G. Brandes, *William Shakespeare* (1898) II 48, who remarks that Hamlet's talk to Ophelia could be translated as 'You are like my mother; you could behave like her.'
5. J. W. von Goethe, *Wilhelm Meister*, IV 14. 'Her whole being hovers in ripe, sweet voluptuousness.' 'Her fancy is moved, her quiet modesty breathes loving desire, and should the gentle Goddess Opportunity shake the tree the fruit would at once fall.'
6. A. C. Bradley, *Shakespearean Tragedy*, 2nd ed. (1905) p. 118.
7. Op. cit. p. 270.
8. Op. cit. p. 128 etc.

9. J. Q. Adams, 'Commentary', in his edition of *Hamlet, Prince of Denmark* (Boston, 1929) p. 255.

10. Sigmund Freud, 'Trauer und Melancholie', in *Vierte Sammlung kleiner Schriften* (1918) ch. 20.

11. F. T. Vischer, 'Hamlet, Prinz von Dänemark', in *Shakespeare Vorträge*, I (1899).

12. Otto Rank, 'Das Schauspiel in Hamlet', in *Imago*, IV 45.

Wolfgang H. Clemen

THE IMAGERY OF *HAMLET*
(1951)

T H E surprisingly new possibilities of language which make this
play appear a turning-point in the development of Shakespeare's
style[1] seem to have their origin in the personality of Hamlet. The
new language comes from him, in him it attains to perfection.
The language of the King and the Queen, of Laertes and
Polonius, although subtly adapted to their character, still treads
the well-worn paths; it is less novel, because the people by whom
it is spoken are not in need of a new form of expression – on the
contrary, they may be more aptly characterized by a conventional mode of speech. But Hamlet's nature can only find expression in a wholly new language. This also applies to the imagery
in the play. It is Hamlet who creates the most significant images,
images marking the atmosphere and theme of the play, which are
paler and less pregnant in the speech of the other characters.
Hamlet's way of employing images is unique in Shakespeare's
drama. When he begins to speak, the images fairly stream to him
without the slightest effort – not as similes or conscious para-
phrases, but as immediate and spontaneous visions.[2] Hamlet's
imagery shows us that whenever he thinks and speaks, he is at
the same time a visionary, a seer, for whom the living things of
the world about him embody and symbolize thought. His first
monologue may show this; the short space of time which lies
between his father's death and his mother's remarriage is to him a
series of pictures taken from real life:

> A little month or ere those shoes were old
> With which she followed my poor father's body
> Like Niobe all tears:　　　　　　　　　　(I ii 147)

>   Ere yet the salt of most unrighteous tears
>   Had left the flushing in her galléd eyes,   (ɪ ii 154)

or a little later, addressed to Horatio:

>   the funeral baked meats
>   Did coldly furnish forth the marriage tables. (ɪ ii 180)

These are no poetic similes, but keen observations of reality. Hamlet does not translate the general thought into an image paraphrasing it; on the contrary, he uses the opposite method: he refers the generalization to the events and objects of the reality underlying the thought. This sense of reality finds expression in all the images Hamlet employs. Peculiar to them all is that closeness to reality which is often carried to the point of an unsparing poignancy.[3] They are mostly very concrete and precise, simple and, as to their subject matter, easy to understand; common and ordinary things, things familiar to the man in the street dominate, rather than lofty, strange or rare objects.[4] Illuminating in this connection is the absence of hyperbole,* of great dimensions in his imagery. In contrast to Othello or Lear, for example, who awaken heaven and the elements in their imagery† and who lend expression to their mighty passions in images of soaring magnificence, Hamlet prefers to keep his language within the scope of reality, indeed, within the everyday world. It is not spacious scenery and nature which dominate in Hamlet's imagery, but rather trades and callings, objects of daily use, popular games and technical terms; his images are not beautiful, poetic, magnificent, but they always hit their mark, the matter in question, with surprisingly unerring sureness. They do not waft the things of reality into a dream-world of the imagination; on the contrary, they make them truly *real*, they reveal their inmost, naked being. All this, the wealth of realistic observation, of real objects, of

---

* If he makes use of hyperbole in v i 275 (at Ophelia's grave) it is to parody Laertes' hyperbolic diction.

† Hamlet, too, invokes God and the heavenly powers, but these invocations never take the form of grandiose images, they are mostly brief and often restricted to mere references (cf. ɪ ii 132, 150, 195; ɪ iv 85; ɪ v 92; v vii 330, 342).

associations taken from everyday life, is enough to prove that Hamlet is no abstract thinker and dreamer. As his imagery betrays to us, he is rather a man gifted with greater powers of observation than the others. He is capable of scanning reality with a keener eye and of penetrating the veil of semblance even to the very core of things. 'I know not seems.'

At the same time, Hamlet's imagery reveals the hero's wide educational background, his many-sidedness and the extraordinary range of his experience.[5] That metaphors taken from natural sciences are specially frequent in Hamlet's language again emphasizes his power of observation, his critical objective way of looking at things.[6] But Hamlet is also at home in classical antiquity or Greek mythology,[7] in the terminology of law,[8] he is not only familiar with the theatre and with acting – as everyone knows – but also with the fine arts,[9] with falconry and hunting,[10] with the soldier's trade and strategy,* with the courtier's way of life. All these spheres disclosing Hamlet's personality as that of a 'courtier, soldier and scholar' (in Ophelia's words, III i 154) are evoked by the imagery which, however, turns them to living account by a fit application to situations, persons and moods. Hamlet commands so many levels of expression that he can attune his diction as well as his imagery to the situation and to the person to whom he is speaking. This adaptability and versatility is another feature in Hamlet's use of language which can also be traced in his imagery.

At the same time, this wide range of imagery can, in certain passages, serve to give relief to his conflicting moods, to his being torn between extremes and to the abruptness of his changes of mood. This characteristic which has been particularly emphasized and partly attributed to 'melancholy' by L. L. Schücking and John Dover Wilson,[11] also expresses itself in the sudden change of language and in the juxtaposition of passages which are sharply contrasted in their diction. With no other character in Shakespeare do we find this sharp contrast between images

* Hamlet speaks of the 'pales and forts of reason' (I iv 28), wonders whether his mother's heart is 'proof and bulwark against sense' (III iv 38; cf. III iv 208).

marked by a pensive mood and those which unsparingly use vulgar words and display a frivolous and sarcastic disgust for the world.[12]

Let us consider further how Hamlet's use of imagery reflects his ability to penetrate to the real nature of men and things and his relentless breaking down of the barriers raised by hypocrisy. Many of his images seem in fact designed to unmask men; they are meant to strip them of their fine appearances and to show them up in their true nature. Thus, by means of the simile of fortune's pipe, Hamlet shows Rosencrantz and Guildenstern that he has seen through their intent, and thus he unmasks Rosencrantz when he calls him a 'sponge', 'that soaks up the king's countenance' (IV ii 15). He splits his mother's heart 'in twain', because he tells her the truth from which she shrinks and which she conceals from herself. And again it is by means of images that he seeks to lead her to a recognition of the truth. He renews the memory of his father in her by means of that forceful description of his outward appearance which could be compared with Hyperion, Mars and Mercury. On the other hand, another series of comparisons seeks to bring home to his mother the real nature of Claudius:

> a mildewed ear,
> Blasting his wholesome brother.   (III iv 64)

> a vice of kings,
> A cutpurse of the empire and the rule,
> That from a shelf the precious diadem stole
> And put it in his pocket –
>
> A king of shreds and patches –   (III iv 98)

So Hamlet sees through men and things. He perceives what is false, visualizing his recognition through imagery.

Hamlet's imagery, which thus calls things by their right names, acquires a peculiar freedom from his feigned madness. Hamlet needs images for his 'antic disposition'. He would betray himself if he used open, direct language. Hence he must speak ambiguously and cloak his real meaning under quibbles and

puns,[13] images and parables. The other characters do not understand him and continue to think he is mad, but the audience can
gain an insight into the true situation. Under the protection
of that mask of 'antic disposition', Hamlet says more shrewd
things than all the rest of the courtiers together.[14] So we
find the images here in an entirely new role, unique in Shakespeare's drama. Only the images of the fool in *King Lear* have a
similar function.

Hamlet suffers an injustice when he is accused of merely
theoretical and abstract speculation which would lead him away
from reality. His thoughts carry further than those of others,
because he sees more and deeper than they, not because he would
leave reality unheeded. It is true that his is a nature more prone to
thought than to action; but that signifies by no means, as the
Hamlet critics would often have us believe, that he is a philosopher
and dreamer and no man of the world. When, in the graveyard
scene, he holds Yorick's skull in his hand, he sees *more* in it than
the others, for whom the skull is merely a lifeless object. And
precisely because he is more deeply moved by the reality and
significance of these earthly remains, his fantasy is able to follow
the 'noble dust of Alexander' through all its metamorphoses. The
comparisons which spring from this faculty of thinking a thing
to the end, as it were, derive in fact from a more intense experience of reality.

It is a fundamental tenet of Hamlet criticism that Hamlet's
over-developed intellect makes it impossible for him to act. In
this connection the following famous passage is generally quoted:

> And thus the native hue of resolution
> Is sicklied o'er with the pale cast of thought,
> And enterprises of great pitch and moment
> With this regard their currents turn awry,
> And lose the name of action.   (III i 84)

The customary interpretation of this passage, 'reflection hinders
action', does it an injustice. For Hamlet does not say 'reflection
hinders action', he simply utters this image. The fact that he does
not utter that general maxim, but this image, makes all the

difference. For this image is the unique and specific form of expression of the thought underlying it, it cannot be separated from it. If we say 'reflection hinders action', we make a false generalization; we replace a specific formulation by an apothegm. And thereby we eradicate in this passage that quality which is peculiarly Shakespeare's or, what is more, peculiarly Hamlet's. Here the image does not serve the purpose of merely casting a decorative cloak about the thought; it is much rather an intrinsic part of the thought.

'Reflection hinders action' – this phrase carries in it something absolute, something damning. We sense a moralizing undertone. Action and reflection are thus conceived of as two mutually inimical abstract principles. But not so in Shakespeare's metaphorical language. 'Native hue of resolution' suggests that Shakespeare viewed resolution as an innate human quality, not as a moral virtue to be consciously striven after. But the Hamlet-criticism of the nineteenth century saw the problem in this light of a moral virtue. We see, then, that a careful consideration of Shakespeare's imagery may sometimes correct false interpretations.[15]

'Reflection hinders action.' Polonius, the sententious lover of maxims, could have said this, for a general saying carries no sense of personal obligation; it places a distance between the speaker and what he would say. But just as it is characteristic of Polonius to utter banalities and sententious effusions,[16] so, too, it is characteristic of Hamlet, to express even those things which would have permitted of a generalizing formulation, in a language which bears the stamp of a unique and personal experience.

Hamlet sees this problem under the aspect of a process of the human organism.[17] The original bright colouring of the skin is concealed by an ailment. Thus the relation between thought and action appears not as an opposition between two abstract principles between which a free choice is possible, but as an unavoidable condition of human nature. The image of the leprous ailment emphasizes the malignant, disabling, slowly disintegrating nature of the process. It is by no mere chance that Hamlet employs just this image. Perusing the description which

the ghost of Hamlet's father gives of his poisoning by Claudius
(I v 63) one cannot help being struck by the vividness with
which the process of poisoning, the malicious spreading of the
disease, is portrayed:

> And in the porches of my ears did pour
> The leperous distilment, whose effect
> Holds such an enmity with blood of man,
> That swift as quicksilver it courses through
> The natural gates and alleys of the body,
> And with a sudden vigour it doth posset
> And curd, like eager droppings into milk,
> The thin and wholesome blood; so did it mine,
> And a most instant tetter barked about
> Most lazar-like with vile and loathsome crust
> All my smooth body.   (I v 63)

A real event described at the beginning of the drama has
exercised a profound influence upon the whole imagery of the
play. What is later metaphor, is here still reality. The picture of
the leprous skin disease, which is here – in the first act – described by Hamlet's father, has buried itself deep in Hamlet's
imagination and continues to lead its subterranean existence, as it
were, until it reappears in metaphorical form.

As Miss Spurgeon has shown, the idea of an ulcer dominates
the imagery, infecting and fatally eating away the whole body; on
every occasion repulsive images of sickness make their appearance.[18] It is certain that this imagery is derived from that one real
event. Hamlet's father describes in that passage how the poison
invades the body during sleep and how the healthy organism is
destroyed from within, not having a chance to defend itself
against attack. But this now becomes the *leitmotif* of the imagery:
the individual occurrence is expanded into a symbol for the
central problem of the play. The corruption of land and people
throughout Denmark is understood as an imperceptible and
irresistible process of poisoning. And, furthermore, this poisoning reappears as a *leitmotif* in the action as well – as a poisoning in the 'dumb-show', and finally, as the poisoning of all the

major characters in the last act. Thus imagery and action
continually play into each other's hands and we see how the term
'dramatic imagery' gains a new significance.

The imagery appears to be influenced by yet another event in
the action underlying the play: Hamlet feels himself to be sullied
by his mother's incest which, according to the conception of the
time, she committed in marrying Claudius. For him this is a
poisoning idea which finds expression in his language. Professor
Dover Wilson has defended the reading of the Second Quarto
with convincing arguments:[19]

> O, that this too too sullied flesh would melt,
> Thaw and resolve itself into a dew!   (I ii 129)

It is therefore probable that this idea is present in Hamlet's mind
at many moments when images of decay and rot appear in his
language.

The *leitmotif* occasionally appears in a disguised form at a
point where it seems to have no real connection with the main
issue of the play, for instance, in the following passage:

> So, oft it chances in particular men,
> That for some vicious mole of nature in them,
> As in their birth, wherein they are not guilty
> (Since nature cannot choose his origin),
> By the o'ergrowth of some complexion,
> Oft breaking down the pales and forts of reason,
> Or by some habit, that too much o'er-leavens
> The form of plausive manners – that these men,
> Carrying I say the stamp of one defect,
> Being nature's livery, or fortune's star,
> His virtues else be they as pure as grace,
> As infinite as man may undergo,
> Shall in the general censure take corruption
> From that particular fault: the dram of evil
> Doth all the noble substance of a doubt,
> To his own scandal.   (I iv 23)

Hamlet has spoken of the excessive revels and drinking-bouts
among his people and has said that this was disparaging to the

Danes in the eyes of the other peoples. Then follows this general reflection. The question arises: why does Hamlet speak in such detail of these matters here? For at this point in the play he has as yet heard nothing of his uncle's murderous deed. And still he touches in this speech upon that *leitmotif* of the whole play; he describes how human nature may be brought to decay through a tiny birth-mark, just as from one 'dram of evil'* a destructive effect may spread over the whole organism. *O'er-leavens* already points to *sicklied o'er*, and, as in the passage discussed, the notion of the human body is in the background. As in later passages, the balance of the powers in man is the theme here, and 'corruption', a basic motif in the whole play, already makes its appearance. This general reflection on gradual and irresistible infection is made in passing, as it were. Thus Shakespeare makes use of every opportunity to suggest the fundamental theme of the play. When the King says to Laertes in the fourth act:

> There lives within the very flame of love
> A kind of wick or snuff that will abate it,

the same motif occurs again: corruption through a 'dram of evil'.

The following passage, too, from Laertes' words of warning to his sister, has never been examined for its value as 'dramatic presaging'.

> The canker galls the infants of the spring
> Too oft before their buttons be disclosed,
> And in the morn and liquid dew of youth
> Contagious blastments are most imminent. (I iii 39)

It is no mere chance that this sententious little image,[20] which is so neatly woven in and so conventional, touches upon a motif later to be worked out more clearly. The worm in the bud, like ulcer and eruption, is also an irresistible force destroying the organism from within. Light is cast upon this early passage

---

* The emendation *evil* has been accepted by several editors, e.g. by John Dover Wilson in the 'New Shakespeare' edition.

when, in the last act, it is said of Claudius: 'this canker of our nature' (v ii 69). But here we still know nothing of the coming developments. The image is a faint warning, preparing the way, together with other hints, for the future.

The Pyrrhus episode[21] which the first Player recites before Hamlet contains features which are also of importance for the theme of the play. For here it is related of Pyrrhus with vigorous emphasis how 'A rouséd vengeance sets him new awork' (ii ii 492). For Hamlet it must be a gentle warning that vengeance calls forth so bloody a deed in another without delay. On the other hand, the previous lines described Pyrrhus as being in suspense, unable to act, 'neutral to his will' as Hamlet still is:

> So as a painted tyrant Pyrrhus stood,
> And like a neutral to his will and matter,
> Did nothing.   (ii ii 484)

The mention of 'strumpet Fortune' and the picture of her broken wheel rolled 'down the hill of heaven' at the end of this passage, is likewise a hint; in the third act this image of the wheel plunging down from the height, reappears in the conversation between Rosencrantz and the King:

> The cess of majesty
> Dies not alone; but like a gulf doth draw
> What's near it with it. O, 'tis a massy wheel
> Fixed on the summit of the highest mount,
> To whose huge spokes ten thousand lesser things
> Are mortised and adjoined, which when it falls,
> Each small annexment, petty consequence,
> Attends the boist'rous ruin.   (iii iii 15)

Through these images, which are also spun out from a more general reflection, the coming catastrophe is already significantly foreshadowed.

The imagery in Shakespeare's tragedies often shows how a number of other images are grouped around the central symbol which express the same idea, but in quite other terms. Several degrees, as it were, of the metaphorical expression of a fundamental idea may be distinguished. Besides images which express a motif with the greatest clarity and emphasis, we find others which utter the thought in a veiled and indirect manner. An examination of the way in which the images are spread over the play, can reveal how subtly Shakespeare modifies and varies according to character and situation.

The most striking images of sickness, which Miss Spurgeon has already listed, make their first appearance, significantly enough, in the second half of the play, and most notably in the scene in which Hamlet seeks to bring his mother to a change of heart. Here the plainness and clarity of the images is meant to awaken the conscience of the Queen; they can scarcely be force-ful enough; 'let me wring your heart', Hamlet has said at the beginning of the meeting. In the first part of the play the atmo-sphere of corruption and decay is spread in a more indirect and general way. Hamlet declares in the first and second acts how the world appears to him:

> . . . ah fie, 'tis an unweeded garden
> That grows to seed, things rank and gross in nature
> Possess it merely.   (I ii 135)

. . . and indeed it goes so heavily with my disposition, that this goodly frame the earth, seems to me a sterile promontory, this most excellent canopy the air, look you, this brave o'erhanging firmament, this majestical roof fretted with golden fire, why it appeareth nothing to me but a foul and pestilent congregation of vapours.   (II ii 301)

The image of weeds, touched upon in the word 'unweeded', is related to the imagery of sickness in Shakespeare's work. It appears three times in *Hamlet*. The ghost says to Hamlet:

> And duller shouldst thou be than the fat weed
> That rots itself in ease on Lethe wharf.   (I v 32)

In the dialogue with his mother, this image immediately follows upon the image of the ulcer:

> And do not spread the compost on the weeds
> To make them ranker.   (III iv 151)

Images of rot, decay and corruption are especially numerous in the long second scene of the second act. There are, for example, Hamlet's remarks on the maggots which the sun breeds in a dead dog (II ii 181), on the deep dungeons in the prison Denmark (II ii 246), on the strumpet Fortune (II ii 238), who reappears in the speech of the first Player (II ii 497), his comparison of himself with a whore, a drab and a scullion (II ii 589).

Seen individually, such images do not seem to be very important. But in their totality they contribute considerably to the tone of the play.

NOTES

1. On the style in *Hamlet*, see L. L. Schücking, *The Meaning of Hamlet* (1937), I i, I iv.

2. The spontaneous and unpremeditated character of Hamlet's imagery will become obvious through a comparison with Claudius' language. Claudius' speeches are studied and give the impression of having been previously prepared. His images often are consciously inserted. Dr Lotte Schmetz notes, in *Sprache und Charakter bei Shakespeare* (Munich thesis, 1949), that while Claudius often uses comparisons, linking object and image by 'as' or 'like', Hamlet's imagination fuses both into a metaphor (cf. IV i 40–4, IV v 93–5 with III ii 76–7, III ii 392–3). Further examples for Claudius' comparisons: III iii 41; IV vii 15; IV vii 86. This is, of course, only one aspect of the manifold differences between Claudius' and Hamlet's language. The whole problem has been exhaustively dealt with in Dr Schmetz's study. For the difference between the imagery of Claudius' public and that of his private language, and for further distinguishing features in Claudius' imagery, see Una Ellis-Fermor, *The Frontiers of Drama* (1945) p. 88.

3. This, as Dr Schmetz notes, gives to Hamlet's language sometimes a brutal violence that expresses itself in the use of forceful metaphors: 'For I mine eyes will rivet to his face' (III ii 83), 'Let me wring your heart' (III iv 35).

4. After completion of the manuscript, the author became acquainted with Professor Mikhail M. Morozow's article, 'The Individualization of Shakespeare's Characters through Imagery', in *Shakespeare Survey* 2 (1949), 83–106. Professor Morozow's more systematic and comprehensive examination of the content of all of Hamlet's images can throw new light on the statements made above

and adds a number of acute observations, which have a bearing on the theory put forward here. Morozow also emphasizes the realistic, common and popular nature of Hamlet's imagery, his faculty to 'see right through people' and his closeness to the common people which does not exclude his scholarship and humanist education.

5. For the following, cf. Dr Schmetz's study and Professor Morozow's article.

6. Cf. III i 118; I v 22, 27, 29; III iv 147. For the disease-imagery, see below.

7. e.g. I ii 140, 149, 153; III ii 82, 283; III iii 56–8; v i 277, 285.

8. v i 96 ff.

9. e.g. his images taken from musical instruments, III ii 68.

10. II ii 382; III ii 349; II ii 434.

11. Cf. Schücking, *The Meaning of Hamlet*, and J. Dover Wilson, *What Happens in Hamlet* (1935).

12. There are many instances for these contrasts in Hamlet's language. Cf. the transition from the famous monologue in III i 56 to his conversation with Ophelia in the same scene (a parallel change in III ii) or cf. IV iii 21: v i 201 ff. Dr Schmetz notes the following instances of Hamlet's use of vulgar words: 'truepenny' (I v 150); 'old mole' (I v 162); 'drab' (II ii 590); 'carrion' (II ii 182); 'Jowls it to the ground' (v i 76); 'Knocked about the mazzard' (v i 87). For further instances of Hamlet's use of coarse and common images, see Morozow's article, p. 95.

13. Through J. Dover Wilson's edition of *Hamlet* (1934) many of these puns and quibbles which so far had remained unintelligible (or were falsely understood) have been cleared up. On the importance of quibbles in *Hamlet*, see Dover Wilson's Introduction, pp. xxxiii ff.

14. Edward Dowden noted this: 'Madness possesses exquisite immunities and privileges. From the safe vantage of unintelligibility he can delight himself by uttering his whole mind and sending forth his words among the words of others, with their meaning disguised, as he himself must be, clothed in an antic garb of parable, dark sayings which speak the truth in a mystery' (*Shakespeare, His Mind and Art* (1877) p. 145). Cf., too, Dover Wilson's Introduction to *Hamlet*, p. xl.

15. Cf. Caroline Spurgeon, *Shakespeare's Imagery* (1935) pp. 318–19.

16. Cf. Edward Dowden: 'his wisdom is not the outflow of a rich or deep nature, but the little, accumulated hoard of a long and superficial experience. This is what the sententious manner signifies' (*Shakespeare, His Mind and Art*, p. 142). Professor John W. Draper, reviewing the divergent interpretations of Polonius' character, gives him a far more favourable treatment and considers him 'not far removed from the Elizabethan ideal of what a courtier, what a father, what a "Worthie

Priuie Counceller" should be' (*The Hamlet of Shakespeare's Audience* (Durham, N.C., 1938) p. 53).

17. For the contemporary scientific background of the disease-imagery in *Hamlet*, see John W. Draper, *The Humors and Shakespeare's Characters* (Durham, N.C., 1945).

18. Spurgeon, *Shakespeare's Imagery*, pp. 316 ff.

19. Cf. the note on this passage on p. 151 of Dover Wilson's edition of *Hamlet*: ' "Sullied flesh" is the key to the soliloquy and tells us that Hamlet is thinking of the "kindless" incestuous marriage as a personal defilement. Further, "sullied" fits the immediate context as "solid" does not. There is something absurd in associating "solid flesh" with "melt" and "thaw"; whereas Shakespeare always uses "sully" or "sullied" elsewhere (cf. *1 Henry IV*, II iv 84; *Winter's Tale*, I ii 326) with the image, implicit or explicit, of dirt upon a surface of pure white; and the surface Hamlet obviously has in mind here is snow, symbolical of the nature he shares with his mother, once pure but now befouled.'

20. Dr Schmetz points out that this use of sententious diction betrays a certain immaturity in Laertes, just as his apostrophes at the sight of the mad Ophelia in IV v 154 reveal a hollow pathos, or as his hyperboles at Ophelia's grave impress us as theatrical bombast (V i 245).

21. A new and important interpretation of the 'Player's Speech' is given by Harry Levin in 'An Explication of the Player's Speech', in *Kenyon Review*, XII 2 (1950).

D. G. James

MORAL AND METAPHYSICAL UNCERTAINTY IN *HAMLET* (1951)

W E have, in the first place, to see Hamlet as a man uncertain of his duty in the circumstances in which he finds himself. Ought he to murder the murderer of his father and the seducer of his mother? That is the question:

> To be, or not to be, that is the question,
> Whether 'tis nobler in the mind to suffer
> The slings and arrows of outrageous fortune,
> Or to take arms against a sea of troubles,
> And by opposing, end them. To die, to sleep ...

I am not unaware that I am plunging into, to say the least, debated territory. But it is better, I think, for me to declare myself at once and make clear where, on this battlefield, I stand and fight ... [Dr Johnson's] interpretation of this soliloquy seems to me incomparably the best yet offered. The thought of the soliloquy is not, at the outset, of suicide at all, but of personal immortality: whether we are to be or not to be, to live or in truth to die; and in the context of this thought, which recurs at the conclusion of the lines I quoted (... and by opposing, end them. To die, to sleep ...), Hamlet asks whether it be nobler to suffer the slings of fortune or to take arms against troubles and end them. Hamlet's mind is moving fast: we may read the 'that is the question' as referring both backwards and forwards; and the two questions, Whether we shall live or die? and, Whether it is nobler to suffer or to take arms against our troubles? are tied up with each other and are in Hamlet's mind quite inseparable. Certainly, the thought of suicide occurs later with the talk of a bare bodkin making a quietus for us; this is one way of taking arms against a sea of troubles; and then Hamlet's thought turns at once, again, to death and a life to come. He had spoken first of taking arms against others with the chance that he be killed; and his mind had passed at once to the thought of what might come in another world than this. Now he speaks of killing himself; and now, again, his mind turns to what would come in another world.

> For who would bear the whips and scorns of time . . .
> When he himself might his quietus make
> With a bare bodkin; who would fardels bear . . .
> But that the dread of something after death,
> The undiscovered country, from whose bourn
> No traveller returns, puzzles the will . . . ?

We do offence to the speech, or so it seems to me, unless we see Hamlet contemplating first, the killing of others with perhaps, then, his own death, and second, a suicide; both are ways of taking arms against a sea of troubles; and the taking arms in either form is seen against the fearful background of a world to come in which condign punishment may be inflicted by a righteous God. What kind of an eternity will the taking up of arms, whether against others or oneself, bring one? Therefore the overriding question is, Whether 'tis nobler . . . ? This we must know; for God, if there be a God, may punish us through eternity for a wrong choice. There is the intrinsic ethical question, – Which is in itself nobler? But Hamlet ties up this question along with the thought of eternal sanctions imposed by God. If there were no after-life it would not matter, or matter less, which line he took; but he cannot here, upon this bank and shoal of time, jump the thought of a life to come. There is, then, an ethical question; there is also a metaphysical and religious question; and to neither does he know the answer.

I only emphasize here, in passing, Hamlet's fearful imagination of a life after death. I venture to think we often underrate this. Here, indeed, we need to remember how close these Elizabethan days were to the Middle Ages; here we must hold our modernity in restraint. If we need to illustrate further that in this matter Hamlet was not fetching excuses for delay, we may look at lines Shakespeare wrote in another play a few years later. In *Measure for Measure* the Duke has urged Claudio to be absolute for death: the afflictions of life make death sweet. Later in the same scene, Isabella has told Claudio that 'the sense of death is most in apprehension'. But the reply of Claudio, given indeed to Isabella but coming in effect as a reply both to her and to the Duke, is dreadful in its imagination:

> Ay, but to die, and go we know not where;
> To lie in cold obstruction and to rot . . .
>   . . . and the delighted spirit
> To bathe in fiery floods, or to reside
> In thrilling region of thick-ribbed ice;
> To be imprison'd in the viewless winds,
> And blown with restless violence round about
> The pendent world; or to be worse than worst
> Of those that lawless and incertain thought
> Imagine howling: 'tis too horrible!
> The weariest and most loathed worldly life
> That age, ache, penury and imprisonment
> Can lay on nature is a paradise
> To what we fear of death.

Hamlet too had 'lawless and incertain thought'; and it will not do to say that here, in the face of this, Hamlet is finding extravagant or recondite reasons for his hesitation. Since the days when these lines were written the eschatological imagination has fallen steadily back before the onset of naturalism. A. C. Bradley merits our gratitude, and I should be the last man to speak of him without deep respect; but an English Hegelian would be intelligibly disposed to underrate Hamlet's fear of other worlds and to say that his thought, if it moved on these lines, was a symptom merely of a morbid and diseased state. My own wish is frankly to elevate Hamlet's intellectual distresses to an equality in importance with his emotional state; the strength of the emotional shock he has suffered is equalled by the weakness of his mind in the face of difficult moral and metaphysical issues. Hamlet was, after all, an intellectual. We must bear in mind that Shakespeare was the first to make him a member of a university; and *Hamlet* was acted before the universities of Oxford and Cambridge. . . . But my point is that *Hamlet* is not a tragedy of excessive thought; so far as we are to see the cause of Hamlet's destiny in intellectual terms, it is a tragedy not of excessive thought but of defeated thought. Hamlet does not know; and he knows of no way of knowing. And then comes the line,

> Thus conscience does make cowards of us all;

resolution is sicklied o'er, and enterprise loses the name of action. It is hard to know what it is right to do; and we do not know whether in fact we live after we die, and in a universe in which a moral order asserts itself. No doubt Shakespeare had to be careful how he expressed the issues which confronted Hamlet. But the plain issue was, Does God exist or not? What was at stake in Hamlet's mind was nothing less than the greatest which confronts our mortal minds.

'Conscience does make cowards of us.' There has been, I am aware, much dispute as to what the word means here. For my part, I find not the least difficulty in believing that the word carries both its usual meaning and that of 'reflection and anxious thought'. It is a platitude of Shakespeare study that Shakespeare could, with wonderful ease, charge a word with two or three meanings at once; there is hardly a page of Shakespeare which does not illustrate this; and, in any case, the word 'conscience' means for us all both a command to do what is right and anxious reflection as to what is, in fact, the right thing to do. If I had to choose (what I feel under no compulsion whatever to do) between the two meanings proposed, I should unhesitatingly choose the former and usual meaning. A. C. Bradley was cross (in a footnote) with the *Oxford Dictionary* for giving its authority to construing 'conscience' in this passage as meaning 'moral sense or scrupulousness'; and he declares that 'in this soliloquy Hamlet is not thinking of the duty laid upon him at all'. But how then can he begin to explain the lines,

> Whether 'tis nobler in the mind to suffer . . .
> Or to take arms . . . ?

It is precisely his duty Hamlet thinks of, and of his duty, which he finds it hard to decide, in relation to a possible world to come; and the difficulty of knowing what is right, and the uncertainty of our last destiny, together puzzle and arrest the will. Conscience requires that we do what is right; but then, what *is* right or wrong in these circumstances? Anxious reflection discloses no clear conviction; nor does it provide knowledge of a world to come. This is the moral and metaphysical uncertainty in which Hamlet finds himself. He does not know and cannot find out. Conscience makes demands; but it also provides no clear moral or metaphysical sense. Until he finds himself in this climacteric condition, life has gone on smoothly enough; but now, and suddenly, he knows that he lacks the insight, or the know-ledge, or the faith, which will steady him, and carry him forward in a single and continuous course of action. In this, Hamlet knows he is different from Horatio, whose calm and steadily appointed way of life we are expected to admire. Horatio is precisely one who in suffering all, suffers nothing; he has accepted the first alternative Hamlet had proposed to himself: 'whether 'tis nobler in the mind to suffer the slings and arrows . . .' Horatio has, we are expected to understand, decided that it is nobler so to suffer, and he has taken the buffets and the rewards of fortune with equal thanks; he knows his line and he is steady in it. Hamlet has not decided; and hence his peculiar distress.

It is very important to observe the play here on the word 'suffer'. Horatio is one who suffers everything and suffers nothing. What does this mean? I take it to mean, in the first sense, that Horatio accepts equally the fortunes and misfortunes of life; he embraces his good fortune with restraint and he endures his misfortunes. Therefore, in the second sense, he suffers nothing; he is not put out or mastered by circumstance; he is master of himself and of circumstance; he sustains a steady and imperturbable calm. In the one sense of the word, he takes what comes, without rebellion against it; he does not oppose it to end it; he is thus passive. But in the other sense, he is precisely not passive, but pre-eminently active and creative in his life. Such a steadiness and even tenour, in a philosophy of 'suffering', Hamlet does not possess. Horatio is one who, in suffering all, suffers nothing; Hamlet is one who, in suffering nothing, suffers everything. He is active where Horatio is passive, and passive where Horatio is active. His passivity is of the wrong sort; he is blown about by every gust of passion. But it is the same when he is active: his activity, like his passivity, is an affair of passion merely. Judgement is not in it. He is passion's slave, played on like a pipe, lapsed in time and circumstance, unaccountable, now listless, now violent.

But we must remark how Hamlet speaks of Horatio; he does so in words of passionate admiration. His election had sealed Horatio for himself because in suffering all, Horatio suffered nothing; and it is the man who is not passion's slave whom he would wear in his heart's core. How clearly he would be like Horatio! And yet, in the face of what has happened, ought he to be like Horatio? or ought he not to take up arms against his troubles, and violently end them and perhaps thereby himself? He did not know. The ghost had given Hamlet specific instructions to contrive nothing against his mother:

> . . . leave her to heaven,
> And to those thorns that in her bosom lodge
> To prick and sting her.

But ought he perhaps to leave Claudius to heaven also? When his guilt was proved beyond any doubt, Hamlet still did not kill him; he left him alone, giving a reason, plausible enough in Hamlet's eyes, in the eyes of his audience, and in our eyes, and yet inhabiting a middle region between sincerity and insincerity. We are told that in explaining why he does not there kill the King, Hamlet was sincere; it was a belief of the time. But it was certainly not universal. Claudius at least could have told him it was nonsense; Claudius has just made clear to us what was necessary if he, Claudius, was to win heaven. And could a Hamlet who half his time believed neither in heaven nor hell, sincerely and with a whole mind say these things? He leaves Claudius, and goes off to rage at his mother.

Conscience, says Hamlet, makes cowards of us; we are made afraid by it; and who of us does not know that this is true? In the soliloquy in Act IV (How all occasions do inform against me) the same thought is uppermost. God has given us capability and

god-like reason; we may, Hamlet certainly does not, live in a
bestial oblivion of it. What he charges himself with is excess of
scruple in employing it in his moral difficulties, thinking too
precisely on the event; his scruples, he says, are craven; or at least
they are one part wisdom and three-quarters cowardice:

> A thought which quartered hath but one part wisdom,
> And ever three parts coward.

He is disposed to upbraid himself for letting all things sleep; but
he also acknowledges, even in his bitter reproachment of himself,
that he is at least one-quarter wise in thinking precisely on the
event: he could not do other than think precisely on such
momentous issues. But then, if his precise thinking issues in no
results, no assured decision, no clear path of duty, how can he be
other than afraid of doing one thing rather than the other? He has
cause and will and strength and means to do it; yes, all these he
has; but has he the conscience to do it? That is the question; and
conscience makes cowards of us. But where is a resolution of this
distress to come from? From thinking precisely on the event?
Apparently not; Hamlet is a thinker and has thought enough.
Then let him plunge, and do what no doubt most people would
expect of him; he talks fustian at himself about greatly finding
quarrel in a straw when honour's at the stake; and this in future
will be his line. But will it? Of course not. It is better to have
three-quarters cowardice and one quarter wisdom than four
quarters of bravado and tomfoolery; and Hamlet knows this
well enough. But where and how will he find escape from this
proper and rightminded cowardice? This is his problem; and it
is, I suppose, everybody's problem.

I am aware that I may well be manifesting a deplorable cock-
sureness in all this. But at least I shall make clear what I intend;
and I confess to some impatience with what seems to me the
present-day willingness to give up Hamlet for a mystery. Now
it is true, no doubt, that we must not see the play as merely an
affair of the character of its hero. But few of us will deny that
Hamlet's procrastination is the major fact in the play and that it
was intended by Shakespeare to be so. But are we really to find

his procrastination a mystery and to leave it a mystery? Is there really anything mysterious about a man who has come to no clear and practised sense of life, and who in the face of a shocking situation which quite peculiarly involves him, shuffles, deceives himself, procrastinates, and in his exasperation cruelly persecutes the person he loves best in the world? Is this beyond our understanding? If we fail to understand it, is it not only because it is all so near to us and not because it is far off in Elizabethan times? Conscience, Hamlet said, makes cowards *of us all.* He was thinking of himself not as the exception, but as the rule.

Maynard Mack

THE WORLD OF *HAMLET*
(1952)

My subject is the world of *Hamlet*. I do not of course mean
Denmark, except as Denmark is given a body by the play; and I
do not mean Elizabethan England, though this is necessarily close
behind the scenes. I mean simply the imaginative environment
that the play asks us to enter when we read it or go to
see it.

Great plays, as we know, do present us with something that
can be called a world, a microcosm – a world like our own in
being made of people, actions, situations, thoughts, feelings, and
much more, but unlike our own in being perfectly, or almost
perfectly, significant and coherent. In a play's world, each part
implies the other parts, and each lives, each means, with the life
and meaning of the rest.

This is the reason, as we also know, that the worlds of great
plays greatly differ. Othello in Hamlet's position, we sometimes
say, would have no problem; but what we are really saying is that
Othello in Hamlet's position would not exist. The conception
we have of Othello is a function of the characters who help
define him, Desdemona, honest Iago, Cassio, and the rest; of his
history of travel and war; of a great storm that divides his ship
from Cassio's, and a handkerchief; of a quiet night in Venice
broken by cries about an old black ram; of a quiet night in
Cyprus broken by sword-play; of a quiet bedroom where a
woman goes to bed in her wedding sheets and a man comes in
with a light to put out the light; and above all, of a language, a
language with many voices in it, gentle, rasping, querulous, or
foul, but all counterpointing the one great voice:

Put up your bright swords, for the dew will rust them.

O thou weed
Who art so lovely fair and smell'st so sweet
That the sense aches at thee. . . .

Yet I'll not shed her blood
Nor scar that whiter skin of hers than snow,
And smooth as monumental alabaster.

I pray you in your letters,
When you shall these unlucky deeds relate,
Speak of me as I am; nothing extenuate,
Nor set down aught in malice; then must you speak
Of one that loved not wisely but too well;
Of one not easily jealous, but being wrought,
Perplex'd in th' extreme; of one whose hand,
Like the base Indian, threw a pearl away
Richer than all his tribe. . . .

Without his particular world of voices, persons, events, the world that both expresses and contains him, Othello is unimaginable. And so, I think, are Antony, King Lear, Macbeth – and Hamlet. We come back then to Hamlet's world, of all the tragic worlds that Shakespeare made, easily the most various and brilliant, the most elusive. It is with no thought of doing justice to it that I have singled out three of its attributes for comment. I know too well, if I may echo a sentiment of Mr E. M. W. Tillyard's, that no one is likely to accept another man's reading of *Hamlet*, that anyone who tries to throw light on one part of the play usually throws the rest into deeper shadow, and that what I have to say leaves out many problems – to mention only one, the knotty problem of the text. All I would say in defense of the materials I have chosen is that they seem to me interesting, close to the root of the matter even if we continue to differ about what the root of the matter is, and explanatory, in a modest way, of this play's peculiar hold on everyone's imagination, its almost mythic status, one might say, as a paradigm of the life of man.

The first attribute that impresses us, I think, is mysteriousness. We often hear it said, perhaps with truth, that every great work

of art has a mystery at the heart; but the mystery of *Hamlet* is
something else. We feel its presence in the numberless explanations that have been brought forward for Hamlet's delay, his
madness, his ghost, his treatment of Polonius, or Ophelia, or his
mother; and in the controversies that still go on about whether
the play is 'undoubtedly a failure' (Eliot's phrase) or one of the
greatest artistic triumphs; whether, if it is a triumph, it belongs
to the highest order of tragedy; whether, if it is such a tragedy,
its hero is to be taken as a man of exquisite moral sensibility
(Bradley's view) or an egomaniac (Madariaga's view).

Doubtless there have been more of these controversies and
explanations than the play requires; for in Hamlet, to paraphrase
a remark of Falstaff's, we have a character who is not only mad in
himself but a cause that madness is in the rest of us. Still, the very
existence of so many theories and counter-theories, many of
them formulated by sober heads, gives food for thought.
Hamlet seems to lie closer to the illogical logic of life than
Shakespeare's other tragedies. And while the causes of this situation may be sought by saying that Shakespeare revised the play
so often that eventually the motivations were smudged over, or
that the original old play has been here or there imperfectly
digested, or that the problems of Hamlet lay so close to Shakespeare's heart that he could not quite distance them in the formal
terms of art, we have still as critics to deal with effects, not causes.
If I may quote again from Mr Tillyard, the play's very lack of a
rigorous type of causal logic seems to be a part of its point.

Moreover, the matter goes deeper than this. Hamlet's world is
preëminently in the interrogative mood. It reverberates with
questions, anguished, meditative, alarmed. There are questions
that in this play, to an extent I think unparalleled in any other,
mark the phases and even the nuances of the action, helping to
establish its peculiar baffled tone. There are other questions
whose interrogations, innocent at first glance, are subsequently
seen to have reached beyond their contexts and to point towards
some pervasive inscrutability in Hamlet's world as a whole.
Such is that tense series of challenges with which the tragedy
begins: Barnardo's of Francisco, 'Who's there?' Francisco's of

Horatio and Marcellus, 'Who is there?' Horatio's of the ghost, 'What art thou . . .?' And then there are the famous questions. In them the interrogations seem to point not only beyond the context but beyond the play, out of Hamlet's predicaments into everyone's: 'What a piece of work is a man . . . and yet to me, what is this quintessence of dust?' 'To be, or not to be, that is the question.' 'Get thee to a nunnery, why wouldst thou be a breeder of sinners?' 'I am very proud, revengeful, ambitious, with more offences at my beck, than I have thoughts to put them in, imagination to give them shape, or time to act them in: what should such fellows as I do crawling between earth and heaven?' 'Does thou think Alexander looked o' this fashion i' th' earth? . . . And smelt so?'

Further, Hamlet's world is a world of riddles. The hero's own language is often riddling, as the critics have pointed out. When he puns, his puns have receding depths in them, like the one which constitutes his first speech: 'A little more than kin, and less than kind.' His utterances in madness, even if wild and whirling, are simultaneously, as Polonius discovers, pregnant: 'Do you know me, my lord?' 'Excellent well, you are a fishmonger.' Even the madness itself is riddling: How much is real? How much is feigned? What does it mean? Sane or mad, Hamlet's mind plays restlessly about his world, turning up one riddle upon another. The riddle of character, for example, and how it is that in a man whose virtues else are 'pure as grace', some vicious mole of nature, some 'dram of evil', can 'all the noble substance oft adulter'. Or the riddle of the player's art, and how a man can so project himself into a fiction, a dream of passion, that he can weep for Hecuba. Or the riddle of action: how we may think too little – 'What to ourselves in passion we propose', says the player-king, 'The passion ending, doth the purpose lose'; and again, how we may think too much: 'Thus conscience does make cowards of us all, And thus the native hue of resolution Is sicklied o'er with the pale cast of thought.'

There are also more immediate riddles. His mother – how could she 'on this fair mountain leave to feed, And batten on this moor?' The ghost – which may be a devil, for 'the devil hath power T' assume a pleasing shape'. Ophelia – what does her behavior to him mean? Surprising her in her closet, he falls to such perusal of her face as he would draw it. Even the king at his prayers is a riddle. Will a revenge that takes him in the purging of his soul be vengeance, or hire and salary? As for himself, Hamlet realizes, he is the greatest riddle of all – a mystery, he warns Rosencrantz and Guildenstern, from which he will not have the heart plucked out. He cannot tell why he has of late lost all his mirth, forgone all custom of exercises. Still less can he tell why he delays: 'I do not know Why yet I live to say "This thing's to do," Sith I have cause, and will, and strength, and means, To do 't.'

Thus the mysteriousness of Hamlet's world is of a piece. It is not simply a matter of missing motivations, to be expunged if only we could find the perfect clue. It is built in. It is evidently an important part of what the play wishes to say to us. And it is certainly an element that the play thrusts upon us from the opening word. Everyone, I think, recalls the mysteriousness of that first scene. The cold middle of the night on the castle plat-form, the muffled sentries, the uneasy atmosphere of apprehen-sion, the challenges leaping out of the dark, the questions that follow the challenges, feeling out the darkness, searching for identities, for relations, for assurance. 'Barnardo?' 'Have you had quiet guard?' 'Who hath relieved you?' 'What, is Horatio there?' 'What, has this thing appeared again to-night?' 'Looks 'a not like the king?' 'How now Horatio! ... Is not this something more than fantasy? What think you on 't?' 'Is it not like the king?' 'Why this same strict and most observant watch ...?' 'Shall I strike at it with my partisan?' 'Do you consent we shall acquaint [young Hamlet] with it?'

We need not be surprised that critics and playgoers alike have been tempted to see in this an evocation not simply of Hamlet's world but of their own. Man in his aspect of bafflement, moving in darkness on a rampart between two worlds, unable to reject, or quite accept, the one that, when he faces it, 'to-shakes' his disposition with thoughts beyond the reaches of his soul – com-forting himself with hints and guesses. We hear these hints and guesses whispering through the darkness as the several watchers speak. 'At least the whisper goes so,' says one. 'I think it be no other but e'en so,' says another. 'I have heard' that on the crowing of the cock 'Th' extravagant and erring spirit hies To his confine,' says a third. 'Some say' at Christmas time 'this bird of dawning' sings all night, 'And then they say no spirit dare stir abroad.' 'So have I heard', says the first, 'and do in part believe it.' However we choose to take the scene, it is clear that it creates a world where uncertainties are of the essence.

Meantime, such is Shakespeare's economy, a second attribute of Hamlet's world has been put before us. This is the problematic nature of reality and the relation of reality to appearance. The play begins with an appearance, an 'apparition', to use Marcellus's term – the ghost. And the ghost is somehow real, indeed the vehicle of realities. Through its revelation, the glittering surface of Claudius's court is pierced, and Hamlet comes to know, and we do, that the king is not only hateful to him but the murderer of his father, that his mother is guilty of adultery as well as incest. Yet there is a dilemma in the revelation. For possibly the apparition *is* an apparition, a devil who has assumed his father's shape.

This dilemma, once established, recurs on every hand. From the court's point of view, there is Hamlet's madness. Polonius investigates and gets some strange advice about his daughter: 'Conception is a blessing, but as your daughter may conceive, friend look to 't.' Rosencrantz and Guildenstern investigate and get the strange confidence that 'Man delights not me, no, nor woman neither.' Ophelia is 'loosed' to Hamlet (Polonius's vulgar word), while Polonius and the king hide behind the arras; and what they hear is a strange indictment of human nature, and a riddling threat: 'Those that are married already, all but one, shall live.'

On the other hand, from Hamlet's point of view, there is Ophelia. Kneeling here at her prayers, she seems the image of innocence and devotion. Yet she is of the sex for whom he has already found the name Frailty, and she is also, as he seems either madly or sanely to divine, a decoy in a trick. The famous cry – 'Get thee to a nunnery' – shows the anguish of his uncertainty. If

Ophelia is what she seems, this dirty-minded world of murder, incest, lust, adultery, is no place for her. Were she 'as chaste as ice, as pure as snow', she could not escape its calumny. And if she is not what she seems, then a nunnery in its other sense of brothel is relevant to her. In the scene that follows he treats her as if she were indeed an inmate of a brothel.

Likewise, from Hamlet's point of view, there is the enigma of the king. If the ghost is *only* an appearance, then possibly the king's appearance is reality. He must try it further. By means of a second and different kind of 'apparition', the play within the play, he does so. But then, immediately after, he stumbles on the king at prayer. This appearance has a relish of salvation in it. If the king dies now, his soul may yet be saved. Yet actually, as we know, the king's efforts to come to terms with heaven have been unavailing; his words fly up, his thoughts remain below. If Hamlet means the conventional revenger's reasons that he gives for sparing Claudius, it was the perfect moment not to spare him – when the sinner was acknowledging his guilt, yet unrepentant. The perfect moment, but it was hidden, like so much else in the play, behind an arras.

There are two arrases in his mother's room. Hamlet thrusts his sword through one of them. Now at last he has got to the heart of the evil, or so he thinks. But now it is the wrong man; now he himself is a murderer. The other arras he stabs through with his words – like daggers, says the queen. He makes her shrink under the contrast he points between her present husband and his father. But as the play now stands (matters are somewhat clearer in the bad Quarto), it is hard to be sure how far the queen grasps the fact that her second husband is the murderer of her first. And it is hard to say what may be signified by her inability to see the ghost, who now for the last time appears. In one sense at least, the ghost is the supreme reality, representative of the hidden ultimate power, in Bradley's terms – witnessing from beyond the grave against this hollow world. Yet the man who is capable of seeing through to this reality, the queen thinks is mad. 'To whom do you speak this?' she cries to her son. 'Do you see nothing there?' he asks, incredulous. And she replies: 'Noth-

ing at all, yet all that is I see.' Here certainly we have the imperturbable self-confidence of the worldly world, its layers on
layers of habituation, so that when the reality is before its very
eyes it cannot detect its presence.

Like mystery, this problem of reality is central to the play and
written deep into its idiom. Shakespeare's favorite terms in
Hamlet are words of ordinary usage that pose the question of
appearances in a fundamental form. 'Apparition' I have already
mentioned. Another term is 'seems'. When we say, as Ophelia
says of Hamlet leaving her closet, 'He seemed to find his way
without his eyes', we mean one thing. When we say, as Hamlet
says to his mother in the first court-scene, 'Seems, madam! . . .
I know not "seems" ', we mean another. And when we say, as
Hamlet says to Horatio before the play within the play, 'And
after we will both our judgements join In censure of his seeming',
we mean both at once. The ambiguities of 'seem' coil and uncoil
throughout this play, and over against them is set the idea of
'seeing'. So Hamlet challenges the king in his triumphant letter
announcing his return to Denmark: 'To-morrow shall I beg
leave to see your kingly eyes.' Yet 'seeing' itself can be ambiguous, as we recognize from Hamlet's uncertainty about the
ghost; or from that statement of his mother's already quoted:
'Nothing at all, yet all that is I see.'

Another term of like importance is 'assume'. What we assume
may be what we are not: 'The devil hath power T' assume a
pleasing shape.' But it may be what we are: 'If it assume my
noble father's person, I'll speak to it.' And it may be what we are
not yet, but would become; thus Hamlet advises his mother,
'Assume a virtue if you have it not.' The perplexity in the word
points to a real perplexity in Hamlet's and our own experience.
We assume our habits – and habits are like costumes, as the
word implies: 'My father in his habit as he lived!' Yet these habits
become ourselves in time: 'That monster custom, who all sense
doth eat Of habits evil, is angel yet in this, That to the use of
actions fair and good He likewise gives a frock or livery That
aptly is put on.'

Two other terms I wish to instance are 'put on' and 'shape'.

The shape of something is the form under which we are accustomed to apprehend it: 'Do you see yonder cloud that's almost in shape of a camel?' But a shape may also be a disguise – even, in Shakespeare's time, an actor's costume or an actor's role. This is the meaning when the king says to Laertes as they lay the plot against Hamlet's life: 'Weigh what convenience both of time and means May fit us to our shape.' 'Put on' supplies an analogous ambiguity. Shakespeare's mind seems to worry this phrase in the play much as Hamlet's mind worries the problem of acting in a world of surfaces, or the king's mind worries the meaning of Hamlet's transformation. Hamlet has put an antic disposition on, that the king knows. But what does 'put on' mean? A mask, or a frock or livery – our 'habit'? The king is left guessing, and so are we.

What is found in the play's key terms is also found in its imagery. Miss Spurgeon has called attention to a pattern of disease images in *Hamlet*, to which I shall return. But the play has other patterns equally striking. One of these, as my earlier quotations hint, is based on clothes. In the world of surfaces to which Shakespeare exposes us in *Hamlet*, clothes are naturally a factor of importance. 'The apparel oft proclaims the man,' Polonius assures Laertes, cataloguing maxims in the young man's ear as he is about to leave for Paris. Oft, but not always. And so he sends his man Reynaldo to look into Laertes' life there – even, if need be, to put a false dress of accusation upon his son ('What forgeries you please'), the better by indirections to find directions out. On the same grounds, he takes Hamlet's vows to Ophelia as false apparel. They are bawds, he tells her – or if we do not like Theobald's emendation, they are bonds – in masquerade, 'Not of that dye which their investments show, But mere implorators of unholy suits.'

This breach between the outer and the inner stirs no special emotion in Polonius, because he is always either behind an arras or prying into one, but it shakes Hamlet to the core. Here so recently was his mother in her widow's weeds, the tears still flushing in her gallèd eyes; yet now within a month, a little month, before even her funeral shoes are old, she has married

with his uncle. Her mourning was all clothes. Not so his own, he
bitterly replies, when she asks him to cast his 'nighted colour
off'. 'Tis not alone my inky cloak, good mother' – and not alone,
he adds, the sighs, the tears, the dejected havior of the visage –
'that can denote me truly'.

> These indeed seem,
> For they are actions that a man might play,
> But I have that within which passes show,
> These but the trappings and the suits of woe.

What we must not overlook here is Hamlet's visible attire,
giving the verbal imagery a theatrical extension. Hamlet's
apparel now is his inky cloak, mark of his grief for his father,
mark also of his character as a man of melancholy, mark possibly
too of his being one in whom appearance and reality are attuned.
Later, in his madness, with his mind disordered, he will wear his
costume in a corresponding disarray, the disarray that Ophelia
describes so vividly to Polonius and that producers of the play
rarely give sufficient heed to: 'Lord Hamlet with his doublet all
unbraced, No hat upon his head, his stockings fouled, Ungart'red,
and down-gyvéd to his ankle.' Here the only question will be,
as with the madness itself, how much is studied, how much is
real. Still later, by a third costume, the simple traveler's garb in
which we find him new come from shipboard, Shakespeare will
show us that we have a third aspect of the man.

A second pattern of imagery springs from terms of painting:
the paints, the colorings, the varnishes that may either conceal,
or, as in the painter's art, reveal. Art in Claudius conceals. 'The
harlot's cheek,' he tells us in his one aside, 'beautied with
plast'ring art, Is not more ugly to the thing that helps it, Than is
my deed to my most painted word.' Art in Ophelia, loosed to
Hamlet in the episode already noticed to which this speech of the
king's is prelude, is more complex. She looks so beautiful – 'the
celestial, and my soul's idol, the most beautified Ophelia',
Hamlet has called her in his love letter. But now, what does
beautified mean? Perfected with all the innocent beauties of a
lovely woman? Or 'beautied' like the harlot's cheek? 'I have

heard of your paintings too, well enough. God hath given you one face and you make yourselves another.'

Yet art, differently used, may serve the truth. By using an 'image' (his own word) of a murder done in Vienna, Hamlet cuts through to the king's guilt; holds 'as 'twere the mirror up to nature', shows 'virtue her own feature, scorn her own image, and the very age and body of the time' – which is out of joint – 'his form and pressure'. Something similar he does again in his mother's bedroom, painting for her in words 'the rank sweat of an enseaméd bed', making her recoil in horror from his 'counterfeit presentment of two brothers', and holding, if we may trust a stage tradition, his father's picture beside his uncle's. Here again the verbal imagery is realized visually on the stage.

The most pervasive of Shakespeare's image patterns in this play, however, is the pattern evolved around the three words, show, act, play. 'Show' seems to be Shakespeare's unifying image in *Hamlet*. Through it he pulls together and exhibits in a single focus much of the diverse material in his play. The ideas of seeming, assuming, and putting on; the images of clothing, painting, mirroring; the episode of the dumb show and the play within the play; the characters of Polonius, Laertes, Ophelia, Claudius, Gertrude, Rosencrantz and Guildenstern, Hamlet himself – all these at one time or another, and usually more than once, are drawn into the range of implications flung round the play by 'show'.

'Act', on the other hand, I take to be the play's radical metaphor. It distills the various perplexities about the character of reality into a residual perplexity about the character of an act. What, this play asks again and again, is an act? What is its relation to the inner act, the intent? 'If I drown myself wittingly', says the clown in the graveyard, 'it argues an act, and an act hath three branches, it is to act, to do, and to perform.' Or again, the play asks, how does action relate to passion, that 'lapsed in time and passion' I can let 'go by Th' important acting of your dread command'; and to thought, which can so sickly o'er the native hue of resolution that 'enterprises of great pitch and moment With this regard their currents turn awry, And lose the name of action'; and to words, which are not acts, and so we dare not be content to unpack our hearts with them, and yet are acts of a sort, for we may speak daggers though we use none. Or still again, how does an act (a deed) relate to an act (a pretense)? For an action may be nothing but pretense. So Polonius readying Ophelia for the interview with Hamlet, with 'pious action', as he phrases it, 'sugar[s] o'er The devil himself'. Or it may not be a pretense, yet not what it appears. So Hamlet spares the king, finding him in an act that has some 'relish of salvation in 't'. Or it may be a pretense that is also the first foothold of a new reality, as when we assume a virtue though we have it not. Or it may be a pretense that is actually a mirroring of reality, like the play within the play, or the tragedy of *Hamlet.*

To this network of implications, the third term, play, adds an additional dimension. 'Play' is a more precise word, in Elizabethan parlance at least, for all the elements in *Hamlet* that pertain to the art of the theatre; and it extends their field of reference till we see that every major personage in the tragedy is a player in some sense, and every major episode a play. The court plays, Hamlet plays, the players play, Rosencrantz and Guildenstern try to play on Hamlet, though they cannot play on his recorders – here we have an extension to a musical sense. And the final duel, by a further extension, becomes itself a play, in which everyone but Claudius and Laertes plays his role in ignorance: 'The queen desires you to use some gentle entertainment to Laertes before you fall to play.' 'I . . . will this brother's wager frankly play.' 'Give him the cup.' – 'I'll play this bout first.'

The full extension of this theme is best evidenced in the play within the play itself. Here, in the bodily presence of these traveling players, bringing with them the latest playhouse gossip out of London, we have suddenly a situation that tends to dissolve the normal barriers between the fictive and the real. For here on the stage before us is a play of false appearances in which an actor called the player-king is playing. But there is also on the stage, Claudius, another player-king, who is a spectator of this player. And there is on the stage, besides, a prince who is a

D   J.S.H.

spectator of both these player-kings and who plays with great
intensity a player's role himself. And around these kings and that
prince is a group of courtly spectators – Gertrude, Rosencrantz,
Guildenstern, Polonius, and the rest – and they, as we have come
to know, are players too. And lastly there are ourselves, an
audience watching all these audiences who are also players.
Where, it may suddenly occur to us to ask, does the playing end?
Which *are* the guilty creatures sitting at a play? When is an act
not an 'act'?

The mysteriousness of Hamlet's world, while it pervades the
tragedy, finds its point of greatest dramatic concentration in the
first act, and its symbol in the first scene. The problems of
appearance and reality also pervade the play as a whole, but come
to a climax in Acts II and III, and possibly their best symbol is
the play within the play. Our third attribute, though again it is
one that crops out everywhere, reaches its full development in
Acts IV and V. It is not easy to find an appropriate name for this
attribute, but perhaps 'mortality' will serve, if we remember to
mean by mortality the heartache and the thousand natural shocks
that flesh is heir to, not simply death.

The powerful sense of mortality in *Hamlet* is conveyed to us,
I think, in three ways. First, there is the play's emphasis on
human weakness, the instability of human purpose, the subjection of humanity to fortune – all that we might call the aspect of
failure in man. Hamlet opens this theme in Act I, when he describes how from that single blemish, perhaps not even the
victim's fault, a man's whole character may take corruption.
Claudius dwells on it again, to an extent that goes far beyond the
needs of the occasion, while engaged in seducing Laertes to step
behind the arras of a seemer's world and dispose of Hamlet by a
trick. Time qualifies everything, Claudius says, including love,
including purpose. As for love – it has a 'plurisy' in it and dies of
its own too much. As for purpose – 'That we would do We
should do when we would: for this "would" changes, And hath
abatements and delays as many As there are tongues, are hands,
are accidents, And then this "should" is like a spendthrift sigh,
That hurts by easing.' The player-king, in his long speeches to

his queen in the play within the play, sets the matter in a still darker light. She means these protestations of undying love, he knows, but our purposes depend on our memory, and our memory fades fast. Or else, he suggests, we propose something to ourselves in a condition of strong feeling, but then the feeling goes, and with it the resolve. Or else our fortunes change, he adds, and with these our loves: 'The great man down, you mark his favourite flies.' The subjection of human aims to fortune is a reiterated theme in *Hamlet*, as subsequently in *Lear*. Fortune is the harlot goddess in whose secret parts men like Rosencrantz and Guildenstern live and thrive; the strumpet who threw down Troy and Hecuba and Priam; the outrageous foe whose slings and arrows a man of principle must suffer or seek release in suicide. Horatio suffers them with composure: he is one of the blessed few 'Whose blood and judgement are so well co-medled, That they are not a pipe for Fortune's finger To sound what stop she please'. For Hamlet the task is of a greater difficulty.

Next, and intimately related to this matter of infirmity, is the emphasis on infection – the ulcer, the hidden abscess, 'th' imposthume of much wealth and peace, That inward breaks, and shows no cause without Why the man dies'. Miss Spurgeon, who was the first to call attention to this aspect of the play, has well remarked that so far as Shakespeare's pictorial imagination is concerned, the problem in *Hamlet* is not a problem of the will and reason, 'of a mind too philosophical or a nature temperamentally unfitted to act quickly', nor even a problem of an individual at all. Rather, it is a condition – 'a condition for which the individual himself is apparently not responsible, any more than the sick man is to blame for the infection which strikes and devours him, but which, nevertheless, in its course and development, impartially and relentlessly, annihilates him and others, innocent and guilty alike'. 'That', she adds, 'is the tragedy of Hamlet, as it is perhaps the chief tragic mystery of life.' This is a perceptive comment, for it reminds us that Hamlet's situation is mainly not of his own manufacture, as are the situations of Shakespeare's other tragic heroes. He has inherited it; he is 'born to set it right'.

We must not, however, neglect to add to this what another student of Shakespeare's imagery has noticed – that the infection in Denmark is presented alternatively as poison. Here, of course, responsibility is implied, for the poisoner of the play is Claudius. The juice he pours into the ear of the elder Hamlet is a combined poison and disease, a 'leperous distilment' that curds 'the thin and wholesome blood'. From this fatal center, unwholesomeness spreads out till there is something rotten in all Denmark. Hamlet tells us that his 'wit's diseased', the queen speaks of her 'sick soul', the king is troubled by 'the hectic' in his blood, Laertes meditates revenge to warm 'the very sickness in my heart', the people of the kingdom grow 'muddied, Thick and unwholesome in their thoughts'; and even Ophelia's madness is said to be 'the poison of deep grief'. In the end, all save Ophelia die of that poison in a literal as well as figurative sense.

But the chief form in which the theme of mortality reaches us, it seems to me, is as a profound consciousness of loss. Hamlet's father expresses something of the kind when he tells Hamlet how his 'most seeming-virtuous queen', betraying a love which 'was of that dignity, That it went hand in hand even with the vow I made to her in marriage', had chosen to 'decline Upon a wretch whose natural gifts were poor To those of mine'. 'O Hamlet, what a falling-off was there!' Ophelia expresses it again, on hearing Hamlet's denunciation of love and woman in the nunnery scene, which she takes to be the product of a disordered brain:

> O, what a noble mind is here o'erthrown!
> The courtier's, soldier's, scholar's, eye, tongue, sword,
> Th' expectancy and rose of the fair state,
> The glass of fashion, and the mould of form,
> Th' observed of all observers, quite quite down!

The passage invites us to remember that we have never actually seen such a Hamlet – that his mother's marriage has brought a falling off in him before we meet him. And then there is that further falling off, if I may call it so, when Ophelia too goes mad – 'Divided from herself and her fair judgement, Without the which we are pictures or mere beasts'.

Time was, the play keeps reminding us, when Denmark was a different place. That was before Hamlet's mother took off 'the rose From the fair forehead of an innocent love' and set a blister there. Hamlet then was still 'th' expectancy and rose of the fair state'; Ophelia, the 'rose of May'. For Denmark was a garden then, when his father ruled. There had been something heroic about his father – a king who met the threats to Denmark in open battle, fought with Norway, smote the sledded Polacks on the ice, slew the elder Fortinbras in an honorable trial of strength. There had been something godlike about his father too: 'Hyperion's curls, the front of Jove himself, An eye like Mars . . . , A station like the herald Mercury.' But, the ghost reveals, a serpent was in the garden, and 'the serpent that did sting thy father's life Now wears his crown'. The martial virtues are put by now. The threats to Denmark are attended to by policy, by agents working deviously for and through an uncle. The moral virtues are put by too. Hyperion's throne is occupied by 'a vice of kings', 'a king of shreds and patches'; Hyperion's bed, by a satyr, a paddock, a bat, a gib, a bloat king with reechy kisses. The garden is unweeded now, and 'grows to seed, things rank and gross in nature Possess it merely'. Even in himself he feels the taint, the taint of being his mother's son; and that other taint, from an earlier garden, of which he admonishes Ophelia: 'For virtue cannot so inoculate our old stock, but we shall relish of it.' 'Why wouldst thou be a breeder of sinners?' 'What should such fellows as I do crawling between earth and heaven?'

'Hamlet is painfully aware', says Professor Tillyard, 'of the baffling human predicament between the angels and the beasts, between the glory of having been made in God's image and the incrimination of being descended from fallen Adam.' To this we may add, I think, that Hamlet is more than aware of it; he exemplifies it; and it is for this reason that his problem appeals to us so powerfully as an image of our own.

Hamlet's problem, in its crudest form, is simply the problem of the avenger: he must carry out the injunction of the ghost and kill the king. But this problem, as I ventured to suggest at the outset, is presented in terms of a certain kind of world. The

ghost's injunction to act becomes so inextricably bound up for
Hamlet with the character of the world in which the action must
be taken – its mysteriousness, its baffling appearances, its deep
consciousness of infection, frailty, and loss – that he cannot come
to terms with either without coming to terms with both.

When we first see him in the play, he is clearly a very young
man, sensitive and idealistic, suffering the first shock of growing
up. He has taken the garden at face value, we might say, supposing mankind to be only a little lower than the angels. Now, in
his mother's hasty and incestuous marriage, he discovers evidence
of something else, something bestial – though even a beast, he
thinks, would have mourned longer. Then comes the revelation
of the ghost, bringing a second shock. Not so much because he
now knows that his serpent-uncle killed his father; his prophetic
soul had almost suspected this. Not entirely, even, because he
knows now how far below the angels humanity has fallen in his
mother, and how lust – these were the ghost's words – 'though
to a radiant angel linked, Will sate itself in a celestial bed And
prey on garbage'. Rather, because he now sees everywhere, but
especially in his own nature, the general taint, taking from life its
meaning, from woman her integrity, from the will its strength,
turning reason into madness. 'Why wouldst thou be a breeder of
sinners?' 'What should such fellows as I do crawling between
earth and heaven?' Hamlet is not the first young man to have felt
the heavy and the weary weight of all this unintelligible world;
and, like the others, he must come to terms with it.

The ghost's injunction to revenge unfolds a different facet of
his problem. The young man growing up is not to be allowed
simply to endure a rotten world, he must also act in it. Yet how
to begin, among so many enigmatic surfaces? Even Claudius,
whom he now knows to be the core of the ulcer, has a plausible
exterior. And around Claudius, swathing the evil out of sight, he
encounters all those other exteriors, as we have seen. Some of
them already deeply infected beneath, like his mother. Some
noble, but marked for infection, like Laertes. Some not particularly corrupt but infinitely corruptible, like Rosencrantz and
Guildenstern; some mostly weak and foolish like Polonius and

Osric. Some, like Ophelia, innocent, yet in their innocence still serving to 'skin and film the ulcerous place'.

And this is not all. The act required of him, though retributive justice, is one that necessarily involves the doer in the general guilt. Not only because it involves a killing; but because to get at the world of seeming one sometimes has to use its weapons. He himself, before he finishes, has become a player, has put an antic disposition on, has killed a man – the wrong man – has helped drive Ophelia mad, and has sent two friends of his youth to death, mining below their mines, and hoisting the engineer with his own petard. He had never meant to dirty himself with these things, but from the moment of the ghost's challenge to act, this dirtying was inevitable. It is the condition of living at all in such a world. To quote Polonius, who knew that world so well, men become 'a little soiled i' th' working'. Here is another matter with which Hamlet has to come to terms.

Human infirmity – all that I have discussed with reference to instability, infection, loss – supplies the problem with its third phase. Hamlet has not only to accept the mystery of man's condition between the angels and the brutes, and not only to act in a perplexing and soiling world. He has also to act within the human limits – 'with shabby equipment always deteriorating', if I may adapt some phrases from Eliot's 'East Coker', 'In the general mess of imprecision of feeling, Undisciplined squads of emotion.' Hamlet is aware of that fine poise of body and mind, feeling and thought, that suits the action to the word, the word to the action; that acquires and begets a temperance in the very torrent, tempest, and whirlwind of passion; but he cannot at first achieve it in himself. He vacillates between undisciplined squads of emotion and thinking too precisely on the event. He learns to his cost how easily action can be lost in 'acting', and loses it there for a time himself. But these again are only the terms of every man's life. As Anatole France reminds us in a now famous apostrophe to Hamlet: 'What one of us thinks without contradiction and acts without incoherence? What one of us is not mad? What one of us does not say with a mixture of pity, comradeship, admiration, and horror, Goodnight, sweet Prince!'

In the last act of the play (or so it seems to me, for I know there can be differences on this point), Hamlet accepts his world and we discover a different man. Shakespeare does not outline for us the process of acceptance any more than he had done with Romeo or was to do with Othello. But he leads us strongly to expect an altered Hamlet, and then, in my opinion, provides him. We must recall that at this point Hamlet has been absent from the stage during several scenes, and that such absences in Shakespearean tragedy usually warn us to be on the watch for a new phase in the development of the character. It is so when we leave King Lear in Gloucester's farmhouse and find him again in Dover fields. It is so when we leave Macbeth at the witches' cave and rejoin him at Dunsinane, hearing of the armies that beset it. Furthermore, and this is an important matter in the theatre – especially important in a play in which the symbolism of clothing has figured largely – Hamlet now looks different. He is wearing a different dress – probably, as Granville-Barker thinks, his 'sea-gown scarfed' about him, but in any case no longer the disordered costume of his antic disposition. The effect is not entirely dissimilar to that in *Lear*, when the old king wakes out of his madness to find fresh garments on him.

Still more important, Hamlet displays a considerable change of mood. This is not a matter of the way we take the passage about defying augury, as Mr Tillyard among others seems to think. It is a matter of Hamlet's whole deportment, in which I feel we may legitimately see the deportment of a man who has been 'illuminated' in the tragic sense. Bradley's term for it is fatalism, but if this is what we wish to call it, we must at least acknowledge that it is fatalism of a very distinctive kind – a kind that Shakespeare has been willing to touch with the associations of the saying in St Matthew about the fall of a sparrow, and with Hamlet's recognition that a divinity shapes our ends. The point is not that Hamlet has suddenly become religious; he has been religious all through the play. The point is that he has now learned, and accepted, the boundaries in which human action, human judgment, are enclosed.

Till his return from the voyage he had been trying to act

beyond these, had been encroaching on the role of providence, if I may exaggerate to make a vital point. He had been too quick to take the burden of the whole world and its condition upon his limited and finite self. Faced with a task of sufficient difficulty in its own right, he had dilated it into a cosmic problem – as indeed every task is, but if we think about this too precisely we cannot act at all. The whole time is out of joint, he feels, and in his young man's egocentricity he will set it right. Hence he misjudges Ophelia, seeing in her only a breeder of sinners. Hence he misjudges himself, seeing himself a vermin crawling between earth and heaven. Hence he takes it upon himself to be his mother's conscience, though the ghost has warned that this is no fit task for him, and returns to repeat the warning: 'Leave her to heaven, And to those thorns that in her bosom lodge.' Even with the king, Hamlet has sought to play at God. *He* it must be who decides the issue of Claudius's salvation, saving him for a more damnable occasion. Now, he has learned that there are limits to the before and after that human reason can comprehend. Rashness, even, is sometimes good. Through rashness he has saved his life from the commission for his death, 'and praised be rashness for it'. This happy circumstance and the unexpected arrival of the pirate ship make it plain that the roles of life are not entirely self-assigned. 'There's a divinity that shapes our ends, Rough-hew them how we will.' Hamlet is ready now for what may happen, seeking neither to foreknow it nor avoid it. 'If it be now, 'tis not to come – if it be not to come, it will be now – if it be not now, yet it will come – the readiness is all.'

The crucial evidence of Hamlet's new frame of mind, as I understand it, is the graveyard scene. Here, in its ultimate symbol, he confronts, recognizes, and accepts the condition of being man. It is not simply that he now accepts death, though Shakespeare shows him accepting it in ever more poignant forms: first, in the imagined persons of the politician, the courtier, and the lawyer, who laid their little schemes to 'circumvent God', as Hamlet puts it, but now lie here; then in Yorick, whom he knew and played with as a child; and then in Ophelia. This last death tears from him a final cry of passion, but the striking contrast between his behavior and Laertes's reveals how deeply he has changed.

Still, it is not the fact of death that invests this scene with its peculiar power. It is instead the haunting mystery of life itself that Hamlet's speeches point to, holding in its inscrutable folds those other mysteries that he has wrestled with so long. These he now knows for what they are, and lays them by. The mystery of evil is present here – for this is after all the universal graveyard, where, as the clown says humorously, he holds up Adam's profession; where the scheming politician, the hollow courtier, the tricky lawyer, the emperor and the clown and the beautiful young maiden, all come together in an emblem of the world; where even, Hamlet murmurs, one might expect to stumble on 'Cain's jaw-bone, that did the first murder'. The mystery of reality is here too – for death puts the question, 'What is real?' in its irreducible form, and in the end uncovers all appearances: 'Is this the fine of his fines, and the recovery of his recoveries, to have his fine pate full of fine dirt?' 'Now get you to my lady's chamber, and tell her, let her paint an inch thick, to this favour she must come.' Or if we need more evidence of this mystery, there is the anger of Laertes at the lack of ceremonial trappings, and the ambiguous character of Ophelia's own death. 'Is she to be buried in Christian burial when she wilfully seeks her own salvation?' asks the gravedigger. And last of all, but most pervasive of all, there is the mystery of human limitation. The grotesque nature of man's little joys, his big ambitions. The fact that the man who used to bear us on his back is now a skull that smells; that the noble dust of Alexander somewhere plugs a bunghole; that 'Imperious Caesar, dead and turned to clay, Might stop a hole to keep the wind away'. Above all, the fact that a pit of clay is 'meet' for such a guest as man, as the gravedigger tells us in his song, and yet that, despite all frailties and limitations, 'That skull had a tongue in it, and could sing once'.

After the graveyard and what it indicates has come to pass in him, we know that Hamlet is ready for the final contest of mighty opposites. He accepts the world as it is, the world as a duel, in which, whether we know it or not, evil holds the poisoned rapier and the poisoned chalice waits; and in which, if we win at all, it

costs not less than everything. I think we understand by the close
of Shakespeare's *Hamlet* why it is that unlike the other tragic
heroes he is given a soldier's rites upon the stage. For as William
Butler Yeats once said, 'Why should we honor those who die on
the field of battle? A man may show as reckless a courage in
entering into the abyss of himself.'

H. D. F. Kitto

HAMLET AS RELIGIOUS DRAMA (1956)

THE first thing that strikes us, or should strike us, when we contemplate the play is that it ends in the complete destruction of the two houses that are concerned. The character of Hamlet and the inner experience that he undergoes are indeed drawn at length and with great subtlety, and we must not overlook the fact; nevertheless, the architectonic pattern just indicated is so vast as to suggest at once that what we are dealing with is no individual tragedy of character, however profound, but something more like religious drama; and this means that unless we are ready, at every step, to relate the dramatic situation to its religious or philosophical background – in other words, to look at the play from a point of view to which more recent drama has not accustomed us – then we may not see either the structure or the meaning of the play as Shakespeare thought them.

Why do Rosencrantz and Guildenstern die, and Ophelia, and Laertes? Are these disasters casual by-products of 'the tragedy of a man who could not make up his mind'? Or are they necessary parts of a firm structure? Each of these disasters we can refer to something that Hamlet has done or failed to do, and we can say that each reveals something more of Hamlet's character; but if we see no more than this we are short-sighted, and are neglecting Shakespeare's plain directions in favour of our own. We are told much more than this when we hear Horatio, and then Laertes, cry 'Why, what a king is this!', 'The king, the king's to blame'; also when Guildenstern says, with a deep and unconscious irony, 'We here give up ourselves...', and when Laertes talks of 'contagious blastments'. Shakespeare puts before us a group of young people, friends or lovers, none of them wicked, one of them at least entirely virtuous, all surrounded by the poisonous air of Denmark (which also Shakespeare brings frequently and vividly before our minds), all of them brought to death because of its evil influences. Time after time, either in some significant patterning or with some phrase pregnant with irony, he makes us see that these people are partners in disaster, all of them borne down on the 'massy wheel' to 'boist'rous ruin'.

In this, the natural working-out of sin, there is nothing mechanical. That is the philosophic reason why character and situation must be drawn vividly. Neither here nor in Greek drama have we anything to do with characters who are puppets in the hands of Fate. In both, we see something of the power of the gods, or the designs of Providence; but these no more override or reduce to unimportance the natural working of individual character than the existence, in the physical world, of universal laws overrides the natural behaviour of natural bodies. It is indeed precisely in the natural behaviour of men, and its natural results, in given circumstances, that the operation of the divine laws can be discerned. In *Hamlet*, Shakespeare draws a complete character, not for the comparatively barren purpose of 'creating' a Hamlet for our admiration, but in order to show how he, like the others, is inevitably engulfed by the evil that has been set in motion, and how he himself becomes the cause of further ruin. The conception which unites these eight persons in one coherent catastrophe may be said to be this: evil, once started on its course, will so work as to attack and overthrow impartially the good and the bad; and if the dramatist makes us feel, as he does, that a Providence is ordinant in all this, that, as with the Greeks, is his way of universalising the particular event.

Claudius, the arch-villain, driven by crime into further crime, meets at last what is manifestly divine justice. 'If his fitness speaks . . .' says Hamlet; the 'fitness' of Claudius has been speaking for a long time. At the opposite pole stands Ophelia, exposed to corruption though uncorrupted, but pitifully destroyed as the chain of evil uncoils itself. Then Gertrude, one of Shakespeare's most tragic characters: she is the first, as Laertes is the last, to be tainted by Claudius; but while he dies in forgiveness and reconciliation, no such gentle influence alleviates her end. In the bedchamber scene Hamlet had pointed out to her the hard road to amendment; has she tried to follow it? On this, Shakespeare is silent; but her last grim experience of life is to find that 'O my dear Hamlet – the drink, the drink! I am poisoned' – poisoned, as she must realise, by the cup that her new husband had prepared for the son whom she loved so tenderly. After her own sin, and as a direct consequence of it, everything that she holds dear is blasted. Her part in this tragedy is indeed a frightening one. She is no Claudius, recklessly given to crime, devoid of any pure or disinterested motive. Her love for her son shines through every line she speaks; this, and her affection for Ophelia, show us the Gertrude that might have been, if a mad passion had not swept her into the arms of Claudius. By this one sin she condemned herself to endure, and, still worse, to understand, all its devastating consequences: her son driven 'mad', killing Polonius, denouncing herself and her crime in cruel terms that she cannot rebut, Ophelia driven out of her senses and into her grave – nearly a criminal's grave; all her hopes irretrievably ruined. One tragic little detail, just before the end, shows how deeply Shakespeare must have pondered on his Gertrude. We know that she has seen the wild struggle in the graveyard between Laertes and Hamlet. When the Lord enters, to invite Hamlet to the fencing-match, he says: 'The queen desires you to use some gentle entertainment to Laertes before you fall to play.' 'She well instructs me,' says Hamlet. What can this mean, except that she has vague fears of Laertes' anger, and a pathetic hope that Hamlet might appease it, by talk more courteous than he had used in the graveyard? It recalls her equally pathetic wish that Ophelia's beauty and virtue might 'bring him to his wonted way again'. The mischief is always much greater than her worst fears. We soon see how Hamlet's gentle entertainment is received by Laertes; and she, in the blinding flash in which she dies, learns how great a treachery had been prepared against her Hamlet.

We cannot think of Gertrude's death, and the manner of it, without recalling what the Ghost had said: Leave her to Heaven. But if we are to see the hand of Providence – whatever that may

signify – in her death, can we do other with the death of Polonius?
A 'casual slaughter'? A 'rash and bloody deed'? Certainly; and
let us by all means blame Hamlet for it, as also for the callousness
with which he sends Rosencrantz and Guildenstern to their
doom; but if we suppose that Shakespeare contrived these things
only to show us what Hamlet was like, we shall be treating as
secular drama what Shakespeare designed as something bigger.
In fact, Hamlet was *not* like this, any more than he was, by nature,
hesitant or dilatory; any more than Ophelia was habitually mad.
This is what he has become. The dramatist does indeed direct us
to regard the killing of Polonius in two aspects at once: it is a
sudden, unpremeditated attack made by Hamlet, 'mad', on one
who he hopes will prove to be Claudius; and at the same time it
is the will of Heaven:

> For this same lord,
> I do repent; but heaven hath pleased it so,
> To punish me with this, and this with me,
> That I must be their scourge and minister.

Surely this is exactly the same dramaturgy that we meet in
Sophocles' *Electra*. When Orestes comes out from killing his
mother, Electra asks him how things are. 'In the *palace*',* he says,
'all is well – if Apollo's oracle was well.' Perhaps it was a 'rash
and bloody deed'; it seems to bring Orestes little joy. We may
think of it what we like; Sophocles does not invite us to approve,
and if we suppose that he does, we have not understood his
play, or his gods. Apollo approves, and Orestes, though he acts
for his own reasons, is the gods' 'scourge and minister'. Polonius,
no unworthy Counsellor of this King, a mean and crafty man
whose soul is mirrored in his language no less than in his acts,
meets a violent death while spying; and that such a man should
so be killed is, in a large sense, right. Hamlet may 'repent';
Orestes may feel remorse at a dreadful act, but in each case
Heaven was ordinant.

The death of Laertes too is a coherent part of this same pattern.

* I italicise this word in order to represent Sophocles' untranslate-
able μέν, which suggests a coming antithesis that in fact is not expressed.

To this friend of Hamlet's we can attribute one fault; nor are we taken by surprise when we meet it, for Shakespeare has made his preparations. Laertes is a noble and generous youth, but his sense of honour has no very secure foundations – and Polonius' fare-well speech to him makes the fact easy to understand. His natural and unguarded virtue, assailed at once by his anger, his in-complete understanding of the facts, and the evil suggestions of Claudius, gives way; he falls into treachery, and through it, as he comes to see, he is 'justly killed'.

Of Rosencrantz and Guildenstern, two agreeable though un-distinguished young men, flattered and suborned and cruelly destroyed, there is no more to be said; but there remains Hamlet, last and greatest of the eight. Why must he be destroyed? It would be true to say that he is destroyed simply because he has failed to destroy Claudius first; but this is 'truth' as it is under-stood between police-inspectors, on duty. The dramatic truth must be something which, taking this in its stride, goes much deeper; and we are justified in saying 'must be' since this cata-strophe too is presented as being directed by Providence, and therefore inevitable and 'right'. If 'there is special providence in the fall of a sparrow', there surely is in the fall of a Hamlet.

Of the eight victims, we have placed Claudius at one pole and Ophelia at the other; Hamlet, plainly, stands near Ophelia. In both Hamlet and Ophelia we can no doubt detect faults: she ought to have been able to see through Polonius, and he should not have hesitated. But to think like this is to behave like a judge, one who must stand outside the drama and sum up from a neutral point of view; the critic who tries to do this would be better employed in a police-court than in criticism. We must remain within the play, not try to peer at the characters through a window of our own constructing. If we do remain within the play, we observe that what Shakespeare puts before us, all the time, is not faults that we can attribute to Ophelia and Hamlet, but their virtues; and when he does make Hamlet do things deserving of blame, he also makes it evident on whom the blame should be laid. The impression with which he leaves us is not the tragedy that one so fine as Hamlet should be ruined by one fault;

it is the tragedy that one so fine should be drawn down into the gulf; and, beyond this, that the poison let loose in Denmark should destroy indiscriminately the good, the bad and the indifferent. Good and bad, Hamlet and Claudius, are coupled in the one sentence 'If his fitness speaks, mine is ready'. That Claudius is 'fit and seasoned for his passage' is plain enough; is it not just as plain that Hamlet is equally 'ready'? What has he been telling us, throughout the play, but that life can henceforth have no meaning or value to him? Confronted by what he sees in Denmark, he, the man of action, has been reduced to impotence; the man of reason has gone 'mad'; the man of religion has been dragged down to 'knavery', and has felt the contagions of Hell. There is room, though not very much, for subtle and judicious appraisal of his character and conduct; the core of his tragedy is not here, but in the fact that such surpassing excellence is, like the beauty and virtue of Ophelia, brought to nothing by evil. Through all the members of these two doomed houses the evil goes on working, in a concatenation

> Of carnal, bloody and unnatural acts,
> Of accidental judgements, casual slaughters,
> Of deaths put on by cunning and forced cause,

until none are left, and the slate is wiped clean.

The structure of *Hamlet*, then, suggests that we should treat it as religious drama, and when we do, it certainly does not lose either in significance or in artistic integrity. As we have seen more than once, it has fundamental things in common with Greek religious drama – yet in other respects it is very different, being so complex in form and texture. It may be worth while to enquire, briefly, why this should be so.

One naturally compares it with the two Greek revenge-tragedies, the *Choephori* and Sophocles' *Electra*, but whether we do this, or extend the comparison to other Greek religious tragedies like the *Agamemnon* or *Oedipus Tyrannus* or *Antigone*, we find one difference which is obviously pertinent to our enquiry: in the Greek plays the sin, crime or error which is the mainspring of the action is specific, while in *Hamlet* it is something more general, a quality rather than a single act. Thus, although there are crimes enough in the *Oresteia*, what we are really concerned with, throughout the trilogy, is the problem of avenging or punishing crime. The *Agamemnon* is full of hybris, blind folly, blood-lust, adultery, treachery; but what humanity is suffering from, in the play, is not these sins in themselves, but a primitive conception of Justice, one which uses, and can be made to justify, these crimes, and leads to chaos; and the trilogy ends not in any form of reconciliation or forgiveness among those who have injured each other, nor in any purging of sin, or acceptance of punishment, but in the resolution of the dilemma.

Hamlet resembles the *Choephori* in this, that the murder of a King, and adultery, or something like it, are the crimes which have to be avenged; also that these can be avenged only through another crime, though perhaps a sinless one; but the differences are deep and far-reaching. They are not merely that Orestes kills, and Hamlet shrinks from killing. We may say that both in the Greek trilogy and in Shakespeare's play the Tragic Hero, ultimately, is humanity itself; and what humanity is suffering from, in *Hamlet* is not a specific evil, but Evil itself. The murder is only the chief of many manifestations of it, the particular case which is the mainspring of the tragic action.

This seems to be typical. In the *Antigone* a whole house is brought down in ruin, and, again, the cause is quite a specific one. It is nothing like the comprehensive wickedness of Iago, or the devouring ambition of Macbeth, or the consuming and all-excluding love of Antony and Cleopatra. It is, quite precisely, that Creon makes, and repeats, a certain error of judgment, ἁμαρτία; and I use the phrase 'error of judgment' meaning not that it is venial, nor that it is purely intellectual, but that it is specific. It is not a trivial nor a purely intellectual mistake if a man, in certain circumstances, rejects the promptings of humanity, and thinks that the gods will approve; but this is what Creon does, and the tragedy springs from this and from nothing else. He is not a wicked man – not lecherous or envious or ambitious or vindictive. All this is irrelevant. He is simply the man to make and maintain this one specific and disastrous error.

This contrast between the specific and the general obviously has a close connexion with the contrast between the singleness of the normal Greek tragic structure and the complexity of *Hamlet*. In the first place, since Shakespeare's real theme is not the moral or theological or social problem of crime and vengeance, still less its effect on a single mind and soul, but the corroding power of sin, he will present it not as a single 'error of judgment' but as a hydra with many heads. We have shown, let us hope, how this explains, or helps to explain, such features of the play as, so to speak, the simultaneous presentation of three Creons: Claudius, Gertrude and Polonius, each of them, in his own degree, an embodiment of the general evil. Hence too the richer character-drawing. Claudius is a drunkard, and the fact makes its own contribution to the complete structure; if Sophocles had made Creon a drunkard, it would have been an excrescence on the play. Hence too the frequent changes of scene in the first part of the play; also the style of speech invented for Polonius and Osric. The general enemy is the rottenness that pervades Denmark; therefore it is shown in many persons and many guises.

Then, not only are the sources of the corruption diverse, but so are its ramifications too. We are to see how it spreads, whether from Claudius or from Gertrude or from Polonius, and how it involves one after another, destroying as it goes. To be sure, Greek tragedy shows us something similar – but it is not the same. For example, the condemnation of Antigone leads to the death of Haemon, and that to the death of Eurydice; in the *Oresteia* too there is a long succession of crime. In fact, we remarked above that Claudius recalls the *Agamemnon* and its πρώταρχος ἄτη, the crime that sets crime in motion. So he does; but there is a big difference. Both in *Hamlet* and in the Greek plays crime leads to crime, or disaster to disaster, in this linear fashion, but in *Hamlet* it spreads in another way too, one which is not Greek: it spreads from soul to soul, as a contagion, as when Laertes is tempted by Claudius, or, most notably, when, by his mother's example and Polonius' basely inspired interference, Hamlet's love is corrupted into lewdness, or when he turns against his two compromised friends and pitilessly sends them to death.

Extension of evil in this fashion is, I think, foreign to Greek tragedy. Clearly, it involves a dramatic form which is complexive, not linear and single, like the Greek. Of his successive victims, Sophocles does not even mention Haemon until the middle of the play, and Eurydice not until the end; and the effect is most dramatic. In *Hamlet* there are eight victims, all of whom we have to watch, from time to time, as they become more and more deeply involved.

Further, not only are more people involved at the same time in this more generalised Tragic Flaw, but they are involved more intimately, which again makes for a richer dramatic texture. We may compare Hamlet with Orestes. Externally, they are in a similar position. But when Aeschylus has shown us that Orestes is an avenger pure in heart, and that his dilemma is from every point of view an intolerable one, it is not far wrong to say that his interest in Orestes, as a character, is exhausted; anything more would be unnecessary. Hamlet exists in a different kind of tragedy, one which requires that we should see how the contagion gradually spreads over his whole spirit and all his conduct.

The same contrast exists between Hamlet and Sophocles' Orestes and Electra. She, one might say, is drawn much more intimately than the Orestes of Aeschylus. True; but still she is drawn, so to speak, all at once: there is the situation, here is Electra, and this is the way in which it makes her act. It is not Sophocles' conception to show how her mother's continuing crime gradually warps her mind, by a stealthy growth of evil. If she is warped, it has all happened already. His dramatic interest in the characters of the avengers is focussed on this, that they, being what they are, and being affected by Clytemnestra's crime in this way, will naturally act as they do.

It is, in short, a general statement which I think will bear examination, that Greek tragedy presents sudden and complete disaster, or one disaster linked to another in linear fashion, while Shakespearean tragedy presents the complexive, menacing spread of ruin; and that at least one explanation of this is that the Greek

poets thought of the tragic error as the breaking of a divine law
(or sometimes, in Aeschylus, as the breaking down of a temporary
divine law), while Shakespeare saw it as an evil quality which,
once it has broken loose, will feed on itself and on anything else
that it can find until it reaches its natural end. So, for example, in
Macbeth: in 'noble Macbeth', ambition is stimulated, and is not
controlled by reason or religion; it meets with a stronger
response from Lady Macbeth, and grows insanely into a mon-
strous passion that threatens a whole kingdom. It is a tragic
conception which is essentially dynamic, and demands the very
unhellenic fluidity and expansiveness of expression which the
Elizabethan theatre afforded. Whether this is a reflection of some
profound difference between Greek and Christian thought is a
question which I am not competent to discuss.

T. S. Eliot

THE OPENING SCENE OF *HAMLET*
(1951)

IT is . . . necessary for any long poem, if it is to escape mono-
tony, to be able to say homely things without bathos, as well as to
take the highest flights without sounding exaggerated. And it is
still more important in a play, especially if it is concerned with
contemporary life. The reason for writing even the more pedestrian parts of a verse play in verse instead of prose is, however,
not only to avoid calling the audience's attention to the fact that
it is at other moments listening to poetry. It is also that the verse
rhythm should have its effect upon the hearers, without their
being conscious of it. A brief analysis of one scene of Shakespeare's may illustrate this point. The opening scene of *Hamlet* –
as well constructed an opening scene as that of any play ever
written – has the advantage of being one that everybody knows.

What we do not notice, when we witness this scene in the
theatre, is the great variation of style. Nothing is superfluous,
and there is no line of poetry which is not justified by its dramatic
value. The first twenty-two lines are built of the simplest words
in the most homely idiom. Shakespeare had worked for a long
time in the theatre, and written a good many plays, before
reaching the point at which he could write those twenty-two
lines. There is nothing quite so simplified and sure in his previous work. He first developed conversational, colloquial verse
in the monologue of the character part – Faulconbridge in *King
John*, and later the Nurse in *Romeo and Juliet*. It was a much
further step to carry it unobtrusively into the dialogue of brief
replies. No poet has begun to master dramatic verse until he can
write lines which, like these in *Hamlet*, are *transparent*. You are
consciously attending, not to the poetry, but to the meaning of
the poetry. If you were hearing *Hamlet* for the first time, without

knowing anything about the play, I do not think that it would occur to you to ask whether the speakers were speaking in verse or prose. The verse is having a different effect upon us from prose; but at the moment, what we are aware of is the frosty night, the officers keeping watch on the battlements, and the foreboding of a tragic action. I do not say that there is no place for the situation in which part of one's pleasure will be the enjoyment of hearing beautiful poetry – providing that the author gives it, in that place, dramatic inevitability. And of course, when we have both seen a play several times and read it between performances, we begin to analyse the means by which the author has produced his effects. But in the immediate impact of this scene we are unconscious of the medium of its expression.

From the short, brusque ejaculations at the beginning, suitable to the situation and to the character of the guards – but not expressing more character than is required for their function in the play – the verse glides into a slower movement with the appearance of the courtiers Horatio and Marcellus.

> Horatio says 'tis but our fantasy, . . .

and the movement changes again on the appearance of Royalty, the ghost of the King, into the solemn and sonorous

> What art thou that usurp'st this time of night, . . .

(and note, by the way, this anticipation of the plot conveyed by the use of the verb *usurp*); and majesty is suggested in a reference reminding us whose ghost this is:

> So frowned he once, when in an angry parle
> He smote the sledded Polacks on the ice.

There is an abrupt change to staccato in Horatio's words to the Ghost on its second appearance; this rhythm changes again with the words

> We do it wrong being so majestical
> To offer it the show of violence,
> For it is as the air, invulnerable,
> And our vain blows malicious mockery.

The scene reaches a resolution with the words of Marcellus:

> It faded on the crowing of the cock.
> Some say that ever 'gainst that season comes
> Wherein our Saviour's birth is celebrated
> This bird of dawning singeth all night long, . . .

and Horatio's answer:

> So have I heard and do in part believe it.
> But look, the morn in russet mantle clad
> Walks o'er the dew of yon high eastward hill.
> Break we our watch up.

This is great poetry, and it is dramatic; but besides being poetic and dramatic, it is something more. There emerges, when we analyse it, a kind of musical design also which reinforces and is one with the dramatic movement. It has checked and accelerated the pulse of our emotion without our knowing it. Note that in these last words of Marcellus there is a deliberate brief emergence of the poetic into consciousness. When we hear the lines

> But look, the morn in russet mantle clad
> Walks o'er the dew of yon high eastward hill,

we are lifted for a moment beyond character, but with no sense of unfitness of the words coming, and at this moment, from the lips of Horatio. The transitions in the scene obey laws of the music of dramatic poetry. Note that the two lines of Horatio which I have quoted twice are preceded by a line of the simplest speech which might be either verse or prose:

> So have I heard and do in part believe it,

and that he follows them abruptly with a half line which is hardly more than a stage direction:

> Break we our watch up.

It would be interesting to pursue, by a similar analysis, this problem of the double pattern in great poetic drama – the pattern which may be examined from the point of view of stagecraft or from that of the music. But I think that the examination of this one scene is enough to show us that verse is not merely a formalization, or an added decoration, but that it intensifies the drama. It should indicate also the importance of the unconscious effect of the verse upon us. And lastly, I do not think that this effect is felt only by those members of an audience who 'like poetry' but also by those who go for the play alone. By the people who do not like poetry, I mean those who cannot sit down with a book of poetry and enjoy reading it: these people also, when they go to a play in verse, should be affected by the poetry. And these are the audiences whom the writer of such a play ought to keep in mind.

Harry Levin

THE ANTIC DISPOSITION
(1959)

> To define true madness,
> What is't but to be nothing else but mad?

HAMLET'S state of mind is one of those questions upon which all the doctors have disagreed. Even professional alienists have offered their diagnoses; yet discussion has been no more conclusive, and definition no less redundant or circular, than the rhetorical question posed by Polonius (II ii 93–4). At one extreme the answer has been bounded by unequivocal statements in the sources that, as the English translation of Belleforest puts it, 'Hamblet counterfeited the madman'.[1] At the other it has been bemused by the assumption, which proved particularly congenial to romantic actors like Edwin Booth, that Hamlet was really the victim of the mental disease he claimed to be simulating; in other words, his pretence was pretended, a ruse of madman's cunning. Continental observers have diagnosed it as 'the first and greatest manifestation of the English malady, Spleen'.[2] Consultation with contemporaneous authorities on medicine and psychology has illuminated, if not solved, the problem.[3] Hamlet was suffering, so they inform us, from 'melancholy adust' – or, as we might say, having a nervous breakdown. The Elizabethan term, although it depends upon an outmoded physiological concept, is scarcely less precise than our modern expression. Both imply that Hamlet's case is not chronic, that since his father's death his conduct has been uncharacteristic, and that he is not his courtly, scholarly, soldierly self during the interval when we are his witnesses. Hamlet himself is quite explicit upon this point; and in his Third Soliloquy, the single occasion on which he refers to melancholy, he couples it with weakness (II ii 605). That it is symptomatic of an underlying malaise, which has an objective and external cause, his sharpest observer, Claudius, is all too well aware:

> There's something in his soul,
> O'er which his melancholy sits on brood. (III i 167–8)

Something turns out to be nothing less than revenge, deeply motivated and deviously hatched. However, the motive for Hamlet's eccentric behavior is not that of his legendary proto-type, whose father had been openly slain and whose own life would be directly threatened if he were not considered a harmless madman. Hamlet stands in need of a new *persona*, once the Ghost has excited his suspicions, not so much in order to feel his way as to speak his mind with impunity. 'Give thy thoughts no tongue' is the first commandment in the world of Polonius (I iii 59). From the outset Hamlet feels constrained to hold his tongue, to keep his counsel in soliloquy (I ii 159); with his fellow courtiers, as with the players, gradually he learns to 'show fairly outwards' (II ii 377–8). The mere show of mourning, he has retorted to Gertrude, is far surpassed by the actuality of his grief. She had begun by asking him to 'cast thy nighted colour off' (I ii 68). He will comply, with a vengeance, when he decides to 'put an antic disposition on' (I v 172). Claudius will all but under-stand, in wondering 'why he puts on this confusion' (III i 2); and Hamlet will employ the same verb, *put on*, in exhorting Gertrude to assume a virtue she may not possess (III iv 165). Attributes and attitudes are habitually put on and taken off, as if they were clothes, in Shakespeare's imagery. In *1 Henry IV* the Prince serves notice that he will soon 'throw off' his 'loose behaviour' (I ii 232). He too must play an assumed part, as Falstaff jocosely reminds him: 'Thou art essentially mad without seeming so' (II iv 540–1). Hamlet reverses that outlook in a moment of hectic irony, by telling Gertrude to tell Claudius

> That I essentially am not in madness,
> But mad in craft. (III iv 187–8)

Madness, as the abandonment of reason, is a constant danger throughout the play, from Horatio's desperate warning against

the Ghost (I iv 69–74) through Hamlet's disingenuous apology
to Laertes (v II 228–37). Yet Hamlet is clearly thoughtsick rather
than brainsick – neurotic rather than psychotic, to state the
matter in more clinical terms. In his battle of wits with Rosencrantz and Guildenstern, he is led to affirm that his 'wit's
diseased' (III ii 322–3); but he has already come closer to the
mark in characterizing himself as 'mad north-north-west' (II ii
382). He is, indeed, what circumstance has made him, a mono-
maniac. He can distinguish shrewdly enough between a hawk
and a handsaw, or expatiate with lucidity and brilliance upon
many another theme. But his obsession with his mother's marriage and his hostility against his uncle are forbidden themes
which he may not harp on unless he is granted a certain license,
not to say licentiousness. This 'crafty madness' provides him
with a means of expressing pent-up emotions, which are communicated to the audience through asides and soliloquies, but
which can find no release until they reach the other characters
through a sequence of sharply pointed *contretemps*. Thus his
denunciation of feminine frailty, though its appropriate target
will be Gertrude, first falls upon the bewildered ears of the
innocent Ophelia, who thereupon concludes that he is mad. His
intelligence has never been keener than when he soliloquized a
few moments before; while her pronouncement, 'O, what a
noble mind is here o'erthrown!', will reverberate ironically; for it
is her reason which will be sacrificed, 'Like sweet bells jangled,
out of tune and harsh' (III i 153–61).

One way or another, it is not surprising that the play should
have become a byword for preoccupation with insanity. Three of
Shakespeare's contemporaries burlesqued it in *Eastward Ho*,
where a footman named Hamlet calls for 'my lady's coach', and
is asked by a tankard-bearer: 'Are you mad?' (III ii 4, 6). Mallarmé recalls a production at a French provincial theater, which
was billed as *Hamlet, ou le Distrait*.[4] A recent study of 'madness
as a theatrical medium' dates its English popularity during the
early years of the seventeenth century from Shakespeare's
example.[5] In this respect, however, as in so many others, Shakespeare in turn was following the example of that most popular of

all Elizabethan or Jacobean plays, *The Spanish Tragedy, or Hieronimo's Mad Again.* Kyd's subtitle suggests that interest centered upon the fits and remissions of the hero's lunacy. Shakespeare's first tragic hero, Titus Andronicus, crudely observes that precedent; though he is undoubtedly driven insane, he goes on having his lucid intervals, and 'his feigned ecstasies' as well (IV iv 21). When, 'to feed his brainsick humours', Tamora and her sons disguise themselves as personifications of Revenge, Murder, and Rapine, he recognizes her as Lear will recognize Gloucester: 'I know thee well enough' (v ii 71, 21). And Titus knows well enough how to complete the Senecan catastrophe by serving the sons to their mother baked in a pie. These formalities are duly matched by the rant and bombast of the style. All of *Titus Andronicus,* except for two brief scenes of intentional comedy, is written in the blank verse standardized by the Tragedy of Revenge.

Here again, the pattern seems to have been laid down by *The Spanish Tragedy,* wherein, when Hieronimo's wife *'runs lunatic',* her ravings are grandiose, formal, and operatic (III viii). This is true of her husband in the original version, as of Greene's frenzied protagonist in *Orlando Furioso,* and of all stock pre-Shakespearean madmen. But it is a far cry from Hieronimo's vein of plangent lamentation to the anonymous passages added later in a tersely modulated prose. These additions, notably the Painter's Scene, render the moods and changes of derangement far more vividly than Kyd's stilted pentameters, and may well register the influence of *Hamlet* on the revision of the older work. Credit for the actual innovation should be accorded to Marlowe's *1 Tamburlaine,* wherein the distraught Zabina anticipates Ophelia with a good-night speech in distracted prose (IV ii 247–56).[6] Prose, with its pedestrian functions, is inherently a comic idiom, whereas the tragic note is traditionally sounded in verse. When the two modes converge, the result is what neo-classical critics of the Elizabethans deplored, the intermingling of hornpipes with funerals. For the romantics, it was the special glory of Shakespeare to unite the grotesque with the sublime, to catch the complexities of mixed emotion. The paradoxical hints in the opening speech of Claudius, 'mirth in funeral . . . dirge in marriage' (i ii 12), are poignantly acted out in the graveyard and in Ophelia's mad scenes, where snatches of ribald balladry make their subconscious comment on unfulfilled love. 'Thoughts and remembrance fitted' lend pertinence to her unshaped use of speech, while the symbolism of the flowers sets up a series of personal associations, making her case history 'a document in madness' (IV v 177–8).

Similarly, blank verse breaks down into fragmentary prose, which compulsively recapitulates the psychological situation, in the somnambulism of Lady Macbeth or the delirium of King Lear. The latter has two companions in aberration: the half-witted Fool, whose prose is half-crazy, half-comic, and Edgar impersonating Tom of Bedlam. That impersonation had living models which Edgar describes (II iii 13–20), as well as a dramatic forerunner in Diccon the Bedlam, or Vice, of *Gammer Gurton's Needle*. Furthermore, Edgar seems to have worked up his imprecations from a pamphlet by Samuel Harsnett on popery, just as Doll Common in Jonson's *Alchemist* – when she is supposed to be crazed by religious fanaticism – reels off a memorized page or two from Hugh Broughton's scriptural prophecies. This is an easier way of playing insane than Hamlet's, since he is compelled to sustain both sides of his dual role. Up to the end of the First Act, when the Ghost teaches him the grim lesson he writes upon his tables – the difference between *seems* and *is* as personified by the hypocritical Claudius – Hamlet speaks blank verse in all sincerity and sanity. Thereafter, as he warns Horatio and Marcellus in 'wild and whirling words', he is to undergo a transformation (I v 133). Throughout the rest of the play, until his feelings come to the surface again in the last act, his medium for dialogue is his own kind of antic prose. The exceptions to this rule are consistent: the soliloquies and his confidential interviews with Horatio and the Queen. Characteristically he shifts into verse when the others leave the stage:

Ay, so, God bye to you.
                    Exeunt ROSENCRANTZ *and* GUILDENSTERN

> Now I am alone.
> O, what a rogue and peasant slave am I! ...   (II ii 552–3)

Conversely, when he and Horatio are joined by the others, he
maneuvers a quick change into prose:

> They are coming to the play. I must be idle.
> Get you a place.
> *King.*   How fares our cousin Hamlet?
> *Hamlet.* Excellent i' faith, of the chameleon's dish, I eat the air,
>   promise-crammed, you cannot feed capons so.
> (III iv 88–92)

And Claudius is forced, against his habit, to continue more or
less in Hamlet's medium. Hamlet forces the same shift upon his
interlocutors in both the Fishmonger Scene and the Schoolfellow
Scene. It also occurs at a crucial point in the Nunnery Scene,
where, since he has been soliloquizing, and since he almost trusts
Ophelia, he prolongs his greeting to her in verse. The fact that
he switches with 'Ha, ha! are you honest?' supports the argument
that he has just then caught a glimpse of the skulking Polonius
(III i 103). Consequently Hamlet's distrust of Ophelia is confirmed;
and henceforth he will address her too with bitterly cynical gibes.
  Prose, for her, will give voice to authentic madness. He
employs it for his histrionic escapade, though he finds it useful for
other purposes when 'the wind is northerly' (v II 99–100): to
parody the affectation of Osric, or to speculate on the human
condition in language which moves from Florio's Montaigne
toward the King James Bible. The main effect is to isolate Hamlet
from everyone whose discourse runs in the expected rhythms,
so that we are continually and painfully reminded of his exceptional predicament. Since the implicit distinction between the
exterior and the inward man is marked in much the same fashion
by Shakespeare's fellow playwrights, especially Marston, we may
regard the device as a convention. As such, it is thrown into sharp
relief in *The Malcontent*, where the titular character, Malevole, is
actually Duke Altofront in disguise. With his confidant, Celso,
he may talk in blank verse; but at the entrance of an old courtier
who resembles Polonius, the stage-direction reads: '*Bilioso re-*

entering, Malevole shifteth his speech' (i i 255). What he says in
prose is 'halter-worthy' yet privileged. 'He is free as air; he blows
over every man' (i i 42). Yet his railing is merely a source of
amusement to the corrupted courtiers. It is significant that
Malevole, like Hamlet, like most of Marston's heroes, and like
so many protagonists of Jacobean drama, is a disinherited prince.
Elizabethan heroics were exerted, more characteristically, to gain
a crown; but disinheritance is the typical posture, and courtly
intrigue the conventional plot, from the last years of Elizabeth's
reign – with their disillusionment over the downfall of Essex – to
the closing of the theaters and the dethronement of the Stuarts
at mid-century.

The *maladie du siècle* was that self-conscious melancholy which
even Jonson's gulls made a point of cultivating, which Shakespeare's Jaques exhibited so complacently – and so invectively,
since it protected his sensibilities with the weapons of satire,
keen and critical. Malevole-Altofront is a satirical commentator,
as well as a princely revenger; under the former aspect he has
much in common with Asper-Macilente in *Every Man Out of his
Humour*, and with the other spokesmen of Jonson's Comical
Satires. The stage – the stage that Hamlet walked – had become,
in the reverberating phraseology of Davies of Hereford, 'a soiled
glasse . . .'

> Where each man *in* and *out of*'s humour pries
> Upon himselfe, and laughs untill he cries.[7]

Shakespeare did not hold himself altogether aloof from this
notorious War of the Theaters. *As You Like It* amiably satirizes
the would-be satirist; *Troilus and Cressida* sounds the abysmal
depths of detraction. *Hamlet*, which is closely related to these
two plays in its composition, goes out of its way to take note of
the controversy between the child actors and the public troops.
The book that Hamlet reads, or so he professes, was composed
by a 'satirical rogue' (ii ii 197). Because it appears to reflect
against old men, it has been identified with the Tenth Satire of
Juvenal. But Hamlet's conclusion, that crabbed age goes back-
ward, is more suggestive of Erasmus' devastating paragraph on

second childhood in *The Praise of Folly*.⁸ Whoever the rogue
may have been, the innuendo is lost on Polonius, perplexed as
he is by the method in Hamlet's madness. Such 'pregnant . . .
replies' have 'a happiness' that reason could hardly attain.
Possibly they bear some resemblance to those 'happy unhappy
answers' with which the comedian Tarlton used to make Queen
Elizabeth laugh.⁹ Hamlet's pithy repartee becomes more grimly
enigmatic and less politely ironic, increasingly rude to his
enemies as the play progresses. He becomes a master of the trope
that rhetoricians defined under the heading of *sarcasmus:*
Susenbrot's '*iocus cum amaritudine*', Puttenham's 'bitter taunt',
Peacham's 'dispytefull frumpe'.¹⁰

Now Hamlet disapproves of comedians who attract attention
by speaking 'more than is set down for them' (III ii 38). Yet his
own performance *ad libitum*, during the presentation of the play-
within-the-play, is aptly compared by Francis Fergusson to the
improvised antics of a 'night-club entertainer'.¹¹ In his manic
phase, after the success of the entertainment, Hamlet momen-
tarily toys with the notion of turning actor; and he displays the
showman's aplomb when, by acting out the object-lessons of the
recorder and of the cloud, he tells off Rosencrantz, Guildenstern,
and Polonius. He does not put them out of their humors, in the
Jonsonian sense; nothing short of their deaths, in just consequence of their deceptions, will accomplish that end. Rather, he
indulges his own humor – and that of the audience; for, as the
other Johnson pointed out, 'the pretended madness of Hamlet
causes much mirth'.¹² Too many subsequent Hamlets, perhaps,
have tended to overemphasize the solemnity of the part. After
all, the pseudo-lunatic is conventionally a figure of comedy,
which tends to bring out idiosyncrasies of character through its
very appeal to social norms. A classic instance is the misplaced
twin, in the *Menaechmi* of Plautus, whose bewilderment gets
temporarily diagnosed as insanity. His exact symptoms reappear
not only in *The Comedy of Errors* (IV iv 53–4) but also in Ben
Jonson's *Silent Woman* (IV iv 56–8). They are aggravated in
Twelfth Night, when Malvolio is confined and examined. But
when Menaechmus was treated as a madman, he ended by living

E   J.S.H.

up to the accusation, insulting his brother's wife and father-in-law as Hamlet insults Ophelia and Polonius.

> Quid mihi meliust, quam quando illi me insanire praedicant,
> ego med adsimulem insanire, ut illos a me absteream?
>
> (831–2)

In reverse order Hamlet goes through those motions; and when he takes off his antic disposition, in the Closet Scene, it is difficult for him to convince Gertrude that he is sane. Both positions could easily be reduced to a comic level: the plight of the man who is generally misunderstood and the pose of the man who deliberately invites misunderstanding. *Hamlet* abounds in what – if it were an Elizabethan comedy – might have been designated as *errors* or *supposes*, misconceptions contrived and coincidental. Even the Ghost raises the question of a possible disguise, and Polonius dies a martyr to mistaken identity. Such questions could not be resolved by a happy ending, as they are in the first part of Dekker's *Honest Whore*, where a visit to an Italianate Bedlam clears up both the feigned madness of Bellafront and the suspected madness of Candido. We attain the *reductio ad absurdum* in the underplot of Middleton's *Changeling*, which also takes place in a madhouse; there the changeling, who counterfeits a madman because he is in love with the doctor's wife, discovers that a fellow inmate is a rival doing the same thing for the same reason. With the lady joining the masquerade, the lunatics and pseudo-lunatics dance 'a wild distracted measure', which counterpoints the serious plot and completes the title's parallel between loss of mind and change of heart. A similar dance in Webster's *Duchess of Malfi* is supposed to exercise a homeopathic effect upon the melancholia of the Duchess. This treatment, in Ford's *Lover's Melancholy*, is elaborated into a masque, wherein the *dramatis personae* systematically represent the types that Burton had recently analyzed in his *Anatomy of Melancholy*.

By this time, the early Caroline period, the complaint is epidemic. 'Our commonwealth is sick . . . ,' declares an adviser of the bookish prince in *The Lover's Melancholy*, 'The court is now turned antic, and grows wild' (II i 553–7). Contemplating 'the madness of the times', a reduced courtier wonders, 'Why should not I . . . be mine own antic?' (1 i 251–4). And he proceeds to condense his worldly wisdom into an aphorism:

> He that pursues his safety from the school
> Of court, must learn to be madman or fool. (1 i 258–9)

This is a narrower choice than that between folly and knavery, which had so often confronted the protagonists in Jacobean tragedies of revenge. They usually chose as does Vindice-Piato in *The Revenger's Tragedy*:

> And therefore I'll put on that knave for once,
> And be a right man then, a man o' the time;
> For to be honest is not to be i' the world. (1 i 101–3)

Accordingly he plays the double agent, the revenger who becomes a villain in the very process of revenging the villainy he has been taught. But, since he has a genuine score to pay off, he is less completely villainous than Webster's agents, who seem to be disaffected intellectuals, Iago-like malcontents whose professional cynicism operates under a protective coloring of Hamlet-like prose. 'I do put on this feigned garb of mirth', hisses Flamineo in *The White Devil*, 'To gull suspicion' (III i 30–1). In short, it is axiomatic with Hamlet's successors that the honest man can hardly survive to perform his mission at court, unless he disguises his personality with a mask of some sort, preferably foolish; the more outspoken he is, the better it suits him to be – like Feste in *Twelfth Night* – 'an allow'd fool' (1 v 101). Hamlet, indeed, has an immediate predecessor, the exiled son of the Duke of Genoa in *Antonio's Revenge*, who literally dons a fool's habit and blows soap-bubbles. For his apologia he resorts to a commonplace as ancient as Aeschylus: 'He is not wise that strives not to seem fool' (IV i 25).[13]

Antonio's self-justification, 'This coxcomb is a crown', has its Shakespearean counterpart in the mockery of Jaques: 'Motley's the only wear' (II vii 34). Jaques himself does not put on the coxcomb or motley; he wistfully envies the conversational liberties that Touchstone's professional garb allows him to take.

Between Touchstone and Jaques, between the fool and what Hamlet would call 'the Humorous Man' (II ii 326), there seems to be a special affinity, as there is between Passarello and Malevole in *The Malcontent.*[14] A similar relationship is presented, by Chapman in *A Humorous Day's Mirth*, between Labesha, the fool who repines against fortune, and Dowsecer, the young moralist in love. Hamlet, in his virtual isolation, differs from other humorous men; and unlike King Lear, he is not companioned by a fool. Yet the play, like the others that Shakespeare was writing at this period, has its fool's part; and, in view of its pervasive concern with death, it seems appropriate that this particular fool should have been dead and buried for three-and-twenty years. The skull that – in lieu of a coxcomb – personifies Yorick, the late king's jester, has become a mark of identification for Hamlet; it quickly became a standard property in plays like *The Honest Whore* and *The Revenger's Tragedy*. Since Yorick is a *muta persona*, whose gibes and gambols and songs are conspicuous by their silence, they are anticipated by the riddles and gags and equivocations of the Clown as First Gravedigger. The Prince plays straight man to him, eliciting – for the benefit of Shakespeare's English audience – the remark that Hamlet's madness will not be noticed in England: 'There the men are as mad as he' (v i 149–50).

What follows, when the clown identifies Yorick, is the gloomiest of recognition-scenes. The fool's traditional function has been to demonstrate that the other person, whatever his pretensions to wit may be, is likewise a fool; their dialectic, be it erratic or subtle, inevitably terminates with *tu quoque*. Here, however, the poles of the argument are no longer wisdom and folly but life and death. After rushing from his interview with Gertrude to hide the body of Polonius, Hamlet had diverted his conversation from the carnal to the charnel. He had responded to queries about his victim with a political pun on the Diet of Worms and a metaphysical conceit about royal flesh successively feeding a worm, a fish, and a beggar (IV iii 26–30). That speculation will be exemplified in his sorites on Alexander and his lines upon Caesar (v i 207–10), just as the generalizations about mortality will be brought home with shocking concreteness by Ophelia's funeral. Contrary to Hamlet's impression, the Grave-digger had some feeling for his business when he sought to lighten it by singing the song entitled 'The Aged Lover Renounceth Love'. Meanwhile, in the mode of Lucian speculating over the skulls and bones of Greek heroes and heroines, Hamlet satirically evokes the wasted lives of politicians, courtiers, and other ranks of society.[15] He summons them, as it were, to a dance of death, which culminates in the evocation of Yorick; whereupon, to Hamlet's *ubi sunt?* the death's-head replies *tu quoque*. 'Now get you to my lady's chamber, and tell her, let her paint an inch thick, to this favour she must come' (187–8). Hamlet's meditation thus develops the metaphor that Richard II adumbrates, when he personifies Death as 'the antic'[16] who scoffs and grins at the pomp of kings (III ii 162).

In *Der bestrafte Brudermord* there is a live jester who bears the illusory name of Phantasmo; while in the *moralité* of Jules Laforgue, Yorick appears as Hamlet's elder half-brother; but, with Shakespeare, Yorick's role is posthumous. Hence, in his mortal absence, his former playfellow wears the comic mask. Hamlet, like Robert the Devil in the legend, becomes a court jester. He is not one to suffer other fools gladly; the very word sets the keynote for his relations with Polonius; and if Rosencrantz does not comprehend him, it is because 'a foolish speech sleeps in a knavish ear' (IV ii 24–5). On the other hand, he can complain to Horatio, 'They fool me to the top of my bent' (III ii 386). The sight of the apparition makes us 'fools of nature' (I iv 54), even as – for the dying Hotspur – life is 'time's fool' (v iv 81) and Romeo himself is 'fortune's fool' (III i 141). So Hamlet, at the court where he cannot be king, must perforce be fool, an artificial fool pretending to be a natural. His assumption of foolishness is the archetypal feature of his story, as it has come down from primitive legend. In fact, his name derives from the Old Norse Amloði, which means 'a fool, a ninny, an idiot' – and, more especially, a Jutish trickster who feigns stupidity.[17] His Latin chronicler brings out analogies between his adventures and those of the Roman Brutus, whose name is also indicative of

the brutal guise under which he must conceal his wiles.[18] Shakespeare, in refining upon such raw materials, utilized his mastery
of those conventions which made the fool so strategic a figure on
the Elizabethan stage.[19] The comment of Gilbert Murray is
penetrating: 'It is very remarkable that Shakespeare, who did
such wonders in his idealized and half-mystic treatment of the
real Fool, should also have made his greatest tragic hero out of a
Fool transfigured.'[20]

A fool transfigured or else a wise man denatured; for Murray
might well have gone on to note that Hamlet is re-enacting the
classical *eiron*, the Socratic ironist who practices wisdom by
disclaiming it. More immediately, Shakespeare was dramatizing
the humanistic critique of the intellect, as it had been genially
propounded by Erasmus, to whom life itself was a kind of
comedy, wherein 'men come foorthe disguised one in one arraie,
an other in an other, eche plaiying his parte . . . And all this is
dooen under a certaine veile or shadow, whiche taken awaie
ones, the plaie can no more be plaied.'[21] When Hamlet, after
playing hide-and-seek, is captured and brought in attended by
guards, his self-humiliation seems complete: the noble mind
overthrown, the capability and godlike reason thwarted by
animal passion. But we should not forget that he is stooping to
folly in the grand Erasmian manner, and that self-criticism is a
premise which enables him to criticize others. 'The fool doth
think he is wise', in the saying of Touchstone, 'but the wise man
knows himself to be a fool' (v i 33–5). The advantages of this
viewpoint, as originally eulogized in the *Encomium Moriae*,
were versified by Jonson for the misbegotten chorus of his
Volpone.[22]

> Fools, they are the only nation
> Worth men's envy and admiration . . .
> E'en his face begetteth laughter,
> And he speaks truth free from slaughter.
>
>   (I ii 66–7, 74–5)

Hamlet's complexity is compounded of many simples: the
frustrated scholar, the unwilling courtier, the mourner who be-

comes a revenger, the lover whose imagination rages like that of the lunatic or the poet, and still others – not least, the witty fool. If he has the saturnine temperament, that accords with Ficino's vindication of gloomy genius. Why melancholy men are the wittiest is an inquiry which long ago evoked Aristotle's curiosity.[23] Democritus Junior, who subsumes all such ideas and takes the greatest pains to distinguish among them, conceives his subject as the occupational malady of the intellectuals; and yet, he admits, such contagion is universal. 'For indeed who is not a fool, melancholy, mad? – *Qui nil molitur inepte*, who is not brainsick? Folly, melancholy, madness are but one disease...' To sum it up in a pertinent question: '...what madness ghosts us all?'[24] Against this context of prevailing unreason, Hamlet stands apart, a solitary sane individual in – shall we say, with Middleton? – *A Mad World, my Masters*. Or should we say, with Dame Purecraft in *Bartholomew Fair*, for whom the madman Troubleall is the one man of principle in a concourse of knaves: 'The world is mad in error, but he is mad in truth' (IV vi 159–60). To that extent, the madness of Hamlet has its parallels in the maladjustment of Don Quixote, the misanthropy of Alceste, and the idiocy of Prince Myshkin.[25]

NOTES

1. *The Sources of Hamlet*, ed. Sir Israel Gollancz (1926) p. 193.

2. Friedrich Gundolf, *Shakespeare und der Deutsche Geist* (Godesberg, 1947) p. 31.

3. The most recent and comprehensive discussion is that of Lawrence Babb, *The Elizabethan Malady: A Study of Melancholy in English Literature from 1580 to 1642* (East Lansing, 1951).

4. Stéphane Mallarmé, *Divagations* (1922) p. 371.

5. R. R. Read, *Bedlam on the Jacobean Stage* (Cambridge, Mass., 1952) p. 5.

6. By the time of *A New Way to Pay Old Debts* (1633), this convention seems to have come full circle; Sir Giles Overreach raves in Marlovian blank verse.

7. John Davies of Hereford, *Complete Works*, ed. A. B. Grosart (Edinburgh, 1878) II 76.

8. *The Praise of Folie*, trans. Sir Thomas Chaloner (1549) B iv; see also F ii.

9. Quoted from Thomas Fuller by Enid Welsford, *The Fool: His Social and Literary History* (1935) p. 282.

10. T. W. Baldwin, *William Shakespere's Small Latine and Lesse Greeke* (Urbana, 1944) II 144–5.

11. *The Idea of a Theater* (New York, 1953) p. 134.

12. *The Plays of William Shakespeare*, ed. Samuel Johnson (1765) VIII 311.

13. Cf. *Prometheus Bound*, I 387.

14. E. E. Stoll, 'Shakespeare, Marston, and the Malcontent Type', in *Modern Philology* III 3 (June 1906) 1–23. Other scholars have not accepted Professor Stoll's early dating of *The Malcontent*, but they have not discredited his emphasis on the role.

15. *Dialogues of the Dead*, XVIII.

16. 'Antic' is here a substantive meaning *buffoon*, according to Schmidt, whereas Hamlet uses it as an adjective which means *fantastic*. However, Hamlet's usage carries an overtone of the buffoon's part he is about to assume. The three wayfarers in Peele's *Old Wives' Tale* are respectively named Antic, Frolic, and Fantastic. From the fact that the first drops out of the dialogue, it is to be inferred that he takes a leading part in the play-within-the-play.

17. J. V. Jensen, 'Hamlet', in *London Mercury*, XI 65 (March 1925) 510–11.

18. Gollancz, op. cit., 28–33.

19. This view, essentially a renewal of Johnson's, was reasserted by the dramatic critic John Corbin in his Harvard undergraduate honors essay, *The Elizabethan Hamlet: A Study of the Sources, and of Shakespeare's Environment, to Show that the Mad Scenes Had a Comic Aspect now Ignored* (1895). Later studies, delving more deeply into Shakespeare's background, tend to confirm the thesis of Corbin's subtitle.

20. *The Classical Tradition in Poetry* (Cambridge, Mass., 1927) p. 213. Cf. Wolfgang Clemen, *The Development of Shakespeare's Imagery* (1951) p. 110.

21. Op. cit. E iii^v.

22. Cf. Harry Levin, 'Jonson's Metempsychosis', in *Philological Quarterly*, XII 3 (July 1943) 231–9.

23. The texts of Aristotle and Ficino are reprinted by Erwin Panofsky and Fritz Saxl in *Dürers Melencolia I: eine quellen- und typengeschichtliche Untersuchung* (Leipzig, 1923) pp. 93–120.

24. Robert Burton, *The Anatomy of Melancholy*, ed. A. R. Shilleto (1893) I 39, 46.

25. Another approach to the problem, via the convention of the Vice, has been taken by Sidney Thomas in *The Antic Hamlet and Richard III* (New York, 1943).

Helen Gardner

THE HISTORICAL APPROACH
TO *HAMLET* (1959)

W E can understand, to a greater or less degree, how men of our
day think if they try to communicate their thoughts to us. I have
no idea how my silent companions in a bus or tube are thinking,
although they, like me, have modern minds. If one speaks to me I
can understand his thought; or, if I do not, I can ask him questions. I may have failed to grasp what he is saying because he has
assumed that I have some information which in fact I do not
possess. He has perhaps listened to the six o'clock news, or seen
something in the stop press of his evening newspaper. Or perhaps he is speaking from assumptions which I do not share.
When I ask him what he means he may tell me that he is a British
Israelite, and then, if I want to understand what he has to say, I
must listen while he explains his tenets to me. Or perhaps his
mind is obsessed by some personal or family trouble, or is
coloured by the circumstances in which he has grown up, and
then I must listen while he explains to me what complex of
feelings and events prompted a remark which it seemed to him
important to make, but whose import I did not grasp. When we
are confronted with the expression of the mind of someone long
dead, embodied in a work of art, the process of coming to understand it seems to me fundamentally the same, although we cannot
ask our questions directly. We have to develop a technique of
questioning, asking questions which arise out of the work itself.
We can only judge whether the answer to any particular question
is a good answer by its consistency with our answers to other
questions.

To illustrate what I mean I am going to consider some questions about *Hamlet*. An example of an unfruitful question, because it is too large and too general and leads inevitably to an

answer which we ought to have known before we asked it, is the
question which some writers seem to feel bound to raise before
they approach a play built on the theme of revenge. What did the
Elizabethans think of the ethics of private revenge? I have read
more than one book in which the author establishes by detailed,
indeed relentless, accumulation of statements by preachers and
moralists that the Elizabethans thought murder unethical and
private revenge sinful. What else should we expect preachers and
moralists to say? Questions which lead us to platitudes and foregone conclusions are not worth asking. We might more profitably
ponder over the temper of mind which lay behind the Bond of
Association of 1584. The councillors who drafted this document,
among them the pious Burghley, and the thousands up and down
the country who signed it, pledged themselves 'in the presence of
the eternal and ever-living God', whom they knew to have
claimed vengeance as his prerogative, that, in the event of an
attack on Elizabeth's person, they would 'prosecute to the death'
any pretended successor to her throne by whom, or for whom,
such an act should be attempted or committed. They swore 'to
take the uttermost revenge on them . . . by any possible means
. . . for their utter overthrow and extirpation'. That is, if Elizabeth were assassinated, Mary Stuart should be murdered, whether
she were a party to the murder of her cousin or not, and beyond
Mary, her son James, as a beneficiary of the crime. 'Discarding
all scruples', comments Sir John Neale, 'they descended to the
utter ruthlessness of their enemies.' These were law-abiding and
God-fearing men. But they believed that the safety of the country
and the preservation of the Protestant religion hung on the single
life of Elizabeth. They were probably right in believing this.
Perhaps if Elizabeth had met the same fate as William the Silent
and Henry of Navarre, and England had fallen into the chaos of
civil and religious wars, the play of *Hamlet*, along with other
precious things, would not exist for us to talk about. We may be
horrified at their forgetting that vengeance was forbidden by
their religion, but we must recognize the appalling nature of their
dilemma.

As an example of a fruitful question which it did not occur to

Bradley to ask I would cite Professor Dover Wilson's question: 'What opinions were current when Shakespeare was writing about the nature of apparitions?' This is a modest question to which an answer can be found, and the answer Professor Dover Wilson found – that there was a conflict of opinion – is an illuminating one. It is consonant with the impression which the whole play makes upon us and adds to our feeling that Hamlet is moving in a world where there are no certainties. It casts light on the relation of Hamlet to Horatio. It gives meaning to a scene which had puzzled all critics, the cellarage scene. And, lastly, it casts a light upon the whole development of the play's action. By showing us how serious and widespread was the debate on the nature of ghosts, it makes us less ready to accept the notion that Hamlet arranges the play scene as an excuse for delaying his revenge. The information which Professor Dover Wilson made available to us strengthens our conception of Hamlet as a man of intellectual integrity and moral sensibility. To give a parallel from our own day: two hundred years hence, when, for all I know, modern psychology will seem as outmoded as alchemy or the theory of the humours, a critic, living in an age of chemical therapy, might fruitfully inquire what were some of the current opinions on the psychiatrist's role in society which might help to explain the rather ambiguous treatment of Reilly in Mr Eliot's comedy *The Cocktail Party*. Mr Eliot, as we are all perfectly aware without considering the matter at all, has been able to exploit for comic purposes our ambivalent feelings about 'mind doctors', as Shakespeare exploited for tragic purposes the conflict of opinion in his day about the reality and reliability of apparitions of departed persons. We are not asking what Mr Eliot's own opinions about psychiatrists are, any more than we are asking whether Shakespeare believed in ghosts. Nor are we asking what attitude the plays demand that we should assume to the interference of Reilly or to the moral authority of the Ghost of Hamlet's father. These are questions which cannot be answered by historical inquiries alone, but historical inquiries can help us to answer them.

A much more complex and delicate question, which takes us

near to the heart of the play, is raised by the complaint which Johnson makes about the plot of *Hamlet*. 'Hamlet is, through the whole play, rather an instrument than an agent. After he has, by the stratagem of the play, convicted the King, he makes no attempt to punish him, and his death is at last effected by an incident which Hamlet has no part in producing.' Bradley's celebrated question, which he thinks anyone would ask on hearing the plot of *Hamlet*, converts Johnson's objection to the conduct of the plot into censure of the conduct of the hero: 'But why in the world did not Hamlet obey the ghost at once, and so save seven of those eight lives?' And a highly unsympathetic aside of Mr Eliot's converts Bradley's complaint at Hamlet's incompetence into a reproach to him for not being aware, as we are, that he 'has made a pretty considerable mess of things'. Mr Eliot's rebuke to Hamlet for 'dying fairly well pleased with himself'[1] is only logical from a severe moralist if we accept that what the play has shown us is the mess which Hamlet has made of things. Mr Eliot might, however, have noticed that it is not merely Hamlet who appears to feel at the close that if only the whole truth were known – as we, the audience, know it – the name which he leaves behind him would not be 'a wounded name'. Horatio's farewell to him and Fortinbras's comment make no suggestion that what we have witnessed is a story of personal failure and inadequacy; and Horatio's summary of what he will tell 'th'yet unknowing world' does not include any hint that these things have come about through the bungling of the dead Prince. No need of extenuation appears to be felt. On the contrary, the play ends with 'the soldiers' music and the rite of war' and a final volley in salute of a dead hero.

The question here, which arises out of the play itself, is how we are to find consistency between the fact of Hamlet's delay, with which he bitterly reproaches himself, the fact, which Johnson pointed out, that the final denouement is not of his making, and the tone of the close of the play, which suggests so strongly that Hamlet has 'parted well and paid his score'. It hardly seems possible to answer this question, as Mr Eliot does, by ascribing to Hamlet at the moment of his death, and by implication to his creator, a moral sensibility inferior to our own. When faced with a contradiction of this kind, the critic is bound to ask himself whether he has got the play out of focus. Is there some element in it which he is unaware of, which will, when perceived, make the close seem a full and fitting close? He needs to discover whether there is any means by which he can decide whether Shakespeare intended his audience to regard Hamlet as having 'made a mess of things'. And he must ask himself whether what Johnson thought an objection to the conduct of the plot, that the hero does so little to forward it, is a real objection: whether it does actually affect the 'satisfaction' which Johnson thought we should feel at the close of the play. The historical fact to which we can turn is that Shakespeare did not invent the plot of *Hamlet*. He chose, presumably because it in some way appealed to his imagination, to remake an older play. And, although this older play no longer exists, there exist other plays on the same kind of subject. A study of these, to see what they have in common with *Hamlet*, may, at the least, suggest to us things which we should take into account in trying to understand the masterpiece which Shakespeare created in this genre. Such a study shows that the answer which Bradley gave to his question 'Why in the world did not Hamlet obey the ghost at once?' is only a partial answer. To Bradley's assertion, 'The whole story turns upon the peculiar character of the hero', we can object that heroes of very different character also fail to act promptly and also involve themselves and others in the final catastrophe. As for Johnson's comment on the conduct of the plot, we can say that the same complaint can be made to some degree against the plots of other revenge tragedies in the period. What Johnson thought to be a weakness in the plot of *Hamlet* appears to be a feature of the plots of other plays of the same kind and may point us towards a reason for their popularity and even towards what attracted Shakespeare in the old play which he remade.

The essence of any tragedy of revenge is that its hero has not created the situation in which he finds himself and out of which the tragedy arises. The simplest of all tragic formulas, that a tragedy begins in prosperity and ends in misery, does not fit revenge tragedies. When the action opens the hero is seen in a situation which is horrible, and felt by him and the audience to be intolerable, but for which he has no responsibility. The exposition of such plays does not display the hero taking a fatal step, but the hero confronted with appalling facts. This is as true in Argos as it is in Denmark. But in Elizabethan revenge plays it is not merely the initial situation which is created by the villain. The denouement also comes about through his initiative. It is not the result of a successfully carried out scheme of the revenger. The revenger takes an opportunity unconsciously provided for him by the villain. Given this opportunity, which he seems unable to create for himself, he forms his scheme on the spur of the moment. Thus, in *The Spanish Tragedy*, Lorenzo, believing himself safe and that the secret of Horatio's murder lies buried with Serberine and Pedringano, feigns reconcilement with Hieronymo and invites him to provide a play for the entertainment of the court. By means of this play Hieronymo achieves his vengeance and brings to light the secret crime of Lorenzo. Similarly, in *Titus Andronicus*, which is obviously modelled on *The Spanish Tragedy*, although it exceeds it in horrors, the denouement comes about because Tamora believes she can deal with the old mad Titus and, through him, with his dangerous son Lucius who threatens her and her husband, the Emperor. Confident in her scheme, she delivers herself and her sons into Titus' hands. Up to the point when she calls upon him, disguised as Revenge, Titus has done nothing but indulge in wild gestures of grief and distraction; just as Hieronymo has done nothing to avenge his son before Lorenzo's initiative suggests to him a way of destroying his enemies and revealing their wickedness. Again, in a play written after *Hamlet*, Tourneur's *The Revenger's Tragedy*, the Duke himself asks Vendice, whose mistress he has poisoned because she would not yield to him, to find him a new mistress. He himself arranges the place, a hidden pavilion, and allows his courtiers to believe that he has gone away, so as to ensure secrecy. He thus provides Vendice with the perfect place and time for his vengeance. It seems as if in plays of this kind it was a necessary part of the total effect that the villain should be to some extent the agent of his own destruction. As initiator of the action he must be the initiator of its resolution. The satisfaction of the close included to a less or greater degree the sombre satisfaction which the Psalmist felt at the spectacle of the wicked falling into pits which they had digged for others. Here, obscurely, the hand of heaven could be felt, as Raleigh felt it in the bloody pageant of history:

Oh by what plots, by what forswearings, betrayings, oppressions, imprisonments, tortures, poysonings, and under what reasons of State, and politique subtlety, have these forenamed Kings, both strangers, and of our owne Nation, pulled the vengeance of GOD upon themselves, upon theirs, and upon their prudent ministers! and in the end have brought those things to passe for their enemies, and seene an effect so directly contrary to all their owne counsels and cruelties, as the one could never have hoped for themselves, and the other never have succeeded, if no such opposition had ever been made. GOD hath said it and performed it ever: *Perdam sapientiam sapientium; I will destroy the wisedome of the wise.*[2]

'In the end' the wicked will destroy themselves and 'purposes mistook' will fall on 'th'inventors' heads'. The hero waits for his opponent, as if for a signal, and the initiative and activity which Johnson expected from the hero of a play seems not to have been required from heroes in situations of this kind. This conception of a hero who is committed to counter-action, and to response to events rather than to the creation of events, is very powerfully rendered by Tourneur in the exposition of *The Revenger's Tragedy*. The personages of court pass across the stage, while Vendice, holding in his hands the skull of his dead mistress, comments on the parade of vicious power and wealth. He is waiting for 'that bald Madam, Opportunity'.

When we turn back from reading these plays to *Hamlet* we see that Shakespeare has very greatly developed this basic element in the revenge play of his day. He has developed it to make clear what in them is confused by sensationalism, and by that moral indignation which so easily converts itself to immorality. Great writers perceive what is only half perceived by their lesser contemporaries and express what in them finds only partial or imperfect expression. In other revenge plays, once the signal is given, the revenger produces a scheme of horror by which he destroys his opponent. He becomes an agent, bent on fulfilling the hateful Senecan maxim that crimes are only to be avenged by greater crimes. The irony is only mild. It is ironic that the villain, acting as if all were well, invites his destroyer to destroy him. Once invited, the hero descends with alacrity to the moral level of his opponent. The vengeance when it comes is as hideous as the original crime, or even more hideous, and the moral feelings of the audience are confused between satisfaction and outrage.[3] In the denouement of *Hamlet* the irony is profound. Claudius, who has arranged the whole performance in order to destroy Hamlet, is himself destroyed and destroys his Queen. He is 'hoist with his own petar'. His tool Laertes acknowledges the justice of his fate as he reveals the plot to which he had consented: 'I am justly killed with mine own treachery.' Claudius himself makes no such acknowledgement. He dies impenitent; there is 'no relish of salvation' in his death. Kyd, with Hieronymo left alive on his hands at the end of the general holocaust, was forced to the weak expedient of making him commit suicide as the only way to preserve any sympathy for him. Hamlet dies as a victim to that constancy to his purposes which has made him 'follow the king's pleasure' throughout. The end comes because he has accepted every challenge: 'If his fitness speaks, mine is ready.' Unlike Hieronymo, Titus, and Vendice, he remains to the last, in his adversary's words, 'most generous, and free from all contriving'. For there is another point in which an Elizabethan tragedy of revenge differs from the legend of Orestes and from the original Hamlet legend. Everyone in Argos is perfectly well aware that Clytemnestra, with the help of her paramour, Aegisthus, murdered her husband, Agamemnon, just as in the old story of Hamlet everyone knows that his uncle Feng is the murderer of his father. In these ancient stories of revenge for blood the criminals are known to be criminals by all their world. They are not 'secret men of blood'. The secrecy with which Kyd invests the murder of Horatio is carried to such fantastic lengths that at one point in the play it appears that the world in general does not even realize that he is dead. In *Hamlet*, as we know it, whether it was so in the old play or not, only his murderer among living men knows at the beginning of the action that Hamlet the elder was murdered. *The Spanish Tragedy* is built on a powerful moral contrast between the treacherous, subtle, politic Lorenzo and the honest man, Hieronymo, who lives by conscience and the law. At the crisis of the play this contrast is blurred and Hieronymo becomes as crafty as his enemy. In *Hamlet* it is preserved to the end, and Hamlet himself is far more of an instrument and far less of an agent than are his fellow revengers.

The view that the revenger's role was essentially a waiting role, that he was committed by the situation in which he found himself to counter-action, and differentiated from his opponent by lack of guile, does not answer the question 'Why does Hamlet delay?' It sets it in a different light. We must still find consistency between his character and his actions, and Bradley's statement that 'the whole story turns on the peculiar character of the hero' retains its truth. But to set *Hamlet* against other plays of its time which handle the same kind of subject is to suggest that however much he may reproach himself with his delay, that delay is part of a pattern which is made clear at the close. To ask 'Why in the world did not Hamlet act at once?' is to fail to grasp the nature of the dilemma which Kyd crudely adumbrated when he set the man of conscience and duty against the conscienceless and treacherous villain. Hamlet's agony of mind and indecision are precisely the things which differentiate him from that smooth, swift plotter Claudius, and from the coarse, unthinking Laertes, ready to 'dare damnation' and cut his enemy's throat in a church. He quickly learns from Claudius how to entrap the unwary and the generous, and betters the instruction. 'He will never have a better opportunity,' say many critics, when Hamlet, convinced of his uncle's guilt and hot for vengeance, comes on Claudius on his knees. Even Browning's ruthless tyrant, after having long schemed his enemy's destruction, shrank back and 'was afraid' when his victim 'caught at God's skirts and prayed'. Do we really want to see Hamlet stab a

defenceless, kneeling man? This 'opportunity' is no opportunity
at all; the enemy is within touching distance, but out of reach.
Hamlet's baffled rage finds an outlet in the speech which shocked
Johnson by its depth of hatred. The speech reveals more than its
speaker's character. Like many soliloquies, it is proleptic. The
moment which Hamlet here declares that he will wait for, the real
opportunity, will come. When Hamlet has gone and Claudius has
risen from his knees, and not before, we know that Claudius
has not found grace. The opportunity which Hamlet awaits
Claudius will now provide. The play has made Hamlet certain
of his uncle's guilt; it has also shown Claudius that his guilt is no
longer his own secret. If he cannot repent, he must, for his own
safety, destroy Hamlet. He will do it in his own characteristic
way, by the hand of an accomplice and by the treacherous man's
characteristic weapon, poison. And Hamlet will destroy Claudius
in his own characteristic way also: by 'rashness' and 'indis-
cretion', and not by 'deep plots'. He will catch him at the moment
when his guilt has been made clear to all the bystanders, so that
as he runs the sword through him he will do so not as an assassin
but as an executioner. The dark and devious world in which
Hamlet finds himself, when he accepts the necessity of obeying
the command of the Ghost, involves all who enter it in guilt.
But Hamlet's most terrible deed, when he allows himself to be
'marshalled to knavery' and is most contaminated by his world,
the sending of the traitors Rosencrantz and Guildenstern to their
deaths, is a spontaneous, savage response to the discovery of
their treachery; and his other crime, the killing of Polonius, with
its consequence in the madness and death of Ophelia, is also
unpremeditated.

In *Othello*, Iago, speaking in the role of an honest man, puts
crudely to his master the code of a soldier:

> Though in the trade of war I have slain men,
> Yet do I hold it very stuff o' the conscience
> To do no contriv'd murder.

Hamlet is fittingly borne 'like a soldier to the stage', because in
the secret war which he has waged he has shown a soldier's

virtues. Pre-eminently he has shown the virtue of constancy. He
has not laid down his arms and quitted the field. For Bradley's
comment, 'Two months have passed and he has done nothing',
we might better say, 'Two months have passed and he is still
there, at his post, on guard.' The play ends with a soldier's
funeral. It opens with sentries at their watch, being relieved. In
his four great tragedies, when his imagination was working at
its highest pitch, Shakespeare relates his beginnings to his ends
particularly closely. Granville Barker pointed out how *King
Lear* ends as it began with Lear and his three daughters on the
stage and with the old king hanging on the hope of words from
Cordelia's lips. Any writer dramatizing Cinthio's story of the
Moor of Venice would end with the midnight scenes of the
attempted murder of Cassio and the death of Desdemona.
Shakespeare has invented a great midnight opening to balance
this close, with brawling in the streets followed by the midnight
scene before the Senate, where, with the approval of Venice,
Othello is united to Desdemona, as in the last scene he is united
to her in death before the eyes of the envoys of Venice. *Macbeth*
begins and ends with battles. It opens with the epic narrative of
the defeat of the thane of Cawdor who had rebelled, and closes
with the defeat of the thane of Cawdor who had usurped. And
here there is contrast. The first thane confessed his treasons 'very
freely' and died well, giving up his life, 'the dearest thing he
owed', 'as 'twere a careless trifle': his successor in the title,
Macbeth, fought desperately to the last to preserve a life which
had become meaningless to him. The opening and the close of
Hamlet have the same kind of relation to each other. The soldier
on guard, who cannot leave his post until he is relieved or given
permission from above, is a metaphor for the soul in this world
which comes very easily to Renaissance writers. Its source is
Cicero's gloss on the 'secret doctrine' which Socrates appealed
to in his argument against suicide in the *Phaedo*.[4] The Red Cross
Knight uses it against Despair:

> The souldier may not move from watchfull sted
> Nor leave his stand, untill his Captain bed.

And Donne, speaking of this world as 'the appointed field', refers to the same commonplace when he chides the 'desperate coward' who yields to the foes of him

> who made thee to stand
> Sentinell in his worlds garrison.

The play of *Hamlet* continually recurs to the thought of suicide, and the temptation to give up the battle of life. Hamlet's first soliloquy opens with the lament that the Almighty has 'fixed his canon 'gainst self-slaughter', and his last action is to snatch the poisoned cup from the lips of Horatio. Within this frame of soldiers on the watch, being relieved, and of a soldier's laying to rest, I do not believe that the Elizabethans thought that they were witnessing a story of personal failure. Nor do I think that we should do so either, unless we are certain of what, in this situation, would be success.

The tragedy of *Hamlet*, and of plays of its kind, of which it is the supreme example, does not lie in 'the unfitness of the hero for his task', or in some 'fatal flaw'. It is not true that a coarser nature could have cleansed the state of Denmark, some 'Hotspur of the North': 'he that kills me some six or seven dozen of Scots at a breakfast, washes his hands, and says to his wife, "Fie upon this quiet life! I want work." ' The tragedy lies in the nature of the task, which only the noble will feel called on to undertake, or rather, in the nature of the world which is exposed to the hero's contemplation and in his sense of responsibility to the world in which he finds himself. *Hamlet* towers above other plays of its kind through the heroism and nobility of its hero, his superior power of insight into, and reflection upon, his situation, and his capacity to suffer the moral anguish which moral responsibility brings. Hamlet is the quintessence of European man, who holds that man is 'ordained to govern the world according to equity and righteousness with an upright heart', and not to renounce the world and leave it to its corruption. By that conception of man's duty and destiny he is involved in those tragic dilemmas with which our own age is so terribly familiar. For how can man secure justice except by committing injustice, and how can he act without outraging the very conscience which demands that he should act?

It will have been apparent for some time that I am coming round to a point where I am demonstrating the historical nature of my own answer to my question. Although I have gone to the Elizabethans to ask how *Hamlet* appeared to audiences which had applauded *The Spanish Tragedy* and *Titus Andronicus*, it is the moral uncertainties and the moral dilemmas of my own age which make me unable to see *Hamlet* in terms of the hero's failure or success in the task which the Ghost lays upon him.

> For this same lord,
> I do repent; but heaven hath pleased it so,
> To punish me with this, and this with me,
> That I must be their scourge and minister.

Hamlet, speaking over the body of one of his victims, Polonius, speaks for all those called on to attempt to secure justice, the supporters of 'just wars' as well as those who fight in them. In trying to set *Hamlet* back into its own age, I seem to have found in it an image of my own time. The Elizabethan Hamlet assumes the look of the Hamlet of the twentieth century.

That the answers we find are conditioned by our own circumstances does not destroy their value. *Hamlet* is not a problem to which a final solution exists. It is a work of art about which questions can always be asked. Each generation asks its own questions and finds its own answers, and the final test of the validity of those answers can only be time. Johnson, Coleridge, Bradley, all tell us things about *Hamlet* which are consistent with the play as we read it. A critic today cannot hope for more than that his questions and answers will seem relevant, and will continue to seem relevant, to others who read and ponder the play. The reward of the historical approach is not that it leads us to a final and infallible interpretation.

NOTES

1. 'Even Hamlet, who has made a pretty considerable mess of things, and occasioned the death of at least three innocent people, and two more insignificant ones, dies fairly well pleased with himself'

('Shakespeare and the Stoicism of Seneca', in *Selected Essays*, 1932). The odd distinction between the innocent and the insignificant has already been commented on. Mr Eliot's general complaint about the death-scenes of Elizabethan tragic heroes, whose apologias he ascribes to the influence of Seneca, ignores the historical fact that this was an age of public executions in which men were judged by the courage and dignity with which they met public death, and when it was thought proper that at this supreme moment of their lives they should submit their case to the judgement of their fellow-men. The best comment on Othello's last speech and Hamlet's entrusting of his cause to Horatio is provided by Sidney's Musidorus and Pyrocles in their condemned cell: 'In this time, place and fortune, it is lawfull for us to speak gloriously.'

2. Preface to *The History of the World* (1614).

3. It has been suggested by F. T. Bowers (*Elizabethan Revenge Tragedy*, 1940) that we are intended to lose sympathy with Hieronymo when, ignoring the command 'Vengeance is mine', he turns to plots himself and undertakes his murderous play. But the final speech of the Ghost makes it quite clear that to Kyd the characters remained to the end divided into sheep and goats. 'Good Hieronymo slaine by himselfe' is to be conducted with the innocent Isabella and his accomplice Bel-Imperia to the Elysian fields, while the rest of the cast are to be haled off to Tartarean regions by Revenge.

4. 'Vetat Pythagoras injussu imperatoris, id est dei, de praesidio et statione vitae decedere' (*De Senectute*, 20); cf. *Phaedo*, 62.

L. C. Knights

HAMLET AND DEATH (1960)

WHAT we have in *Hamlet* – as in *Othello* and, less successfully, in *Timon* – is the exploration and implicit criticism of a particular state of mind or consciousness. It is an extremely complex state of mind, in which reason and emotion, attitudes towards the self and towards other persons and the world at large, are revealed both directly and through a series of encounters; and our business is to see how the different ingredients (so to speak) are related in such a way that a particular judgment or assessment of experience is precipitated. Since that remark sounds formal and moralistic let me add two qualifying statements. The first is that what we have to do with is not a state of mind that can be adequately described in terms of abstract reason. As. J. I. M. Stewart has said, in *Character and Motive in Shakespeare*:

> It is . . . necessary to recognise that the poetic drama, like myth, is part-based upon an awareness, largely intuitive, of the recesses of human passion and motive. . . . Of just what Shakespeare brings from beyond this portal [of the depths of the mind], and how, we often can achieve little conceptual grasp; and often therefore the logical and unkindled mind finds difficulties which it labels as faults and attributes to the depravity of Shakespeare's audience or what it wills. But what the intellect finds arbitrary the imagination may accept and respond to, for when we read imaginatively or poetically we share the dramatist's penetration for a while and deep is calling to deep.

That, I think, is well said. Hamlet's state of mind, the Hamlet consciousness, is revealed not only at the level of formulable motive, but in its obscure depths; and it is revealed through the poetry. In the second place, the judgment of which I spoke is not a matter of formal approval or condemnation of a dramatic

figure conceived as a real person. No doubt it is partly that; but
essentially it is part of an imaginative apprehension of life in
which, with the whole force of our personality ('judgment ever
awake and steady self-possession combined with enthusiasm and
feeling profound or vehement'), we try to see fundamental
aspects of human life in their true status and relationships. And
what we judge, in this sense, is not someone 'out there', but
potentialities of our own being.

In the particular complex of feelings and attitudes that constitute the Hamlet consciousness it is not easy to separate causes
and effects, but I think that most people would agree that what is
emphasized from the opening scenes is a movement of recoil and
disgust of a peculiar intensity. Whether this negative emotion is,
as T. S. Eliot once claimed, 'in excess of the facts as they appear'
is a question that may be waived for the moment. What is
indisputable is that for the greater part of the play it is stronger
than any counterbalancing movements of positive and outgoing
life. And the determining moment, when this imbalance is
accepted as a kind of compulsion, is . . . the encounter with the
Ghost. When Hamlet swears to 'remember' – with such ominous
repetition of the word – he commits himself to a passion that has
all the exclusiveness of an infatuation.

> Remember thee?
> Ay thou poor ghost while memory holds a seat
> In this distracted globe. Remember thee?
> Yea, from the table of my memory
> I'll wipe away all trivial fond records,
> All saws of books, all forms, all pressures past
> That youth and observation copied there,
> And thy commandment all alone shall live
> Within the book and volume of my brain,
> Unmixed with baser matter.

There is . . . a terrible significance in that *all*. Now Hamlet's
exclusive concentration upon things rank and gross and his
consequent recoil from life as a whole determine his attitude to
death, which also is purely one of negation. Some contrasts may
help us here. When T. S. Eliot's 'Little Gidding' was first

published a notable review of that poem, by D. W. Harding, appeared in *Scrutiny* (XI 3: 1943). Speaking of the way in which a sense of spiritual values can reveal a significant pattern in a life which must otherwise appear meaningless and fragmentary, Harding remarked of the closing sections of the poem:

One effect of this view of time and experience is to rob the moment of death of any over-significance we may have given it. For the humanist of Section II life trails off just because it can't manage to endure. For the man convinced of spiritual values life is a coherent pattern in which the ending has its due place and, because it is part of a pattern, itself leads into the beginning. An over-strong terror of death is often one expression of the fear of living, for death is one of the life-processes that seem too terrifying to be borne. In examining one means of becoming reconciled to death, Mr Eliot can show us life, too, made bearable, unfrightening, positively inviting: 'With the drawing of this Love and the voice of this Calling'.

'An over-strong terror of death is often one expression of the fear of living.' There is of course an instinctive recoil from dying, expressed magnificently by Shakespeare in Claudio's outburst – 'Aye, but to die, and go we know not where' – in *Measure for Measure*; but we are speaking now of settled attitudes, and I think it is obvious that strong, unfrightened and affirmative attitudes to death can only exist as part of strong, unfrightened and affirmative attitudes to living. We could cite the superb closing pages of the Second Part of *The Pilgrim's Progress* (of which I remember F. R. Leavis once remarking to me that no civilization could long endure that did not incorporate in itself some comparable affirmative attitudes); but perhaps here Shakespeare is our most relevant witness, and we may recall how in *The Tempest* the sense of wonder and freshness goes with a serene acceptance of the full human condition; indeed that speech in which Prospero speaks of the transience of all things human begins:

> You do look, my son, in a moved sort,
> As if you were dismay'd; be cheerful, sir.

Now for Hamlet, on the other hand, death is mere negation; but at the same time he is fascinated by it, fascinated not merely by 'the dread of something after death', but by the whole process of earthly corruption, as in the long brooding on the skulls in the churchyard, culminating in the gratuitous fantasy of the progress of Alexander:

To what base uses we may return, Horatio! Why may not imagination trace the noble dust of Alexander, till a' find it stopping a bung-hole?

To which, you remember, Horatio replies, "'Twere to consider too curiously, to consider so'; but Hamlet does not heed him. Certainly the facts that Hamlet dwells on here, as he had dwelt on them in connexion with the death of Polonius, are facts that have to be assimilated somehow, but it is the tone and manner that are betraying:

King.   Now, Hamlet, where's Polonius?
Hamlet.   At supper ... Not where he eats, but where a' is eaten – a certain convocation of politic worms are e'en at him: your worm is your only emperor for diet, we fat all creatures else to fat us, and we fat ourselves for maggots ...

and again:

Hamlet.   Dost thou think Alexander looked o' this fashion i' the earth?
Horatio.   E'en so.
Hamlet.   And smelt so? pah!

It need cause no surprise that these attitudes of fascinated revulsion combine with a regressive longing for the death that, from another point of view, appears so repulsive. .... I would ... call attention to the way in which [the 'To be, or not to be' soliloquy] expresses this basic aspect of Hamlet's attitude to death. The speech (if I may make use of what I have written elsewhere) 'is built up on two contrasted sets of metaphors. Life, "this mortal coil", is at best something which hampers and impedes, imposing "fardels" under which we "grunt and sweat";

"the slings and arrows of outrageous fortune", "the thousand natural shocks", and "the whips and scorns of time" present it as an actively hostile force; and in "a sea of troubles" the power that it has to inflict pain is felt as continuous and irresistible like the sea. Death, on the other hand, is presented simply as a relaxing of tension and an abandonment of the struggle. The reiterated "sleep", the soothing "quietus", and the smooth and weighted "consummation" make plain why death is so ardently desired by a spirit which, whether "suffering" or "opposing", feels itself continually on the defensive against a world conceived as entirely hostile.' The essay from which I am quoting I have come to feel as decidedly fragmentary and provisional, but I see no reason to retract the conclusion that what we have here is a quality of moral relaxation, a desire to lapse *back* from the level of adult consciousness. What has to be added is that Hamlet finally accepts death in words of a peculiarly haunting quality ... but it is from the standpoint of a life that has been largely emptied of significance.

John Holloway

HAMLET (1961)

THE current coin of Shakespeare criticism condemns, as is well
known, an approach to the plays through Bradleian 'character-
analysis' (though the critics of this school are not above ingenious interpretations of character themselves when it suits their
purpose). There is, however, a reason for not attempting to
probe the character of Hamlet, besides those which argue in
general against this approach to the plays. It is that, by contrast
with what is often thought, the *character* of this character (if one
may so put it) is not displayed to us with unusual fulness; and
we are not even afforded good reasons for supposing it to be
abnormally intricate. Undoubtedly, Hamlet displays an *intelligence* which is perhaps unsurpassed in drama for its fertility and
intricacy. That is another matter. Again, his consciousness, the
whole working of his mind, is undoubtedly presented to us
throughout the play with unequalled fulness and detail. But
character is not intelligence, and it is not consciousness.

If one wishes to investigate Hamlet's character, there is of
course much to build upon; but since he is often shamming and
sometimes a good deal distracted, there is little cause for surprise
if that evidence is built upon with difficulty. Indeed, an important
general point emerges. No doubt a character in a great play must
be a vivid presence. No doubt also his nature must be such that
what he does and suffers can issue convincingly from what he is,
and be imposed convincingly upon it. But no play has to be seen
as an illustration, articulate in every detail, of all-pervading
causality, of character issuing, at every point, systematically into
action. Perhaps this is a characteristically nineteenth-century way
of seeing drama, as indeed it was in that time a new and exciting
discovery about how to see life. But in essence, a great dramatic

spectacle does not require its audience to form an exact view, in all detail, of the 'characters' of all the major characters. Its momentum is drawn from other and more distinctively dramatic sources.

The present discussion does not begin by raising the matter of Hamlet's character. Yet there is a fact about this play, as about its author's other tragedies, which is so prominent that it ought to be given recognition. It is this. In nearly all of Shakespeare's major tragedies the hero, the protagonist, has a very great and indeed a peculiar prominence. There is no parallel to this in Shakespeare's other plays, not even the most tense and serious of them, like *Measure for Measure* (in its early scenes) or *The Winter's Tale*. Nor is it paralleled in all tragedies by other authors (the contrast with most of Racine's plays, or *The Trojan Women* of Euripides, is plain). But for all that, this prominence is not rightly seen in terms simply of character.

It is rather, that we make contact very directly with the *experience* through which the protagonist passes in the course of the play. The issue is not, what kind of man Hamlet *is*; but what he *does*. Or rather, what he both does and undergoes: how one can describe the whole volume of the experience through which he passes, as one who both acts and suffers the action of others. Because of the peculiar prominence of the protagonist, to see lucidly what he has experienced, in this sense, will in large part be to see our own experience as spectator. By no means, of course, will it be wholly to see this. The spectator enters into the experience of the protagonist; he also stands back from it. But to have diagnosed the experience through which that peculiarly prominent character passes is to have made a start with taking stock of the experience of the spectator himself.

Hamlet's experience in the course of the play does not take him from the top of Fortune's Wheel to the bottom. This would express the facts only crudely and misleadingly. At the beginning, everyone's interest and concern and loyalty is ostensibly (and often truly) centred upon him. All the characters in the first scene turn at the end of it to him as the man to deal with their crisis and the man to whom they are devoted:

Horatio. Let us impart what we have seen to-night
Unto young Hamlet, for upon my life
This spirit dumb to us, will speak to him:
Do you consent we shall acquaint him with it,
As needful in our loves, fitting our duty?

(I i 169–73)

In the scene which follows, Claudius and the Queen, as soon as
the necessary business has been disposed of (it is plain that the
order of events could not have been reversed, save at the expense
of disastrous bathos), both give Hamlet the central place in their
thought and their court, make him the cynosure of Denmark,
and solicit him to accept this kind of position within the society
of which they are the heads:

King.   We pray you throw to earth
This unprevailing woe, and think of us
As of a father, for let the world take note
You are the most immediate to our throne,
And with no less nobility of love
Than that which dearest father bears his son,
Do I impart toward you . . . For your intent
In going back to school in Wittenberg,
It is most retrograde to our desire,
And we beseech you, bend you to remain
Here in the cheer and comfort of our eye,
Our chiefest courtier, cousin, and our son.
Queen. Let not thy mother lose her prayers, Hamlet,
I pray thee stay with us, go not to Wittenberg.
Hamlet. I shall in all my best obey you, madam.
King. Why, 'tis a loving and a fair reply,
Be as ourself in Denmark.   (I ii 106–22)

The King's words bring to notice an important dramatic
principle. To see them as helping to build up the King's character
is to give them the wrong kind of weight. That Claudius has at
first a fund of genuine benevolence towards Hamlet, or that from
the start he is afraid, and full of eagerness to placate and disarm
potential opponents, would be facts (if facts they were) of only
secondary importance. But in Shakespeare, where there is no

dramatic chorus, the characters speak continually, not perhaps out of character (though sometimes they do even this), but independent of their character, as a kind of running implicit chorus. Their words clarify the situation to the spectator. This is the primary function of what Claudius says here. It shows Hamlet's central position.

Each new scene, at the beginning of the play, underlines the same idea. Act I scene iii shows Ophelia in love with Hamlet, and her brother preoccupied with him. In scene iv Hamlet is the only man to whom the Ghost will speak. Early in Act II, Polonius and the King are still preoccupied, and on the face of it bene-volently so, with Hamlet's affairs and with his welfare. Rosen-crantz and Guildenstern are to give him their company and 'draw him on to pleasures'. This is Hamlet's central and especially privileged position as the play opens. He is still what Ophelia calls him a little later when she thinks of the past:

> Th'expectancy and rose of the fair state,
> The glass of fashion, and the mould of form,
> Th'observed of all observers.   (III i 155–7)

Yet, save for the very first scene, this universal deference is real only within limits. It may not be feigned, but there is some-thing ceremonial in it, there is a nuance of withholding the reality of being a central figure. Claudius's concern is real, but even before Hamlet's closing soliloquy, it is clear that the King's motives are not often unmixed. Laertes' preoccupation is also an alienation. Ophelia may love Hamlet, but she abandons him. Polonius at the end of Act II scene i might be said still to be a friend:

> I am sorry that with better heed and judgement
> I had not quoted him. I feared he did but trifle
> And meant to wreck thee, but beshrew my jealousy:
> By heaven it is as proper to our age
> To cast beyond ourselves in our opinions,
> As it is common for the younger sort
> To lack discretion; come, go we to the king.
> This must be known.   (II i 108–15)

Even so, he is soon trying to pick Hamlet's brain for the benefit
of the King and Queen behind the arras. As for Rosencrantz and
Guildenstern, Hamlet constantly wishes to call them 'friends',
and does so over and over; but their friendship, real enough in
the past (II ii 20–1), is now a façade. When Guildenstern has
heard the King's request to sound Hamlet, and replies:

> Heavens make our presence and our *practices*
> Pleasant and helpful to him!   (II ii 38–9)

the italicized word comes with the full Machiavellian ring of its
Elizabethan meaning.[1] It is not long before Hamlet realizes that
he can trust these 'old schoolfellows' only as 'adders fanged'
(III iv 203).

Indeed, as the play progresses, Hamlet is placed more and
more in a characteristic relation: his fellows surround him with
their attentiveness, offer him their conversation and concern
('They fool me to the top of my bent', III ii 386). But it is a
façade more like a strange kind of baiting than genuine concern;
and the note of harshness, of force to be used on the invalid or the
victim if all else fails, is always present and if anything it grows.
With Claudius's soliloquy (IV iii 57–67) revealing his scheme for
Hamlet's assassination in England, with the murderous duel
plotted by Claudius and Laertes (IV vii), and more particularly
with the graveyard scene when Laertes seizes Hamlet by the
throat and says 'The devil take thy soul' (V i 252) – with these,
the covert hostility to Hamlet comes out into the open. Hamlet's
response relates this incident to how Ophelia, Rosencrantz,
Guildenstern and indeed his mother (who also tried to sound
him for the benefit of a hidden listener) have all gone over to the
other side. It is the response of a man who thought mistakenly
that he had a friend:

> Hear you, sir,
> What is the reason that you use me thus?
> I loved you ever, but it is no matter.   (V i 282–4)

Finally – in what is almost a symbolic moment, so brief it is and
yet so significantly placed – Hamlet parts company with Horatio,

rejecting his advice to avoid the duel; Horatio with whom, as with Rosencrantz and Guildenstern, he once rejected any title but that of friend (II ii 225–7; I ii 162–3). Horatio does not speak again until after the lethal blows have been struck; and apart from him, in this crucial scene Hamlet acts in the conspicuous isolation of one who fights in single combat surrounded by those who in one way or another are on the side of the opponent.

This distinguished isolation is aptly expressed in the likeness which the play often throws out for Hamlet: the lonely moon, the single star. As illustrations of this one may count Laertes' 'The chariest maid is prodigal enough / If she unmask her beauty to the moon' (I iii 36–7); Hamlet's own reference, which applies ironically to himself, to 'nature's livery, or fortune's star' (I iv 32); his letter to Ophelia – 'Doubt thou the stars are fire . . . but never doubt I love' (II ii 116); and perhaps, in view of its ironical reference back to his own honesty in a world of intrigue, his words to Laertes before the duel: 'I'll be your foil, Laertes. In mine ignorance / Your skill shall like a star i' th' darkest night / Stick fiery off indeed' (v ii 253–5). The contribution of the imagery is not prominent, but it is there. Yet the whole action of the work progressively bringing out Hamlet's position in its starkest truth, carries – as it should – the main weight.

A part of Hamlet's experience, over the play, is to pass from one of these extreme positions to the other: from centrality to isolation. His experience has that shape, and that measure of integration: and ours has the reflection of it as we watch. As for Hamlet's character, the experience is related less to that than to what overrides it and renders it irrelevant. In this play as in many other tragedies, the experience of the protagonist is not the deployment of a determinate character, but the assumption, and then the enactment, of a determinate *rôle*. Rôle predominates over character, because once it is assumed by an actor, it will be much the same whatever his nature may be. It overrides that nature: the play is its acting out.

At least twice, Hamlet refers explicitly to his having taken on (albeit unwillingly) the task of the revenger whose narrower function may have been to avenge a wronged kinsman, but

whose wider one was to purge from society the evil which it
could not otherwise escape.

> The time is out of joint, O cursèd spite,
> That ever I was born to set it right!   (I v 188–9)

and

> For this same lord,
> I do repent; but heaven hath pleased it so,
> To punish me with this, and this with me,
> That I must be their scourge and minister.   (III iv 172–5)

– both these quotations express the sense on Hamlet's part that
he is discharging a rôle; one which, so far from being a product
of character, is something thrust upon that. Much in the play
confirms this. The scene at the close of Act I scene v is a deliberate
self-dedication, made as conspicuous as possible, to the rôle of a
revenger. Hamlet invents a brief ritual, a ceremony, the grimly
humorous writing of Claudius down in his tablets; and he
follows this with the more conventional ceremony of swearing
the others to be his confederates. The whole . . . has striking
parallels in other plays; its function is to make both conspicuous
and solemn the moment when Hamlet took upon himself the
rôle which henceforth he is to act and suffer.

Much else in his part would have had this recognizable and
conventional quality for the spectator of the time, though
scholarship has now to recover it. This is true of his cynicism
about chastity in women, and about cosmetics; of his passing
references to his own ambition; of his other conventional or
traditional musings, for example on the *de contemptu mundi*
theme, on the arguments for and against suicide and (following
Castiglione) on how and when the honourable man may engage
in violence.[2] The same also applies to his variations of *loci
classici* in Seneca's tragedies: 'I have that within which passes
show', I ii 85: 'Curae leves loquuntur, ingentes stupent', *Hippo-
lytus*, 607; 'I shall win at the odds; but thou wouldst not think
how ill all's here about my heart – but it is no matter . . . Not a
whit, we defy augury', V II 209–17: 'Nihil timendum video, sed

timeo tamen', *Thyestes*, 435. These details all point the same way.

To take them, however, as indications of character (that Hamlet, say, had a tendency to slip into conventionalities in moments of stress) would be ludicrous; to take any of them (say, those about unchastity or honour) as seriously entering the fabric of ideas of the play would not be ludicrous but would be to seek the far-fetched at the expense of the obvious and central. What is central is the recognizable rôle which has been assumed, the situation (familiar in a general way in the very idea of the revenge play and the malcontent) which is progressing phase by phase before our eyes. These details keep those central facts steadily before our attention; they remind constantly of what the events are that have arrested us. We have a recognizable kind of situation, a man engaged in a known career.

With this in mind, Hamlet's soliloquies take on a new appearance. One must bear in mind that they are, after all, easily foremost in bringing the idea of his delay to notice. It is meaningless to see a delay, in a fiction, merely because something that requires doing is not done at once. The story is of its doing. Naturally it will be done at the end of the story, if it is what will end it. A reader or spectator may see procrastination only if the fiction underlines procrastination. In Saxo Grammaticus's account of Hamlet's taking revenge, mere length of time counts for nothing. Hamlet makes his journey to England (which he does not reach at all, of course, in Shakespeare), stays there a whole year, and at the end of the time merely returns 'thirsting to exact the vengeance, *now long overdue*, for his father's murder'.[3] The author does not raise the question of why it was overdue, and it does not raise itself.

In the play, and apart from the soliloquies, the idea that Hamlet delays can be traced only to two passages. The first is the single occasion when we see him reject a real opportunity for the King's death (the latter is praying after the play scene). No weight can be given to this, for what it mainly does is to give a striking theatrical twist: Hamlet seems to have a fine chance to put an end to his own self-anger at delaying; and then, when he thinks twice, it seems to prove no chance at all. The second passage also deserves little stress, for it is merely that the Ghost (III iv 110–11) endorses Hamlet's own suggestions that he has come, his 'tardy son to chide'. Were it not for Hamlet's own soliloquies, whether he delayed or not would barely invite notice.

It is now possible, however, to see the stress on delay in the soliloquies as being not so much for the sake of stressing delay itself, as of showing how the protagonist is preoccupied with his rôle, in order to stress that it *is* a rôle: a recognizable 'part', undertaken by him with what might almost be termed a pre-ordained course and end. This is in fact constantly the burden of the soliloquies. 'But break my heart, for I must hold my tongue' (I ii 159); 'from the table of my memory / I'll wipe away all trivial fond records' (I v 98–9); 'what would he do, / Had he the motive and the cue for passion / That I have?' (II ii 563–5); 'who would fardels bear, / To grunt and sweat under a weary life' (III i 76–7); 'now could I drink hot blood, / And do such bitter business as the day / Would quake to look on' (III iii 393–5); 'Now might I do it pat' (III iv 73); 'I do not know / Why yet I live to say "This thing's to do" ' (IV iv 43–4). In each of the seven soliloquies the idea is clear: Hamlet's life is one to be lived under the imposition of a great task, an imperious demand from outside. The speeches show him for a man taken up with the demands made upon him by that fact.

Of necessity, Hamlet pursues his course as revenger, scourge and minister, within a social group; but that group is not stable, it is itself disintegrating. Admittedly, the play barely invites its audience to see this as the disintegration of a whole society. It is less a political tragedy, and much more, in the wide sense, a domestic one, than *King Lear* or *Macbeth*. Nevertheless, the royal family with its entourage is there as a group: Hamlet is progressively alienated and isolated from it, and in its turn it is breaking into pieces. Ophelia loses her lover, her father, her reason and her life. Claudius is obliged to plan a second assassination; Hamlet brings about the death of his old school-fellows; Laertes plots revolt first, and murder to follow. As the play proceeds, it becomes clear that the audience is invited to widen its gaze beyond the protagonist himself, and to see his increasingly disastrous relation to his fellows as the central case of something happening everywhere.

These fairly obvious facts about the developing spectacle of the play have been given some surprising expression. 'To Hamlet comes the command of a great act – revenge . . . a sick soul is commanded to heal, to cleanse, to create harmony. But good cannot come of evil: it is seen that the sickness of his soul only further infects the state – his disintegration spreads out, disintegrating,' writes Professor Knight; closely echoed by Mr Traversi, who speaks of 'the disease which, emanating from Hamlet himself, expands from his wounded nature to cover the entire action'.[4] Were these references to spreading and expanding to mean only that, at the beginning, Hamlet alone is in an unhappy condition, but that the others become so as the play goes on, little would have been said, and there would be little need to dissent from it. Professor Knight's reference to Hamlet's sick soul 'infecting' the state, however, suggests that Hamlet is to be seen not simply as the first to suffer from what later becomes general, but the cause of that change: in effect, that is, the source of the evil in the play. If something of this kind is meant (which is not wholly clear) one is entitled to see a certain whimsy in the idea that Shakespeare meant his play to depict the harm a society may incur from the disillusion of a man suffering from the familiar Jacobean disease of melancholy; and threw in regicide, usurpation and incest in the royal line to enliven the middle distance: for this is what would follow. But little harm is done by leaving an account of this sort as intact as it starts; so long as one bears in mind how amply the text puts forward another.

This other account is what follows from the most widespread of Elizabethan dramatic ideas in revenge tragedy: 'Blood will have blood.' 'Foul deeds will rise, / Though all the earth o'erwhelm them, to men's eyes', is almost Hamlet's first comment on hearing of the Ghost. He does not mean, of course, that the risen Ghost itself is a foul deed, but that its apparition is the first sign of how some hidden wickedness, its nature yet unknown, is beginning to do what wickedness traditionally does, bring after

itself a train of evil everywhere. The same implication is clear
when the Ghost is seen once more:

> *Horatio.*   Have after – *to what issue will this come?*
> *Marcellus.* Something is rotten in the state of Denmark.
> *Horatio.*   Heaven will direct it.   (I iv 89–91)

At the close of his first soliloquy, Hamlet has uttered the same
inescapable idea:

> O most wicked speed ... to post
> With such dexterity to incestuous sheets!
> It is not, nor it *cannot come to* good.   (I ii 156–8)

Later, Rosencrantz and Guildenstern state the doctrine in all its
formality and solemnity. The passage expressed vital truths and
current dangers in Shakespeare's age, and it will sound banal only
to the brash and heedless modern ear:

> *Guil.* Most holy and religious fear it is
>   To keep those many many bodies safe
>   That live and feed upon your majesty.
> *Ros.* The single and peculiar life is bound
>   With all the strength and armour of the mind
>   To keep itself from noyance, but much more
>   That spirit upon whose weal depends and rests
>   The lives of many. The cess of majesty
>   Dies not alone; but like a gulf doth draw
>   What's near it with it ...
>   ... when it falls,
>   Each small annexment, petty consequence,
>   Attends the boist'rous ruin. Never alone
>   Did the king sigh, but with a general groan.
>   (III iii 8–23)

The stinging irony of these words is plain. Claudius is not the
prop of social weal. He is the very man who knocked that prop
away, and by doing so initiated the movement of the play. These
lines tell us of exactly that progressive 'ruin' which we must see it
enact, as it goes forward, and of exactly what we ought to
recognize as the cause of that ruin. More clearly than almost any-
where in this work, Shakespeare has made characters speak out of

character (for it is scarcely to these two pantaloons that one would turn for the principles of politics) in order that their words may guide our eyes and minds as we watch.

As for the actual quality of that progressive social ruin by which Hamlet is surrounded, we may trace it symbolized, if we wish, in the way that from Act III scene iv on to Act IV scene iv the characters (and indeed men generally) are likened by the imagery of the play more and more to beasts, without that reason which makes men what they are. We may trace it in the appearance of two other conventional ideas of the time, in which rebellion transforms the ordered life of things on land into the savage chaos of the sea, and the order of tradition into the chaos of total new-fangledness:

> *Attend.* The ocean, overpeering of his list,
> Eats not the flats with more impiteous haste
> Than young Laertes in a riotous head
> O'erbears your officers: the rabble call him lord,
> And as the world were now but to begin,
> Antiquity forgot, custom not known,
> The ratifiers and props of every word,
> They cry 'Choose we, Laertes shall be king!'
>
> (IV v 99–106)

We may trace it yet again, if we wish, in how that most rigorous and solemn of duties in an early society, the fitting burial of the dead, begins to be no longer performed (Polonius, IV v 83; Ophelia, v i 229–32); a failure ironically pointing back not to the 'maiméd rites' in the burial of Old Hamlet, but certainly to his sudden and chaotic death ('Unhouseled, disappointed, unaneled', I v 77). We may see this in a sense ultimate sign of social chaos made general and symbolic in Hamlet's meditation (v i) upon how the bodies of the dead, thrown up from their graves (this is the vital point), pass through every kind of wrong and senseless condition.

Finally, this whole movement in the action is symbolized in the spectacular tableau (it comes towards the close of Act v scene i), where the two young men of the play, soon to fight a duel using an unbated and poisoned weapon, stand struggling in the open grave, surrounded by the rituals of death by suicide. But in thus tracing this movement through metaphor and symbol and fantasy and spectacle, we should remember that these things are not its primary vehicle; they help to make the movement pervasive and potent, but it is one which is embodied in the first instance in the action itself.

There are many plays in which, to put the matter baldly, the case of the *dramatis personae* gets worse as the play goes on. In *Hamlet* this occurs, in two ways, with a distinctive nuance. To begin with, over its whole length the play shows this degeneration into universal violence, conspiracy and chaos within the frame of a brilliant, exhilarating and yet (when once it is seen) disturbing and indeed fearful paradox. The world of *Hamlet*, as it declines into tragedy and chaos, yet maintains one part of itself always in a condition of exuberantly febrile life. Whatever else decays, there remains an incessant play and thrust of frenzied intrigue, of plot and counterplot, and on the surface of this, as its overt counterpart, a scintillating texture of intelligence and wit. Largely, this is the incomparable contribution of Hamlet himself; but not only so. Polonius plays his part at the beginning, Osric at the end. The grave-yard scene is almost an emblem of this paradox within the play: Hamlet's last and most extravagant ingenuities flash about that universal death, real on the stage and imagined by the actors, which is the state towards which the people of the play are heading all the time. This staggering hypertrophy of intelligence provides one large part of the delight and excitement; but another part, not exuberant, but none the less powerful for that, lies in our supervening awareness of how this play of wit iridesces upon the great *caput mortuum* which is coming into focus everywhere below it. Here is something surely unique in Shakespeare.

There is something else distinctive of the movement towards disaster in *Hamlet*. It is less sharply distinctive, because it is based upon a traditional conviction which both Shakespeare and others (notably Dante) have drawn upon. But this traditional conviction is worked out (as one could expect from the stress everywhere in this work upon fertile and witty ingenuity) with a complexity, thoroughness and repeated dexterity that have few parallels. The distinctive quality comes to light if the question is asked, *what kind* of event is it which carries the action (as we have seen, the progressive alienation of the dedicated protagonist from a society falling into chaos) stage by stage forward?

It might be the case that no answer could be given to that question; or the answer might be simply, various sorts of things occurring from time to time. But in the present case, the right answer seems somewhat more ambitious. There does seem to be a large design, which draws together most of the steps the play takes forward on its course, making them of one kind, and an illustration of one underlying idea; and we should be encouraged to trust what is suggested by attentive reading, when we notice that this is no distinctively modern pre-occupation. It is no idea coined by our contemporaries and read back into a work that comes from a past age, but one which (valid and massive as it is when recovered) is unfamiliar to us, although it lay at the centre of things in Shakespeare's own time.

A large proportion, perhaps most, of the main events which carry forward the action of this play, seem like chance events. They seem the work of 'Fortune' in her most casual, most random capacity. Polonius (II ii 139–45) misjudges the sincerity of Hamlet's love for Ophelia: it brings about her rejection of him, certainly has an important effect upon Hamlet himself, and plays its part in leading to Ophelia's madness and death. Yet of itself it seems not design, but pure unlucky accident. With it goes Polonius's other accidental error of judgement: that Ophelia's rejection is the cause of Hamlet's madness. This leads, along an improbable route, to the King's first sensing a real danger in Hamlet himself (III i 170). Rosencrantz and Guildenstern have arrived in Denmark at the 'hasty sending' of Claudius; but although they have not come by chance, it is the idea that they are the children of Fortune, of chance, which is strongly stressed at their first meeting with the Prince (II ii 230 ff.). The players arrive (and one must bear in mind that their arrival is what makes possible the play scene and all that follows from it) entirely by chance (II ii 320). It is a chance that the one opportunity Hamlet

had to kill Claudius proved no opportunity at all, because the
King was praying; and another that this too was an error, because
his praying was a sham. The killing of Polonius seems pure
chance ('take thy fortune', III iv 32); and so of course is Hamlet's
meeting at sea with the pirates and subsequent return to Denmark.

All this side of the play seems to be epitomized and symbolized
in the duel, greatest and most mortal of chances, at its end.
Hamlet twice implies that he is himself the minion (darling or
plaything) of Fortune. Speaking to Horatio, he mentions how
men with one decisive defect, though they may be 'nature's
livery, or fortune's star' (I iv 32), cannot but be discredited in the
end. The speech has long been seen to apply ironically to Hamlet
himself. Again, he later extols Horatio for being one of those

> Whose blood and judgement are so well co-medled,
> That they are not a pipe for Fortune's finger
> To sound what stop she please   (III ii 67–9)

– which once more ironically implies that he, lacking Horatio's
stoicism and calm resolve, is exactly such a plaything of Fortune
himself. The idea is confirmed in a later scene, where he reproves
Rosencrantz and Guildenstern for trying to 'sound' him as if he
were a pipe, but only a moment later he says 'they fool me to the
top of my bent', and thus realizes that here too, within limits, he
is Fortune's mere victim. The final arrival of Fortinbras, which
makes possible the close of the play in some sort of order, is
again a pure chance.

Yet what *is* pure chance? The orthodox and traditional view
still had a decisive strength in Pope's time, and permitted him to
write 'All Chance, Direction which thou canst not see'. This to
Shakespeare was a central commonplace: perhaps its most
eloquent and elaborate contemporary expression is the debate
between Pamela and her wicked aunt in Sidney's *Arcadia*.[5] Here
Sidney expends his ingenuity, as *avocatus diaboli*, in arguing that
the seemingly random events of life are truly random; but the
strong emotion and the eloquence appear in Pamela's reply,
which argues that through all randomness runs ultimately, and

decisively, the power and design of Providence. Randomness simply does not exist. All that exists is the operation, sometimes abrupt and direct, sometimes devious and slow, of Divine Justice.

Over and over in *Hamlet*, chance turns into a larger design, randomness becomes retribution. Polonius hides behind the arras so as to enable himself to explain everything: and he is silenced for ever ('thou find'st to be too busy is some danger', III iv 33). Rosencrantz and Guildenstern, bearing the sealed letters which order the death of Hamlet, go by just such letters, in altered form, to their deaths themselves. Hamlet, thinking how he will bring such a reversal about, says,

> Let it work,
> For 'tis the sport to have the enginer
> Hoist with his own petar;   (III iv 205–7)

– but the irony goes further than he sees: he has just afforded such sport himself. Killing Claudius (as he thought) at a time when he could do so scot-free, he has only, in killing Polonius, magnified all his difficulties. Claudius has been moving along just such a self-defeating path from the start, and says so:

> O liméd soul, that struggling to be free,
> Art more engaged ...   (III iii 68–9)

In the end, it is not from Hamlet's rapier that he dies ('O, yet defend me, friends, I am but hurt', v ii 322), but from the poisoned cup that he has himself prepared and that he has just tried to have passed to Hamlet: 'He is justly served, / It is a poison tempered by himself', is Laertes' comment. As for the Queen, her death also comes, as retributively it should, in the intoxication and delight of the wine she has taken at the hand of Claudius. Laertes is the same. The rapier that he intends for Hamlet is that which kills him:

Osric.   How is't, Laertes?
Laertes. Why, as a woodcock to my own springe, Osric!
          I am justly killed by mine own treachery.
                                        (v ii 303–5)

All these things must be in Horatio's mind when, in the closing moments of the play, he says that he will give a public account of the whole bloodthirsty tangle, and culminates his summary of that account by speaking of

> purposes mistook
> Fall'n on th' inventors' heads   (v ii 382–3)

It is the same idea as that with which Dante closes Canto 28 of the *Inferno*: Bertrand de Born, in hell with his head severed forever because he severed father and son in rebellion, says, 'Così s'osserva in me lo contrapasso' (Thus retribution shows itself in me). Here, in this pervasive moving back upon itself of the work of Fortune, until it becomes the work of Destiny, transpires the radical organization and symmetry of the action; and in its repetition, its ingenious observance everywhere, something of what most distinguishes the play.

NOTES

1. Cf. *King John*, IV iii 64; *King Lear*, I ii 170–3.

2.
> Rightly to be great
> Is not to stir without great argument,
> But greatly to find quarrel in a straw
> When honour's at the stake.   (IV iv 53–6)

Cf. Castiglione, *The Courtier*, I: 'Neither let him run rashly into these combats, but when he must needes to save his estimation withall: for . . . he that goeth headlong to these thinges, and without urgent cause, deserveth great blame, although his chance be good. But when a man perceiveth that he is entred so far that hee cannot draw backe without burthen, hee must both in such thinges as hee hath to doe before the combate, and also in the combate, be utterly resolved with himselfe, and always show a readiness and a stomach.' Mr Traversi, writing that 'the two statements thus made (by Hamlet) have the appearance of a noble and consistent attitude based on "honour", but are actually in virtual contradiction' (*An Approach to Shakespeare* (1956 ed.) p. 101), seems not to recognize that Hamlet is uttering a traditional commonplace (nor to comprehend its soundness). The last

sentence of the passage quoted from Castiglione bears plainly upon
part of Polonius's advice to Laertes:

> Beware
> Of entrance to a quarrel, but being in,
> Bear't that th' opposéd may beware of thee.
>
> (I iii 65–70)

3. Saxo Grammaticus, *Historia Danica*, III, trans. O. Elton (1894)
p. 117; italics mine.
4. *The Wheel of Fire* (1930) p. 20; *An Approach to Shakespeare*, p.
95.
5. *Essay on Man*, I 290; *Arcadia* (1590 ed.) III 10.

Patrick Cruttwell

THE MORALITY OF *HAMLET* — 'SWEET PRINCE' OR 'ARRANT KNAVE'? (1963)

W A S Hamlet a good man or was he a bad one?

I cannot think it illegitimate to ask that simple question (though, of course, the answer need not be simple); it is, I believe, a question which every reader or playgoer 'uncorrupted by literary prejudices' asks himself, and which the play as a whole insists that we should ask. But the answers it has received range no less widely than those given to the other questions which play and characters provoke; for the one thing about Hamlet (prince as well as play) on which all writers are in agreement is the unique extent of their disagreement. And disagreements about Hamlet seem to have been of a special kind. They have involved a transference to ourselves, to within ourselves, of problems which should exist only inside the play, with the consequence of an all-befogging emotional subjectiveness. It is plain that this subjectiveness, and the consequent fogging, are often wilful. Many critics have been helpless and puzzled before *Hamlet* because they wanted to be helpless and puzzled, because they found it emotionally pleasurable. Some of them have rationalised this by arguing that it is also aesthetically justifiable, for such was the author's intention – but, be that as it may, this puzzlement about Hamlet has certainly caused, and been caused by, a habit of expanding him from a specific character in a specific play to something wider and vaguer. Hamlet = Everyman; Hamlet = Shakespeare: these have been the favoured expansions – and one may be right in suspecting that lying behind both of them has often been another: Hamlet = Me. The appeal of this last is not hard to guess. Partly a projected masochism – how many of us, in our adolescent moods, have taken to our own wounded sensibilities the cursed spite and the time out of joint! – and partly a projected vanity; for that Hamlet is a 'genius' is a conviction no less widespread than that he is Shakespeare or Everyman. The conviction, I suspect, is largely derived from this sensed kinship with our own self-mirroring daydreams; for, without that aid, would one see more in him than great charm, quick wit, a ranging curiosity of mind and a remarkable articulateness? At least it should rouse our suspicions when we see that the kind of genius which intellectuals attribute to Hamlet is precisely the kind appropriate to intellectuals: what Coleridge called 'the prevalence of the abstracting and generalising habit over the practical'. And one loses count of the later critics who have simply paraphrased Coleridge.

What it all amounts to, then, is that Hamlet is one of the handful of literary creations which have turned into something more than simply characters in a novel or poem or play. He has become a figure of myth; and just as Odysseus is the myth-character of the Traveller, Faust of the Seeker, Quixote of the Knight, and Juan of the Lover, so Hamlet has been made the myth-character of the doubting, self-contemplating Intellectual. It is only appropriate, then, that his outlines should be so much hazier than those of the other myth-characters. The haziness is inherent in the myth and in the manner by which the myth has been made, for Hamlet, the puzzled self-contemplator, has been created through the self-projections of a long line of puzzled self-contemplators. Everything about him has for long been hazy; and why should we expect an exemption from haziness in the moral judgements which men have passed on him?

For the first decades of the play's existence we have no direct evidence; but P. S. Conklin is surely correct in suggesting that 'the early prince was most decidedly a malcontent avenger who still kept the markings of his Kydian ancestry'[1] – for however great or little importance we ascribe to the undoubted existence of that earlier play and earlier prince, it can hardly have had no effect at all. The transforming of the malcontent avenger, 'often bitterly sarcastic, cynical, cruel and obscene' (as Conklin – p. 13 – describes the type) into a character basically sympathetic must have been gradual. One can hardly imagine an actor daring suddenly to present a Coleridgean or Goethean Hamlet, even if he could have conceived it; for I doubt if audiences of the seventeenth century were as ready as are (unfortunately) audiences of the twentieth to accept Shakespearian productions which work on the principle: 'Let's see what the text obviously calls for and then do the opposite.' Gradual the transformation must have been, but not really slow. As early as 1709, it looks as if the seed of a sympathetic Hamlet has been sown; for in that year Steele is talking of his 'noble ardour' and 'generous distress at the death of Ophelia' and praising the veteran Betterton, still acting the part 48 years after Pepys had seen him, for representing '*virtue* . . . on the stage with its proper ornaments'. Through the eighteenth century the debate continued. Johnson assumes that Hamlet is 'represented as a virtuous character', but is aware that some of his actions – notably his stated reason for sparing the king at prayer and his mendacious excuses to Laertes for his behaviour at Ophelia's funeral – are difficult to reconcile with the assumption of goodness. But Johnson does assume this; what he blames is Shakespeare's inconsistent character-drawing. Akenside, as reported by George Steevens, was categorically on the opposite side: 'The conduct of Hamlet was every way unnatural and indefensible, unless he were to be regarded as a young man whose intellects were in some degree impaired by his own misfortunes' – and Steevens supported him, talking of 'the immoral tendency of [Hamlet's] character.' But in spite of Akenside and Steevens, the general run of eighteenth-century comment was towards the totally sympathetic Hamlet of Goethe and Coleridge and the nineteenth century as a whole; this is foreshadowed, as one might expect, by Henry Mackenzie, the Man of Feeling, who talks in 1780 of the prince's 'delicate sensibility'. Through the romantic and Victorian years this tune is sustained, with whatever variations. Hamlet is deeply admired – more than that, he is loved, as the Shakespeare- and Everyman- and Me-identifications thicken and intensify – and as for the awkward episodes, especially his behaviour to Ophelia, these are usually dealt with by accepting Akenside's hint and assuming that

Hamlet's madness was not always or altogether feigned.

Thus the Hamlet of nineteenth-century romanticism was largely the 'sweet' and angel-borne prince of Horatio's farewell. Our own age has queried this, and the Hamlet who is now presented, both on stage and in print, is a figure whose moral effect is much more dubious. In part, no doubt, this has been caused by – or at least gone together with – a revised opinion of the play itself as a work of art. The consensus of earlier judgement gave it as Shakespeare's masterpiece; most of us today, if we don't go as far as Eliot's 'most certainly an artistic failure' (*Selected Essays*, p. 143), do tend to agree with Knights's: 'In the twentieth century, *Hamlet* has yielded to *King Lear* the distinction of being the play in which the age most finds itself' (p. 11). (The present writer feels inclined to disagree – or at least would like to add: 'So much the worse for "the age".') And the fact that the total effect of the play is undoubtedly centred on the name-part to a degree unique in Shakespeare (a fact noted as early as 1710, when Shaftesbury said it had 'only ONE *Character*') – this has meant that any shift in attitude, any uneasiness, towards the play (or the prince) involves a corresponding shift towards the prince (or the play). The moral shift with regard to the prince may give the superficial effect of a return to the original Hamlet, the 'malcontent avenger' of Conklin, and it is true that this figure has been revived, brought back to our notice, whereas for Goethe and Coleridge he had entirely disappeared. But this is only superficial, this impression of a return to the seventeenth century; for although we have readmitted intellectually and recognised historically the 'malcontent avenger', it is quite impossible for the twentieth century to respond to such a type as we may imagine the seventeenth century responded. The latter seems to have regarded the 'malcontent avenger' – Tourneur's Vendice is the perfect specimen – as a type almost on the edge of caricature, to be taken at times with a shudder, at other times with a giggle, but almost never with that fellow-feeling, that degree at least of moral admiration, which true tragedy is usually thought to call for. You could admire a Vendice for his wit, his panache, his conspiratorial ingenuity, and his quickness with dagger or

sword; but you did not admire his goodness, and when he came
to his own sticky end you felt that he had earned it no less,
though no more, than the scoundrels he himself had disposed of.
A response as simple as that is not possible for Hamlet.

The question to be asked, I repeat, is the question: Was
Hamlet a good man or was he a bad one? I shall look at this as it
appears in most of the play's major episodes; but underlying it
throughout, and decisive for our answer, are two other questions.
How do we take his madness – feigned or real, or, if mixed,
mixed in what proportions? And how do we take the obligation
of revenge laid on him by the ghost – as a true moral duty,
recognised as such by the prince himself and to be accepted as
such by us, or as a temptation to wrongdoing?

The former is clearly paramount in deciding Hamlet's moral
responsibility. When, for example, he says to Ophelia: 'I loved
you not', but to Laertes, over her dead body: 'I loved Ophelia' –
when he behaves to her as we see him doing in the nunnery-scene
but also as she reports him to have done before – then surely the
natural and immediate response of most of us is that unless we
can allow him a degree of genuine mental disturbance, the only
possible verdict is Johnson's 'useless and wanton cruelty'. (But
the 'natural and immediate response' is not always the right one.)
And a survey of *Hamlet* commentators would show, I believe,
a certain correlation. Those who like the prince and admire him
as a good man will tend to see a part at least of his madness as
genuine; those who do not will see it all as feigned. We assume,
of course, that in the lost 'Kydian' *Hamlet*, the hero simply put it
on as a trick. But Kyd's own example, *The Spanish Tragedy*, is
enough to show how easily that can slide into something more
than a trick: for the 'mad Hieronymo' of the later additions makes
an effect dramatically indistinguishable from the effect of the real
thing. (Compare Edgar as Tom o'Bedlam: how many producers,
how many actors, how many audiences, really remember that he
is perfectly sane?) The earliest references to 'mad Hamlet' seem
indecisive on the question of real or feigned, but they imply
beyond doubt a great deal of thoroughly extreme behaviour. 'His
shirt he onely weares, Much like mad-Hamlet, thus as passion

tears . . .' (1604). 'If any mad Hamlet hearing this smell villany and rush in by violence . . .' (1609). Conklin suggests (p. 12) that the character as originally played must have had 'comic over-tones' when putting on the 'antic disposition', and there is probably a relic of this as late as 1765, in Johnson's surprising remark: 'The pretended madness of Hamlet causes much mirth.' What seems undeniable is that the prince as originally conceived and played behaved for quite long stretches in a manner utterly different from his behaviour at other times. Whether an audience thought his madness feigned or real – and remember we are criticising a play, not a treatise of psychiatry – the effect was bound to be: 'This isn't the *real* Hamlet!' And for such a way of playing, for such violent alternations of behaviour, the text gives ample warrant, indeed specific instructions. From Hamlet's own 'put an antic disposition on' through Ophelia's description of neglected clothes, physical collapse ('pale as his shirt, his knees knocking each other'), hysterical gestures and deep sighs, and the king's 'transformation . . . Sith nor th'exterior nor the inward man Resembles that it was', to the Queen's 'mad as the sea and wind when both contend', and in many other places, the text is insisting on an extravagance of behaviour which could scarcely be overacted. But no contemporary actor that I have seen – and not many contemporary critics that I have read – pay more than token attention to these unequivocal textual instructions. The modern tendency is to present not a Hamlet who is at times perfectly sane and at other times perfectly lunatic, or behaving as if perfectly lunatic, but a Hamlet who is all the time just a trifle – and part of the time more than a trifle – neurotic. This, I suppose, in the age of Freud, may be expected. Ernest Jones is quite clear about it – 'Hamlet's behaviour is that of a psychoneurotic' – and though Knights may not accept Jones's fully psycho-analytical reading, he can begin a sentence: 'As in many neurotics, Hamlet . . .'[2] – as if this were to be taken for granted. It is, in my own judgement, almost totally wrong.

Right or wrong, it has had a curious effect on the moral issue. If one imagined Hamlet as a real person, outside the theatre and the play, then clearly his moral responsibility would be greatly lessened if he could be thought of as all the time mentally and emotionally disturbed. But the effect of this *in the play* is to keep him all the time before us as a person behaving, if not quite normally, then at least within sight of normality and therefore within reach of moral judgement; whereas if he is allowed now and then to rant and caper, heave profound sighs and wear his stockings down-gyved to the ankles, we forget, in practice, that this is 'feigning' and simply discount it. If – to take a concrete instance – the scene with Ophelia can be played as Aaron Hill in the early eighteenth century suggested – that is, Hamlet must quite unmistakably 'act mad' when she is watching but look sanely miserable when she doesn't see him – then his behaviour to her becomes perfectly plausible. But no modern actor does play the scene in that way. The reasons are clear. Partly it is that our greater reluctance to accept on the stage a 'make-believe' we would not credit offstage renders an acted madness unacceptable; partly that our greater sensitiveness to mental illness makes the mere idea of pretending to be mad more than a little distasteful. So in the names of realism and sensitiveness, Hamlet is never allowed to behave as practically everyone in the play (including himself) assures us he does frequently behave. And this implies a very different Hamlet. Instead of a man sufficiently in command of himself to sustain for long periods an exceedingly difficult masquerade, and sustain it well enough to deceive everybody, we have someone always on the edge of breakdown and sometimes over it. The former, I believe, is a great deal nearer than the latter to Shakespeare's conception: though I must agree with Waldock that here Shakespeare himself is partly to blame.[3] He has not completely 'assimilated, re-explained' the inherited theme of feigned madness into his own creation.

To this it may be said that after all Hamlet does complain, more than once, of 'melancholy'; he does express a deep disgust and weariness of life; and that this indicates a degree of 'madness' that is not 'feigned'. But, as B. L. Joseph[4] and Lily Campbell point out, melancholy to the Elizabethan mind did not necessarily imply a condition in the least resembling what we would call a state of 'neurosis'. It was simply a variety of temperament. It

might occur in a thoroughly vigorous and decisive man of action
– though perhaps (this is my own impression) it was thought
more likely to be the temperament of the scholar, the meditative
man. This is the sense still current in Milton's 'Penseroso', and
that Hamlet was of that kind may have been signalled to an
Elizabethan audience by his 'intent in going back to school in
Wittenberg'. (Most of the contributors to this volume are probably melancholiacs in the Elizabethan sense – but not, I trust,
neurotics.) Shakespeare does show characters who are what we
would call neurotic – Don John of *Much Ado*, Jaques, Angelo,
Leontes, Apemantus – and these are truly unbalanced in ways
that Hamlet is not. They show it by an alienation from reality
which breeds irremovable delusions, violently anti-social behaviour, and above all a tendency to shun and hate their fellow-
creatures. In none of them are the easy sociability, the unforced
authority, the capacity to love and be loved, which Hamlet
shows. And as for the disgust for life which Hamlet expresses,
isn't this very adequately accounted for by what happens to him?
Eliot's famous remark, that 'Hamlet . . . is dominated by an
emotion which . . . is in *excess* of the facts as they appear'
(*Selected Essays*, p. 145), has always, I must confess, filled me
with stupefaction; for when I consider the 'facts' as they did
'appear' to Hamlet – the sudden death of a much-loved father,
followed immediately by the indecently hasty and incestuous
remarriage of his mother to a man whom Hamlet hated and
despised and who then proceeded to cheat him out of the throne,
this followed in turn by the supernatural reappearance of his late
father with the information that Hamlet's stepfather was his
father's murderer and the peremptory command that he, Hamlet,
should set to work at once on vengeance – when I consider all
this, I find it hard to imagine any degree of emotion which ought
to be censured as 'excessive' and I am deep in admiration for the
high behaviour-standards of those critics who find in Hamlet's
occasional outbursts of hysteria evidence that he must be
neurotic. This seeing Hamlet's emotion as 'excessive' and irrational is part, I believe, of that tendency to expand his character
outwards from the play in which it should remain embedded;

what has happened is that because Hamlet has become the great type-figure of intellectual *Weltschmerz*, the very embodiment of 'ich weiss nicht was soll' es bedeuten, dass ich so traurig bin', the fact that he has very good factual and individual reasons for feeling 'traurig' has to be forgotten, and the passages in which disgust for life is most powerfully expressed are read as if they were odes by Leopardi or lyrics by Housman instead of dramatic utterances conditioned by particular moments in a sequence of dramatic events.

If, then, we conclude that Hamlet is not a neurotic, he is a normal man in a situation of intense strain, what effect will this have on the moral question? It must clearly make Hamlet a good deal more culpable when he misbehaves, at least when we reflect about him afterwards, if not when we are actually seeing him on the stage. We can rescue him only on one assumption – that he has had laid on him a moral duty so stern and undeniable as to excuse any behaviour which is directed to its performance. And this brings us to the question of revenge.

The original Hamlet, there is no doubt, was almost nothing but an embodiment of Revenge. Shakespeare's play, as Conklin says, 'had merely made more proverbial still a "Hamlet revenge" fixation which the popular mind already possessed' (p. 11) – a fact attested by a wealth of contemporary allusion on the lines of that in *Westward Ho*: 'Let their husbands play mad Hamlet and cry Revenge.' We cannot tell for how long this Ur-Hamlet held the stage instead of – or together with – his more complex descendant; it looks as if for a time there must have been one Hamlet for the groundlings and another for the highbrows. Waldock seems to me in the right when he suggests (p. 66) that in Shakespeare's handling of his inherited story 'the revenge theme has been considerably damaged'; but, damaged or not, it is still very much there. We cannot ignore it, we must not play down its sometimes unpleasing effects – or play them up, giving them a quality of moral repulsiveness which may not have been meant – for it is this, more than anything else, which has divided the prince's interpreters. Was he right to take the command 'Revenge!' as a true moral duty? Does the play as a whole insist that we should agree with this – as powerfully as the *Choephori*, for instance, insists that Orestes must take vengeance for his father's murder? There is a whole spectrum of answers to these questions – of which we may take Joseph as representative of the one end, Knights and Wilson Knight of the other. Joseph, accepting the revenge-ethic as the ethic which governs the play, argues that 'in a revenge play a nobleman was bound to kill Claudius, and many of Shakespeare's first audiences would have expected this in real life as well' (p. 24). Knights's disagreement is specific: 'We may be told, in *Hamlet* Shakespeare is using the conventions of the revenge play. . . . This has always seemed to me a very rum argument indeed. . . .'[5] Joseph argues that Hamlet is a character 'in the renaissance tradition of honourable and noble behaviour', that in the whole play there is no 'overt statement' against revenge, and that when Hamlet accepts the ghost's command to forget everything but the duty of taking vengeance he is performing a symbolic 'act of forgetting' (pp. 37, 44, 80). Knights replies that a ghost who 'clamours for revenge' must be a ghost concerning whom Shakespeare entertains 'grave doubts' and that Hamlet's acceptance of his command is simply a yielding to temptation (pp. 46–8). Wilson Knight agrees; the ghost's command was 'devilish', he was 'a portent not kind but sinister'.[6]

Disagreement could hardly be more absolute. It is part, of course, of a wider disagreement. Joseph sees the character relatively, in terms partly historical, Knights and Wilson Knight absolutely, in terms entirely moral. My own verdict inclines to agree with Joseph, mainly, I think, because this reading seems to stay more scrupulously within the play itself and within the framework of time and form in which the play was made. Knight's reply to this is that he *is* seeing the play within a 'framework' – and the framework is that of Shakespeare's other plays written in the same period as *Hamlet*. These, he thinks, enforce a morality which exposes the inadequacy, the wrongness of the revenge-ethic; and would Shakespeare, at about the same time, write a play to the opposite effect? But this, I believe, falls into two errors. It minimises the difference between an imaginative artist and a moralising arguer; and it is based on selective reading.

We may be entitled to draw from Isabella's pardoning of Angelo and Cordelia's of Lear the message that forgiveness is better than vengeance; but surely it is equally true that the whole moral weight of *Macbeth* is behind the personal and bloody vengeance which Macduff vows and takes on the man who has killed his wife and children, and the whole moral weight of *Lear* is no less behind Edgar's challenging and killing of Edmund. (Not to mention the action of Lear when he 'killed the slave that was a-hanging' Cordelia.) This reluctance to believe that Shakespeare could possibly have conceived a character who was 'represented as virtuous', in Johnson's words, but who also pursued revenge as a moral duty – and even greater reluctance to believe that Shakespeare could have thought such a character right to do so – springs, to my mind, from the very powerful quasi-pacifist emotions of many twentieth-century liberal intellectuals and especially of those literary critics whose preoccupations are more with morality than with history. They hate the use of physical force; they are enormously suspicious of what were once called the 'military virtues'; they do not like the idea that a poet whom they admire could have admired a fighting-man. It is this which distorts Leavis's view of Othello and Traversi's of Henry V, and it is this which I detect in Knights's phrase 'the *murder* of Rosencrantz and Guildenstern' (p. 33). Murder? Well, yes, in a sense I suppose it was; but I fancy that most readers, when they come to that word, are brought up with a shock – a shock of spontaneous disagreement – which, if they reflect on it, they will explain in words like these: 'Knights has forgotten something. He has forgotten that *Hamlet is at war.*' Shakespeare did his best to remind him, with pointed use of military imagery – 'the enginer / Hoist with his own petar' and 'the pass and fell incensèd points / Of mighty opposites', both of which refer directly to Rosencrantz and Guildenstern – but I suspect that these signposts failed to show the right way because, for this critic, 'war' and 'murder' are emotionally synonymous. They were not so for Shakespeare; nor for Hamlet. And revenge, in effect, was a private war. Does not Bacon's 'wild justice' really say the same?

But could it not still be argued that even if Hamlet, and even if the play of *Hamlet*, accept revenge as a moral duty, nevertheless its execution, and the nasty things that must be done on the way to it, do in fact degrade and contaminate the prince? This is Kitto's argument. Hamlet, he thinks, is paralysed and 'left prostrate' by 'his comprehensive awareness of evil' and 'the destructive power of evil'.[7] Knights finds this inadequate. Part of the corruption is in Hamlet himself, not all in the world around him, and the play 'urges' us to question and criticise 'the attitudes with which Hamlet confronts his world' (p. 34). Does it? I wish I could see just where the play is 'urging' this. The only un-equivocal urgings that I can see are those which – through Hamlet himself – are urging him to get on with the job; other-wise, I should have thought, the overall tone of the play is urging us very strongly to admire this prince, and to sympathise with him, at least, all through. Denial of this implies, of course, that the ending of the play must be totally ironic: not merely Horatio's elegy – which I suppose may be discounted (though against the emotional grain) as the words of a deeply moved friend – but also the verdict of the uninvolved Fortinbras:

> For he was likely, had he been put on,
> To have proved most royal . . .   (v ii 405)

He could never have said that of Knights's Hamlet.

Nor can I believe, in any case, that Elizabethan minds would accept the proposition that a man who pursues a cause just in itself can be corrupted by the pursuit of it. Their minds were more theological than ours, more closely keyed to an ultimate destiny of total black or white, damned or saved. *Respice finem*, they would have said, in every sense; Macbeth and Lady Macbeth are totally ruined, Othello and Leontes temporarily ruined, not because of the terrible things they do, but because the ends for which they do them are wrong. If then we accept, as I have argued we must, Shakespeare's acceptance in *Hamlet* of the ethic of revenge, we must accept also that the man who follows this ethic with courage and responsibility cannot be doing wrong, what-ever mistakes or inevitable damage to others may befall him on the way. And Hamlet does show responsibility, when he doubts the *bona fides* of the ghost and arranges that its story shall be tested. (If only Othello had tested Iago's story with as much responsibility – !)

Nevertheless, it would be absurd to argue that Shakespeare's Hamlet – prince *and* poem – can yield a moral effect as simple as that of *The Spanish Tragedy* or, we may presume, of the original Kydian *Hamlet*. Waldock and Joseph are right, I believe, when they point out (p. 22, etc.; p. 37) that there are no signs from Hamlet of conscientious scruples about undertaking the task of revenge, and no other expressions of such feelings in the play: but is it not strange that there should be none? For both play and character are notably Christian. The ghost's speech about Purgatory; the wonderful lines of Marcellus describing the miracles at Christmas; the King at prayer; the burial of Ophelia; Hamlet's references to Christian doctrine on suicide: these give the play terms of reference much more specifically Christian than those of the other tragedies. And yet the completely anti-Christian ethic of revenge is never, as it were, tested by, never even brought up against, this Christian world in which it lives. It is this which makes the moral effect so much more ambiguous than that of a play which is revenge-play and nothing else, such as *The Spanish Tragedy*; for in that the moral universe is completely pagan, and the fact that the story is supposed to be set in Christian Spain is simply forgotten. This, too, invalidates Kitto's reading of *Hamlet* as a 'religious drama', one which shows 'the natural working-out of sin' and the 'operation of the divine laws' (pp. 329–30). Such words would apply only to dramas where the religious basis was clear-cut and single; but what we have in *Hamlet* is an extraordinary muddle of *two* moralities, one avowed, the other not avowed, but both playing heavily and continuously on the central character. This, I believe, is very largely responsible both for Hamlet's own confusions and for the confusions of his critics; it is certainly responsible for one or two crucially ambiguous episodes – and above all for that in which Hamlet spares the King at prayer because he thinks that if he kills him then, his victim will go straight to heaven. Nothing poor Hamlet ever did has brought down on his head so much critical obloquy as the not-doing of this. Johnson was deeply shocked: 'too horrible to be read or to be uttered' was his verdict on the speech – and if we believe, as we certainly should, that Hamlet meant what he said, then we ought indeed to be shocked. But the irony is that Hamlet is here behaving as he does because he is a Christian, convinced, as most believers then were, of the vital importance of 'dying well'. The pagan revenger could have taken his vengeance then and there – the only vengeance available to a pagan, the bringing to an end of bodily life – if he were not also a Christian believer.

How aware was Shakespeare of this moral muddle at the core of his play? And how aware was Hamlet that his behaviour as revenger and his beliefs as Christian were scarcely compatible? We shall never be able to answer these questions; but it is a fact that in the Renaissance the Christian ethic which says: 'Vengeance is mine, saith the Lord; I will repay' and the ethic of personal revenge co-existed side by side not merely as ways in which men actually behaved but as accepted, one might almost say respectable, moralities. (They continued to do so, of course, till much later: revenge became duelling, a narrower code but recognisably the same.) Whether the play intends this or not, the curious spectacle it presents of two rival moralities going their ways apparently without noticing each other is no bad representation of the actual contemporary state of affairs outside the theatre; and Hamlet himself, morally divided so perfectly that he does not seem aware of the division, may have seemed to many young men of the early 1600s a remarkably penetrating analysis of a young man like themselves. It is certain that his character 'caught on' with a speed and intensity unrivalled by any other dramatic creation of the age; his presence, his attendant aura of madness and mortality, and his peculiar tone which blends wit and pathos, cynicism and sentiment, brutality and tenderness, are everywhere in the Jacobean poets and dramatists. When a character 'catches on' like this, it is safe to assume that it does so because some element in the age feels itself fixed or embodied in this character. The level on which this is felt may be entirely superficial, of no permanent interest; and then one has the kind of creation (Byron's

Corsair, for instance, and perhaps Osborne's Jimmy Porter) which enjoys at first a great brief vogue and baffles posterity ever after. But in any case the understanding of such characters should start from understanding their original affinities; and one may begin to understand the 'moral flavour' of Hamlet's personality by trying to see him as he may have been seen by the well-born young intellectuals of the early 1600s. What would they have found interesting and notable in this figure of the theatre? Where might they have thought themselves represented?

They might have noted at once that Hamlet is a student as well as a prince – and not only a temporary, youthful student but one who, at the age of thirty and when heir presumptive to the throne, is still anxious to go 'back to school in Wittenberg'. This would have been unusual in any age; it may have seemed even more unusual then, when the division between university and world, scholar and man of the world, still had much of the medieval strictness. Here, perhaps, was a sign pointing to a temperament which did not naturally crave a life of activity but rather one of contemplation. The strange action with which Hamlet strives to control his hysteria immediately after the ghost has left him – the taking out of his tables and writing in them – and the imagery he uses at the same moment – 'within the book and volume of my brain' – these may have seemed entirely appropriate to such a temperament. Only a very powerful conviction of duty would induce a man like this to embark on a course of action and violence; he was all the more to be admired for forcing himself to do it. When the story moved on to the 'delays' and to Hamlet's self-reproaches for them, a contemporary audience would not, I think, have responded as Goethe and Coleridge did and concluded that Hamlet was *unfit* for action. They would have seen, on the contrary, just as Fortinbras did, that he was thoroughly fit for it; they would have concluded – correctly, to my mind – that what Hamlet showed, because of his temperament, was an unusual degree of reluctance and repugnance rather than unfitness. For another thing they would have noted was Hamlet's fastidiousness; this they would have picked up early on from the prince's disgust at the drunkenness of the Danish court, and that would have helped them to see him, for a certain disdain for the life of the court was one of the marks of the years round 1600. It can be found in Donne's lines of reminiscence written to Sir Henry Wotton:

> Beleeve mee Sir, in my youths giddiest dayes,
> When to be like the Court, was a playes praise,
> Playes were not so like Courts, as Courts' are like playes,

and again through Donne in such a 'Paradoxe' as the one entitled *Why are Courtiers sooner Atheists than Men of other Conditions?* In expression, at least, this disillusion was ironic and 'sophisticated' rather than serious, though perhaps it was a symptom of something serious. It mocked rather than sought to reform; it would have been sorry at heart to lose its targets. Its characteristic tone was exactly that of Hamlet on Osric and Polonius – the satire of one who is, or poses as, an insider, mocking what he is part of. When this spirit ranged wider than the court, one finds a 'no-nonsense' Old Tory pose in comment on social changes; Hamlet has it in his jest about the toe of the peasant and the courtier's kibe, and below this lay a bewildered disgust, as in Raleigh's *The Lie*, Shakespeare's own 66th Sonnet ('Tir'd with all these . . .'), and Hamlet's 'Denmark's a prison'. But this was rarely allowed free and simple expression. In a manner which may be thought very upper-class English, it hid itself as a rule under an edgy flippancy, of which Hamlet's talk with Rosencrantz and Guildenstern gives the tone – quick, bawdy, cynical. It was based, like Donne's poems, on a parody of scholastic chop-logic, as Hamlet recognises when he gives it up with 'by my fay, I cannot reason' (II ii 268); and the flippancy was always liable to suggest – as does 'Denmark's a prison' – that it might be more than flippancy. This was the characteristic mood of the intelligent young men of the time – a mood which is always uncertain what attitude to take or what pose to strike. Knights notes it in Hamlet – with great dislike – when he talks (p. 65) of his taking 'refuge in postures' and being rarely sincere; but this seems to me unnecessarily hostile, for it is a matter of uncertainty rather than of insincerity.

It is when involved with sex that the uncertainty shows itself most vividly; and this may explain – if not entirely excuse – Hamlet's behaviour to Ophelia and his mother. He has for women that extraordinary mixture of attitudes – some completely incompatible with each other but all, it seems, held together by the same person – of which the classic expression is Donne's *Songs and Sonets*. (I trust these references to Donne will not lead me to be accused of saying that Hamlet – or Shakespeare – is 'like' Donne; his name recurs simply because we know far more about him, he has left incomparably more lively evidence behind him, than any other young man of his kind and time.) Among this chaos of contradictory attitudes were these. There was a cynical disbelief in the possibility of women's being chaste. There was a contempt for the old-style high-falutin lyrical courtship – Hamlet's 'Doubt thou the stars are fire...' is his mocking expression of that – but there was certainly also a sneaking regret for the loss of it. There was a habit of confident generalising about the nature of women; Hamlet's 'frailty thy name is woman' (1 ii 146) comes from the same stable as Donne's 'No where Lives a woman true, and faire'. All this was sometimes conventional jesting; sometimes the desperate lashing-out of men who had been really hurt; sometimes an understandable and salutary reaction from the absurdities of 'courtly love'; sometimes the degenerate descendant of the anti-feminism of the medieval church. The language and tone of the last were certainly used, whether or not the thing was believed in, to give a quasi-theological justification; when Hamlet says to Ophelia: 'Get thee to a nunnery, why wouldst thou be a breeder of sinners?' (III i 121), he is giving advice which many a Father of the Church had given before him, and for the same reason. (Incidentally, it is quite wrong to think that Ophelia's unhappiness during this dialogue is caused by her thinking the prince is behaving cruelly. He may be doing so; but she does not think so. She is unhappy because she thinks he is mad.) Similarly with Hamlet's response to his mother's remarriage. What really catches him on the raw about this is neither its incestuousness (though that certainly counts for more than the modern reader is likely to allow), nor the fact that it is with a man whom he detests, but the fact that it, and its hastiness, prove Gertrude's sexuality to be rampantly alive. When he says to her: 'You cannot call it love, for at your age The hey-day in the blood is tame, it's humble...' (III iv 68), he is saying what he desperately wishes were true, but knows is not true. We tend to interpret this disgust on Freudian lines, as if it were entirely caused by Gertrude's being Hamlet's mother; but in fact this feeling that there is something wrong, something indecent, in a middle-aged woman's having sexual desires was very strong and widespread. It is expressed directly in Lear's hysteria:

> Behold yond simpering dame,
> Whose face between her forks presageth snow,
> That minces virtue, and does shake the head
> To hear of pleasure's name:
> The fitchew, nor the soiled horse, goes to it
> With a more riotous appetite ...

It was part of the traditional medieval-clerical way of feeling about sex; it is given savagely disgusted expression in Dunbar's *Twa Mariit Wemen and the Wedo*, and the Wyf of Bath's prologue is one long comic refutation of it. And even in our own time, only a few years ago, a Pope gave it as his opinion that though widows were allowed to remarry, it would be better if they didn't. A reader of the twentieth century is certainly entitled to feel, if he wishes, that the responses to sex which Hamlet's behaviour seems to show were deplorable and wrong; I do not think he is entitled to conclude that Hamlet himself was peculiarly culpable or unbalanced, or that Hamlet's creator intended him to appear so.

In some other things less vital, the young men of the time might have found themselves in Hamlet. There is his lively, intimate, very knowledgeable interest in the popular theatre – yet it is an interest spiced with the highbrow's mockery. When he says: 'The adventurous Knight shall use his foil and target, the Lover shall not sigh gratis, the Humorous Man shall end his part

in peace, the Clown shall make those laugh ... etc.' (II ii 324),
we are prepared for his preferring the play which 'pleased not the
million' but did please Hamlet himself and an élite of 'others'; and
the combination is exactly that of – shall we say the egghead of
1963 who professes an admiration for *Coronation Street*? – well,
certainly, it is exactly the combination of the young gentlemen of
the Inns of Court round the year 1600. So, I suspect, is Hamlet's
attitude to war and the military qualities. This comes out, of
course, in the scene (IV iv) in which he meets the captain of
Fortinbras's army. His response to that is curious. It is partly
critical, that all this courage and all this bloodshed should be for
what is not worth more than an 'egg-shell'. But together with the
criticism, and apparently overcoming it, are agreement and
admiration; for the action of this army is seen as an example of the
use of 'that capability and god-like reason' which Hamlet feels he
himself is not using. Knights is quite sure (p. 81) not only that
Hamlet himself is wrong to feel this, but that Hamlet's creator
agreed and intended us to agree. It is possible, though personally
I doubt it, for I do not think that Shakespeare regarded his
creations in the critical evaluating way suggested by Knights's
phrase for Hamlet's soliloquy in this scene; it 'contains', he
thinks, 'a firm though implicit placing judgement' – of Shakespeare on Hamlet, that is, as if Shakespeare were a contributor to
Scrutiny and Hamlet were Dylan Thomas. But what I do feel
clear about is that Hamlet is here responding exactly as the young
volunteers who pestered Elizabeth's military expeditions responded; he dreams of a military simplicity and certainty as
solution for the complexities of his problem just as Donne, in *The
Calme*, meditated on what might have been his reasons for joining
the Islands Voyage:

> Whether a rotten state, and hope of gaine,
> Or to disuse mee from the queasie paine
> Of being belov'd, and loving, or the thirst
> Of honour, or faire death, out pusht mee first ...

One of the odd things about Hamlet's character – and one of
the things which make it so often possible to compare him with

a real person such as Donne – is that in practice we continually forget that *he is a prince*. Something seems to have almost obliterated that great difference between royalty and the rest which real life, at that time, certainly preserved and which is normally visible even in the Shakespearian drama itself. We do not have with Hamlet, as we do with Prince Hal, a deliberate 'stepping-down', and in fact we are never able to forget Prince Hal's rank, for he himself never forgets it. It is a matter with Hamlet of a relaxed informality of manner and an easy colloquialism of tone; they contrast very strongly, as I am sure they are meant to, with the formality of Claudius, the affectations of Osric, and the pomposity of Polonius. A great deal of Hamlet's attractiveness has always depended on this; all through the centuries readers and spectators alike have felt for him, as for no other character, I suspect, a delusion of equality and intimacy, and they have been all the more pleased with this delusion because they remembered, at moments, whom they were feeling it for. (We can be snobs in our imaginations just as much as in our lives.) We nowadays may take this rather for granted; but for Hamlet's first audiences it must have come as something of a shock and a great deal of a delight. He must have seemed in this respect a remarkably, perhaps a daringly, 'contemporary' creation, an embodiment of that phenomenon which men in the last years of Elizabeth and first years of James were all aware of, whether they approved of it or not: a loosening of the old-style formality, a relaxing of the starched Tudor stiffness. There is no need to believe the old story that Polonius was intended as a caricature of Burghley in order to feel that he could well have been played so as to suggest it.

Hamlet, then, was a very 'contemporary' character. But this character Shakespeare put in a setting almost as incongruous as he could have found. Whether he did this knowingly or not, no one can say. I should say not; it was rather the inherent effect of taking over an old story for new times. But I am sure that it is here, in this continuous incongruity between central character and setting, that the clue lies to the moral problems which play and character present. For, first of all, he is made a prince, heir

G   J.S.H.

presumptive to the throne; the would-be scholar, the quick-witted affable talker, is put in a position where tradition required of him gravity, haughtiness, aloofness. (Of which expected distance Polonius's warning-off of Ophelia is a symptom: 'Lord Hamlet is a prince out of thy star' (II ii 141).) And then he is placed, this fastidious hater of debauchery and lover of the theatre, in a court peculiarly sombre, sordid and tasteless; and there, against his expressed desire, he is forced to remain. There comes to him next a direct supernatural intervention – one which he must and does believe in (for under his flippant wit he is a believing Christian) but which shocks him with doubts and questions as it would not have shocked the credulity of earlier ages or simpler types. And finally, there is imposed on him the demand of Revenge. This he accepts as a moral duty, for he has enough in him of the inherited concept of a prince's and a gentle-man's honour; but though his reason and his conscience tell him Yes, his nerves tell him No. It is not that he cannot do it; he can, and knows he can. Nor is it that he does not want to through some delicate reluctance to kill in general or some Freudian reluctance to kill his 'father-uncle' in particular. It is the whole life of action, violence, intrigue and public duty that he is reluctant to enter; he would rather be in Wittenberg, with his books. What he really is, is a conscript in a war. He has done things, as we all do in wars, he would rather not have done; but he believes it to be a just war, and all in all, he has borne himself well. That this was how Shakespeare saw it, the ending of the play convinces me; for why else should

> The soldiers' music and the rite of war
> Speak loudly for him?

NOTES

1. P. S. Conklin, *A History of Hamlet Criticism, 1601–1821* (1947) p. 9.

2. *Explorations*, cited in *Readings on the Character of Hamlet 1661–1947*, ed. C. C. H. Williamson (1950) p. 753.

3. A. J. A. Waldock, *Hamlet: A Study in Critical Method* (1931) p. 68.

4. See *Conscience and the King* (1953) p. 26 etc.

5. L. C. Knights, *An Approach to Hamlet* (1960) pp. 45–6.

6. *The Wheel of Fire* (1959 ed.) p. 42.

7. H. D. F. Kitto, *Form and Meaning in Drama* (1960) pp. 290, 327–8.

Jan Kott

HAMLET OF THE MID-CENTURY (1964)

I

THE bibliography of dissertations and studies devoted to *Hamlet* is twice the size of Warsaw's telephone directory. No Dane of flesh and blood has been written about so extensively as Hamlet. Shakespeare's prince is certainly the best-known representative of his nation. Innumerable glossaries and commentaries have grown round Hamlet, and he is one of the few literary heroes who live apart from the text, apart from the theatre. His name means something even to those who have never seen or read Shakespeare's play. In this respect he is rather like Leonardo's 'Mona Lisa'. We know she is smiling even before we have seen the picture. Mona Lisa's smile has been separated from the picture, as it were. It contains not only what Leonardo expressed in it, but also everything that has been written about it. Too many people – girls, women, poets, painters – have tried to solve the mystery of that smile. It is not just Mona Lisa that is smiling at us now, but all those who have tried to analyse or imitate that smile.

This is also the case with *Hamlet* – or rather with *Hamlet* in the theatre. For we have been separated from the text, not only by Hamlet's 'independent life' in our culture, but simply by the size of the play. *Hamlet* cannot be performed in its entirety, because the performance would last nearly six hours. One has to select, curtail and cut. One can perform only one of several *Hamlet*s potentially existing in this arch-play. It will always be a poorer *Hamlet* than Shakespeare's *Hamlet* is; but it may also be a *Hamlet* enriched by being of our time. It *may*, but I would rather say it *must* be so.

For *Hamlet* cannot be played simply. This may be the reason why it is so tempting to producers and actors. Many generations have seen their own reflection in this play. The genius of *Hamlet* consists, perhaps, in the fact that the play can serve as a mirror. An ideal *Hamlet* would be one most true to Shakespeare, and most modern at the same time. Is this possible? I do not know. But we can only appraise any Shakespearian production by asking how much there is of Shakespeare in it, and how much of us.

What I have in mind is not a forced topicality, a *Hamlet* that would be set in a cellar of young existentialists. *Hamlet* has been performed, for that matter, in evening dress and in circus tights; in medieval armour and in Renaissance costume. Costumes do not matter. What matters is that through Shakespeare's text we ought to get at our modern experience, anxiety and sensibility.

There are many subjects in *Hamlet*. There is politics, force opposed to morality; there is discussion of the divergence between theory and practice, on the ultimate purpose of life; there is the tragedy of love as well as family drama; political, eschatological and metaphysical problems are considered. There is everything you want, including deep psychological analysis, a bloody story, a duel, and general slaughter. One can select at will. But one must know what one selects, and why.

II

The *Hamlet* produced in Cracow a few weeks after the Twentieth Congress of the Soviet Communist Party lasted exactly three hours. It was light and clear, tense and sharp, modern and consistent, limited to one issue only. It was a political drama *par excellence*. 'Something is rotten in the state of Denmark' – was the first chord of *Hamlet*'s new meaning. And then the dead sound of the words 'Denmark's a prison' three times repeated. Finally the magnificent churchyard scene, with the gravediggers' dialogue rid of metaphysics, brutal and unequivocal. Gravediggers know for whom they dig graves. 'The gallows is built stronger than the church,' they say.

'Watch' and 'inquire' were the words most commonly heard from the stage. In this performance everybody, without exception, was being constantly watched. Polonius, minister to the royal murderer, even sends a man to France after his own son. Was Shakespeare not a genius for our time? Let us listen to the minister:

> Inquire me first what Danskers are in Paris,
> And how, and who, what means, and where they keep,
> What company, at what expense, and finding
> By this encompassment and drift of question
> That they do know my son, come you more nearer
> Than your particular demands will touch it.   (II i)

At Elsinore castle someone is hidden behind every curtain. The good minister does not even trust the Queen. Let us listen to him again:

> 'Tis meet that some more audience than a mother,
> Since nature makes them partial, should o'erhear
> The speech of vantage.   (III iii)

Everything at Elsinore has been corroded by fear: marriage, love and friendship. Shakespeare, indeed, must have experienced terrible things at the time of Essex's plot and execution, since he came to learn so well the working of the Grand Mechanism [of history]. Let us listen to the King talking to Hamlet's young friends:

> I entreat you both,
> That being of so young days brought up with him,
> And sith so neighboured to his youth and haviour,
> That you vouchsafe your rest here in our court
> Some little time, so by your companies
> To draw him on to pleasures, and to gather
> So much as from occasion you may glean
> Whether aught to us unknown afflicts him thus,
> That opened lies within our remedy.   (II ii)

The murderous uncle keeps a constant watchful eye on Hamlet. Why does he not want him to leave Denmark? His presence at court is inconvenient, reminding everybody of what they would like to forget. Perhaps he suspects something? Would it not be better not to issue him with a passport and keep him at hand? Or does the King wish to get rid of Hamlet as soon as possible, but has given way to the Queen, who wants to have her son near her? And the Queen? What does she think about it all? Does she feel guilty? What does the Queen know? She has been through passion, murder and silence. She had to suppress everything inside her. One can sense a volcano under her superficial poise.

Ophelia, too, has been drawn into the big game. They listen in to her conversations, ask questions, read her letters. It is true that she gives them up herself. She is at the same time part of the Mechanism and its victim. Politics hangs here over every feeling, and there is no getting away from it. All the characters are poisoned by it. The only subject of their conversation is politics. It is a kind of madness.

Hamlet loves Ophelia. But he knows he is being watched; moreover – he has more important matters to attend to. Love is gradually fading away. There is no room for it in this world. Hamlet's dramatic cry: 'Get thee to a nunnery!' is addressed not to Ophelia alone, but also to those who are overhearing the two lovers. It is to confirm their impression of his alleged madness. But for Hamlet and for Ophelia it means that in the world where murder holds sway there is no room for love.

Hamlet was performed in Cracow in 1956 unequivocally and with a terrifying clarity. Doubtless it was a simplified *Hamlet*. But it is equally certain that this interpretation was so suggestive that when I reached for the text after the performance, I saw in it only a drama of political crime. To the classic question, whether Hamlet's madness is real or feigned, the Cracow production gave the following reply: Hamlet feigns madness, he puts on, in cold blood, a mask of madness in order to perform a *coup d'état*; Hamlet is mad, because politics is itself madness when it destroys all feeling and affection.

I have nothing against such an interpretation. And I am not sorry for all the other Hamlets: for the moralist unable to draw a clear-cut line between good and evil; for the intellectual unable to find a sufficient reason for action; for the philosopher to whom the world's existence is a matter of doubt.

I prefer the youth deeply involved in politics, rid of illusions, sarcastic, passionate and brutal. A young rebel who has about him something of the charm of James Dean. His passion sometimes seems childish. No doubt he is more primitive than all previous Hamlets. Action, not reflection, is his forte. He is wild and drunk with indignation. The Polish Hamlet after the Twentieth Party Congress. One of many. He does not yet experience deep moral doubts, but he is not a simpleton. He wants to know if his father has really been murdered. He cannot fully trust the Ghost, or any ghosts for that matter. He looks for more convincing evidence, and that is why he arranges a psychological test by staging the crime that has been committed. He loathes the world, and that is why he sacrifices Ophelia. But he does not flinch from a *coup d'état*. He knows, however, that a *coup* is a difficult affair. He considers all the pros and cons. He is a born conspirator. 'To be' means for him to revenge his father and to assassinate the King; while 'not to be' means to give up the fight.

It is significant that very similar conclusions have been reached by Hans Reichenbach, who in the last book published before his death, entitled *The Rise of Scientific Philosophy*, unexpectedly devotes two pages to Hamlet's soliloquy. Reichenbach was one of the most outstanding modern neo-positivists and concerned himself with the application of the theory of anticipation to particular branches of science. In Hamlet's soliloquy he sees an inner dialogue between logician and politician. It is the law of averages applied to the moral justification of an act. Without war and postwar experiences the learned neo-positivist would never have written those two pages.

But the *Hamlet* I saw in Cracow was modern not only because the problems of the play have been brought up to date. It was modern in its psychological and dramatic qualities. Action developed under great stress, similar to that experienced by us in real life. This production, deprived of the great soliloquies and of narrative quality, was marked by a violence typical of modern conflicts. Political, erotic and career motives intermingle, reactions are brutal, solutions are quickly effected. In this *Hamlet*

there were even the 'black-outs' of modern political cabaret, and
great ironic humour. Let us quote Shakespeare:

King.   Now, Hamlet, where's Polonius?
Hamlet. At supper.
King.   At supper? where?
Hamlet. Not where he eats, but where a' is eaten.   (IV iii)

This joke might have been taken out of the Little Vocabulary
of the Surrealists. It is in the same style and has two meanings,
one of which is derisive the other cruel. Or let us take the short
lesson in political opportunism which might serve as model for a
real satirical cabaret. This is how Shakespeare puts it:

Hamlet.   Do you see yonder cloud that's almost in shape of a
             camel?
Polonius. By th'mass and 'tis, like a camel indeed.
Hamlet.   Methinks it is like a weasel.
Polonius. It is backed like a weasel.
Hamlet.   Or, like a whale?
Polonius. Very like a whale.   (III ii)

III

Hamlet is like a sponge. Unless produced in a stylized or anti-
quarian fashion, it immediately absorbs all the problems of our
time. It is the strangest play ever written; by its very imperfec-
tions. *Hamlet* is a great scenario, in which every character has a
more or less tragic and cruel part to play and has magnificent
things to say. Every character has an irrevocable task to fulfil, a
task imposed by the author. This scenario is independent from
the characters; it has been devised earlier. It defines the situations,
as well as the mutual relations of the characters; it dictates their
words and gestures. But it does not say who the characters are.
It is something external in relation to them. And that is why the
scenario of *Hamlet* can be played by different sorts of characters.

An actor always enters a ready part, written not only for him.
In this respect *Hamlet* does not, of course, differ from other plays.
At the first rehearsal the actors sit at a table. 'You will be the
king,' says the producer, 'you will be Ophelia, and you will be

Laertes. We shall now read the play.' So far so good. But in the play itself similar things happen. Hamlet, Laertes, Ophelia also have to play parts imposed on them, parts against which they revolt. They are actors in a drama they do not always wholly understand, in which they have become involved. The scenario dictates the actions of the *dramatis personae*, but does not dictate the motives underlying the actions, i.e. the psychology. This is true of life as well as of the theatre.

A secret organization is preparing an action. The plan has been carefully worked out: place, time-table, direction of retreat. Then the parts have to be distributed. You will stand on that corner and raise your handkerchief when you see the grey car. You will go to Z and bring a case with grenades to house no. 12. You will shoot in direction W and escape in direction M. The tasks have been allotted, the parts taught. Even gestures have been defined. But the evening before, the boy who is to shoot in direction N could have read Rimbaud or drunk vodka, or both. He may be a young philosopher or just a teddy-boy. The girl who is to bring grenades may be having an unhappy love affair, or may be a good-time girl, or possibly both. The plan of action will not be altered because of that. The scenario remains unchanged.

Hamlet can be summarized in a number of ways: as a historical chronicle, as a thriller, or as a philosophical drama. They will probably be three different plays, though all three have been written by Shakespeare. But if the summary is fair, the scenarios of the three plays will be the same. Except that every time there will be a different Ophelia, Hamlet and Laertes. The parts are the same, but performed by different actors.

Let us have a look at the scenario. For after all Shakespeare had written, or rather re-written, an old scenario and the parts in it. But he did not distribute the parts. This has been done anew in every age. Every age has its own Poloniuses, Fortinbrases, Hamlets and Ophelias. Before they enter the stage, they have to go to dressing-rooms. But let them not stay there too long. They may put on huge wigs, shave off their moustaches or stick on beards, put on medieval-looking tights or throw Byronic capes over their shoulders; they may play in armour or in tails. This does not really make much difference, on condition that their make-up is not overdone; for they must have modern faces. Otherwise they would perform a costume piece, instead of *Hamlet*.

Bertolt Brecht wrote in his *Little Organum for the Theatre*:

The theatre should always be mindful of the needs of its time. Let us take, as an example, the old play of *Hamlet*. I believe that in view of the bloody and gloomy times in which I am writing this, in view of the criminal ruling classes and general despair of reason . . . the story of this play may be read thus: It is a time of war. Hamlet's father, the king of Denmark, had, in a victorious war of plunder, killed the king of Norway. While the latter's son, Fortinbras, is preparing himself for a new war, the king of Denmark is also killed, by his brother. The brothers of the dead kings, having become kings themselves, conclude peace with each other. Norwegian troops, on their way to a war of plunder against Poland, have been permitted to cross Danish territory. Just at this time, the warlike father's ghost asks young Hamlet to revenge the crime committed on himself. After some hesitation as to whether he should add one bloody deed to another, Hamlet – willing even to go into exile – meets at the sea shore young Fortinbras and his troops on their way to Poland. Following his example he turns back, and, in a scene of barbaric slaughter, kills his uncle, his mother, and himself, leaving Denmark to the Norwegians. Thus we observe how, in these circumstances, the young man, already somewhat stout, badly misuses his new knowledge acquired at Wittenberg university. This knowledge gets in the way when it comes to resolving the conflicts of the feudal world. His reason is impractical when faced with irrational reality. He falls a tragic victim to the discrepancy between his reasoning and his action.

Brecht was writing his *Little Organum* in the years of the Second World War. No wonder that in Shakespeare's tragedy he saw, above all, armies devastating the country, wars of aggression, the powerlessness of reason. Hamlet's personal drama or Ophelia's misfortunes were made insignificant by the events of history. Brecht was sensitive to the politics in *Hamlet*. He was more interested in the sequences of historical conflict than in the depths of the Prince of Denmark's soul. The point of departure of Polish productions of *Hamlet* in 1956 and 1959 was very similar, however they might have differed from Brecht's concepts. *Hamlet* was a political play in 1956, and remained such in 1959, although the Prince of Denmark had by then become a much more complex personality and had passed through new experiences.

Let us have a look at the scenario in order to find out what parts it contains, knowing that they will be played by modern characters. *Hamlet*, envisaged as a scenario, is the story of three young boys and one girl. The boys are of the same age. They are called Hamlet, Laertes, Fortinbras. The girl is younger, and her name is Ophelia. They are all involved in a bloody political and family drama. As a result, three of them will die; the fourth will, more or less by chance, become the king of Denmark.

I have deliberately written that they are involved in a drama. For none of them has chosen his part; it is imposed on them from outside, having been conceived in the scenario. The scenario has to be played to the end, no matter who Hamlet, Ophelia, and the other characters are. I am not concerned at the moment with what the scenario itself is supposed to be. It may be the Mechanism of history, fate, or the human condition, depending on how we want to envisage *Hamlet*. *Hamlet* is a drama of imposed situations, and here lies the key to modern interpretations of the play.

The King, the Queen, Polonius, Rosencrantz and Guildenstern have been clearly defined by their situations. It may be a tragic situation, as in the case of the Queen; or grotesque, as in the case of Polonius. But character and situation are closely connected. Claudius does not play the part of a murderer and a king. He *is* the murderer and the king. Polonius does not play the part of a despotic father and a king's councillor. He *is* the despotic father and the king's councillor.

It is different with Hamlet. He is more than the heir to the throne who tries to revenge himself for the murder of his father. The situation does not define Hamlet, or at any rate does not define him beyond doubt. The situation has been imposed on him. Hamlet accepts it, but at the same time revolts against it. He accepts the part, but is beyond and above it.

In his student days Hamlet had carefully studied Montaigne. It is with Montaigne's book in his hand that he chases the medieval ghost on the terraces of Elsinore castle. The ghost has hardly disappeared when Hamlet writes on the book's margin that 'one may smile, and smile, and be a villain'. Shakespeare has thrust the most attentive of Montaigne's readers back into the feudal world. He has also set a mousetrap for him.

'Poor boy with a book in his hand . . .' Thus was Hamlet described in 1904 by Stanislaw Wyspiański, painter, dramatist, designer, whom Gordon Craig used to call the most universal artist of the theatre. Wyspiański made the Polish Hamlet walk round the renaissance galleries of Cracow's Royal Castle. The scenario of history imposed on the Polish Hamlet at the turn of the century a duty to struggle for the nation's liberation. That particular Hamlet used to read Polish romantic poets and Nietzsche. He experienced his powerlessness as a personal failure.

Every Hamlet has a book in his hand. What book does the modern Hamlet read? Hamlet in the Cracow production of late autumn 1956 read only newspapers. He shouted that 'Denmark's a prison' and wanted to improve the world. He was a rebellious ideologist and lived only for action. Hamlet in the Warsaw production of 1959 was full of doubts again; and again he was the 'poor boy with a book in his hand'. We can easily visualize him in black sweater and blue jeans. The book he is holding is not by Montaigne, but by Sartre, Camus or Kafka. He studied in Paris, or Brussels, or even – like the real Hamlet – in Wittenberg. He returned to Poland three or four years ago. He very much doubts if the world can be reduced to a few simple statements. Occasionally he is tormented by thoughts of the fundamental absurdity of existence.

This latest, the most modern of Hamlets, returned to the country at a moment of tension. His father's ghost demands revenge. His friends expect him to fight for succession to the throne. He wants to go away again. He cannot. Everybody

involves him in politics. He has been trapped into finding himself
in a compulsory situation; a situation he does not want, but which
has been thrust upon him. He is looking for inner freedom and
does not want to commit himself. At last he accepts the choice
imposed on him; but only in the sphere of action. He is committed, but only in what he does, not in what he thinks. He
knows that all action is clear-cut, but he refuses to let his thought
be thus limited. He does not want practice to be equated with
theory.

He is inwardly starved. He considers life to be a lost cause from
the outset. He would rather be excused from this big game, but
remains loyal to its rules. He knows that 'though man does not
do what he wants, he is responsible for his life'. And that 'it does
not matter what has been made of us; what matters is what we
ourselves make of what has been made of us'. Sometimes he
thinks himself an existentialist; at other times – just a marxist who
has revolted. But he knows that 'death transforms life into
destiny'. He has read Malraux's *La Condition Humaine*.

This attitude of the modern Hamlet is a defence of his inner
freedom. This Hamlet fears, most of all, a clear-cut definition.
But act he must. Ophelia may have a hair-do like Leonardo's
'Lady with a Weasel', or her hair may be let down loose; she may
wear a pigtail, or a pony-tail. But she, too, knows that life is a
hopeless business from the start. So she does not want to play
her game with life at too high a stake. It is the events that compel
her to over-play. Her boy friend has been involved in high politics. She has slept with him. But she is a daughter of a minister of
the crown, an obedient daughter. She agrees to her conversation
with Hamlet being overheard by her father. Maybe she wants to
save Hamlet. But she falls into the trap herself. The events have
driven her into a blind alley from which there is no way out. An
ordinary girl, who loved her boy, has been given by the scenario
of history – a tragic part.

IV

Traditional nineteenth-century Hamletology devoted itself
almost exclusively to the study of the problem of who Hamlet

really was. The traditional scholars charged Shakespeare with having written an untidy, inconsistent and badly constructed masterpiece. Whereas modern essays consider *Hamlet* from a theatrical standpoint. *Hamlet* is not a philosophical, moral or psychological treatise; it is a piece for the theatre, that is to say, a scenario with parts. If this is so, then one must begin with Fortinbras, who plays a decisive role, as far as the scenario of *Hamlet* is concerned.

Let us imagine a modern producer starting analytical rehearsals of *Hamlet*. He has seated his actors round a table and told them: 'We are going to do a play by Shakespeare called *Hamlet*. We will try to do it as honestly as we can. That means we are not going to alter the text. We will try to give as much text as can be put over in three and a half hours. We will reflect on every cut. We will try to show a modern *Hamlet*. We will try to break with nineteenth-century naturalism and be content with a back-cloth, rostrum and two chairs on either side of the stage. We will endeavour to design colourful renaissance costumes. But these costumes will be worn by us, modern people. You must not throw your hands up in the air, walk on tiptoes or on stilts. The world shown in this scenario is cruel, but every one of us has experienced the cruelty of the world. Some people revolt against this cruelty, others accept it as a law; but both are crushed by it.'

An elderly actor who is to play Polonius will, perhaps, ask at this point: 'Is *Hamlet* a political play?'

'I don't know,' the producer will probably reply. 'This depends on what Denmark means to these three young people here.' And he will point out a young girl who is to play Ophelia, the young actor who is just trying on the green costume of Laertes, and Hamlet, who is sitting anxiously in the corner looking at his silver medallion. Then, maybe, the producer will be lost in thought for a while and say quietly to himself: 'Perhaps it depends on who our Fortinbras will be?'

In all modern analyses of *Hamlet* (H. Granville-Barker, F. Fergusson, J. Paris) the character of Fortinbras has been brought to the foreground. In structural interpretations *Hamlet* is a drama of analogical situations, a system of mirrors, in which the same problem is in turn reflected tragically, pathetically, ironically and grotesquely: three sons who have lost their fathers, one after the other, or Hamlet's and Ophelia's madness. In predominantly historical interpretations *Hamlet* is a drama of power and heredity. In the first instance Fortinbras is one of Hamlet's 'doubles', '*alter egos*', 'mediums'. In the other he is the heir to the throne of Denmark; the man who has broken the chain of crime and revenge, who has restored order to the Danish kingdom. This order may be understood as the restoration of moral law, or as the *neue Ordnung in Europa*. The ending of the tragedy has been interpreted in both ways. For if one wishes to place *Hamlet*'s moral conflicts in a historical context, no matter whether renaissance or modern, one cannot ignore the part played by Fortinbras.

The difficulty is that in the text of the play Fortinbras is only broadly sketched. On the stage he appears only twice: for the first time in act four, when he and his troops are on the way to Poland; for the second time when he comes to claim the throne after the general slaughter. But young Fortinbras is mentioned many times. His father has been killed in a duel by Hamlet's father. The fathers of all the young people in this play – Hamlet, Laertes and Ophelia – have been murdered. Spectators get confused when tracing the history of young Fortinbras. From the opening scene we learn that he wants to wage war against Denmark; then he fights with the Poles for a piece of land hardly worth having; at the end he appears in Elsinore. It is he who speaks the final words of this cruel drama.

Who is this young Norwegian prince? We do not know. Shakespeare does not tell us. What does he represent? Blind fate, the absurdity of the world or the victory of justice? Shakespearian scholars have made a case for all these interpretations in turn. The producer has to decide. Fortinbras is a young, strong and cheerful fellow. On his arrival he delivers a speech to this effect: 'Take away these corpses. Hamlet was a good boy, but he is dead. Now I shall be your king. I have just remembered that I happen to have certain rights to this crown.' Then he smiles and is very pleased with himself.

A great drama has been concluded. People fought, plotted, killed one another, committed crimes for love, and went mad for love. They told amazing things about life, death and human fate. They set traps for each other, and fell into them. They defended their power or revolted against power. They wanted to build a better world or just save themselves. They all stood for something. Even their crimes had a certain greatness. And then a vigorous young lad comes, and says with a charming smile: 'Take away these corpses. Now I shall be your king.'

QUESTIONS

1. Dr Johnson gives to *Hamlet* 'the praise of variety'. How great a variety do you find in the play?

2. What are the external obstacles to Hamlet's achievement of his revenge? At what points in the play would the action have developed differently if there had been no other obstacles than these?

3. On what occasions does Hamlet act in a ruthless fashion? How profoundly do his deeds on these occasions affect our estimate of him?

4. What evidence does the play contain for saying that Hamlet delays in seeking his revenge? How much of this evidence consists of utterances made by Hamlet himself in soliloquy? How much weight ought we to attach to such utterances?

5. 'O, what a noble mind is here o'erthrown!' exclaims Ophelia. Would its nobility have been evident without Ophelia's assurance?

6. Discuss the change which many critics find in Hamlet on his return from his sea voyage.

7. G. Wilson Knight describes Claudius as a 'good and gentle king'; L. C. Knights calls him a 'slimy beast'. Give your own view.

8. 'Frailty thy name is woman!' Compare and contrast Hamlet's attitudes to Gertrude and Ophelia.

9. Describe the court society presented in *Hamlet*. By what means are its qualities and defects imposed upon our imaginations?

10. What significance do you find in the fact that the play contains three young men whose fathers die by violence: Hamlet, Laertes, and Fortinbras?

11. For what purposes does Shakespeare use prose in this play? How does he adapt his prose to these purposes?

12. What would the play lose if it were not a poetic play?

13. What is contributed to the play by the thoughts on death which are so frequent in it?

14. What role may be ascribed to Providence in *Hamlet*?

SELECT BIBLIOGRAPHY

ANTHOLOGIES OF CRITICISM

Readings on the Character of Hamlet 1661–1947, ed. C. C. H. Williamson (Allen & Unwin, 1950).

The following refer to Shakespeare's plays generally; they are more accurate textually than is Williamson's collection:

Shakespeare Criticism: A Selection, ed. D. Nichol Smith (World's Classics: Oxford U.P., 1916).

Shakespeare Criticism 1919–35, ed. Anne Ridler (World's Classics: Oxford U.P., 1936).

Shakespeare Criticism 1935–60, ed. Anne Ridler (World's Classics: Oxford U.P., 1963).

CRITICISM SINCE 1945

Salvador de Madariaga, *On Hamlet* (Hollis & Carter, 1948). He sees Hamlet as an egoistic Renaissance prince.

Francis Fergusson, *The Idea of a Theater* (Princeton U.P. and Oxford U.P., 1949). Replies to T. S. Eliot on *Hamlet.*

Ernest Jones, *Hamlet and Oedipus* (Gollancz, 1949).

E. M. W. Tillyard, *Shakespeare's Problem Plays* (Chatto & Windus, 1950). Associates *Hamlet* with Shakespeare's dark comedies.

Wolfgang H. Clemen, *The Development of Shakespeare's Imagery* (Methuen, 1951).

D. G. James, *The Dream of Learning* (Clarendon Press, 1951).

Maynard Mack, 'The World of Hamlet', in *Yale Review,* XLI (1951–2) 502–23.

Peter Alexander, *Hamlet, Father and Son* (Clarendon Press, 1955). Questions current assumptions regarding Shakespeare's conception of tragedy.

H. D. F. Kitto, *Form and Meaning in Drama* (Methuen, 1956).

Shakespeare Survey 9, ed. Allardyce Nicoll (Cambridge U.P., 1956). *Hamlet* is the central theme of this collection of essays by various contributors. The volume contains Clifford Leech's excellent survey, 'Studies in *Hamlet*, 1901–1955'.

T. S. Eliot, 'Poetry and Drama' (1951), in *On Poetry and Poets* (Faber & Faber, 1957).

Harry Levin, *The Question of Hamlet* (Oxford U.P., 1959).

Helen Gardner, *The Business of Criticism* (Oxford U.P., 1959).

L. C. Knights, *An Approach to Hamlet* (Chatto & Windus, 1960).

John Holloway, *The Story of the Night* (Routledge & Kegan Paul, 1961).

Stratford-upon-Avon Studies 5: Hamlet, ed. J. R. Brown and Bernard Harris (Arnold, 1963). Ten new essays by various hands. Includes Patrick Cruttwell's 'The Morality of *Hamlet* – "Sweet Prince" or "Arrant Knave"?'

Jan Kott, *Shakespeare our Contemporary* (Methuen, 1964).

Terence Hawkes, *Shakespeare and the Reason* (Routledge & Kegan Paul, 1964). Interprets *Hamlet* and other plays in the light of the medieval and Renaissance distinction between a higher and a lower reason.

Martin Holmes, *The Guns of Elsinore* (Chatto & Windus, 1964). Sheds light on particular passages by reference to Elizabethan sources of knowledge about Denmark.

P. R. Grover, 'The Ghost of Dr. Johnson: L. C. Knights and D. A. Traversi on *Hamlet*', in *Essays in Criticism*, XVII (1967) 143-57.

NOTES ON CONTRIBUTORS

WOLFGANG H. CLEMEN. Professor of English Philology in the University of Munich. Author of *The Development of Shakespeare's Imagery* (1951), *English Tragedy before Shakespeare* (1961).

PATRICK CRUTTWELL. Formerly Professor of English at Kenyon College, Ohio. Author of *The Shakespearean Moment* (1954).

T. S. ELIOT (d. 1965). Major English poet and critic. His early essay on *Hamlet* (1919) has been the starting-point of much subsequent discussion.

HELEN GARDNER. Was Merton Professor of English Literature at Oxford, until 1975. Author of *The Art of T. S. Eliot* (1949), *The Business of Criticism* (1960), *Religion and Literature* (1971); editor of the poems of Donne (1952, 1965).

JOHN HOLLOWAY. Professor of Modern English at Cambridge (1972-82). Author of *The Victorian Sage* (1953), *The Story of the Night* (1961) and several volumes of verse.

D. G. JAMES. Winterstoke Professor of English in the University of Bristol, 1942-52; Vice-Chancellor of the University of Southampton, 1952-65. Author of *Scepticism and Poetry* (1937), *The Dream of Learning* (1951), *Matthew Arnold and the Decline of English Romanticism* (1961).

ERNEST JONES (d. 1958). A disciple of Freud, he introduced the study of psycho-analysis into Great Britain and the United States. Author of twelve books and many monographs.

H. D. F. KITTO. Literary critic and classical scholar, for many years Professor of Greek in the University of Bristol. Author of

Greek Tragedy (1939), *The Greeks* (Pelican, 1951), *Form and Meaning in Drama* (1956), and works on Sophocles.

L. C. KNIGHTS. King Edward VII Professor of English Literature at Cambridge, 1965–73. Author of *Drama and Society in the Age of Jonson* (1937), *Explorations* (1946), *Some Shakespearean Themes* (1959), *An Approach to Hamlet* (1960), *Further Explorations* (1965).

JAN KOTT. Professor of Literature in the University of Warsaw. Author of *Shakespeare Our Contemporary* and of Polish versions of individual plays

HARRY LEVIN. Professor of English and Comparative Literature at Harvard. Author of *James Joyce: a Critical Introduction* (1941), *Christopher Marlowe: the Overreacher* (1952), *The Question of Hamlet* (1959), *The Myth of the Golden Age in the Renaissance* (1969) and many other books.

MAYNARD MACK. Sterling Professor of English at Yale. Editor of *An Essay of Man* in the 'Twickenham' Pope (1950); author of *King Lear in Our Time* (1965).

INDEX

References to *Hamlet* and to its protagonist are naturally too numerous to be recorded here. References to other characters in the play are recorded only when they involve comments on the way these characters are presented in it.